THE COUNTRY LIFE
COLLECTOR'S
POCKET BOOK

THE COUNTRY LIFE
COLLECTOR'S
POCKET BOOK

G. BERNARD HUGHES

Illustrations by Therle Hughes

COUNTRY LIFE
LONDON · NEW YORK · SYDNEY · TORONTO

Published for Country Life Books by
The Hamlyn Publishing Group Limited
London · New York · Sydney · Toronto
Hamlyn House, Feltham, Middlesex, England
© Copyright G. Bernard Hughes 1963
ISBN 0 600 43055 3

Printed and bound in Great Britain by
Hazell Watson & Viney Limited
Aylesbury, Bucks

9th impression 1970

Contents

Introduction

This book is designed for the pocket rather than the book-shelf. Its aim is to be an on-the-spot reference in the sale-rooms, at exhibitions, in show-piece country house and back-street curio shop—wherever beginner-collectors fore-gather to share their absorbing hobby. Words are pruned to a minimum of essential facts aided by drawings which are an integral part of the survey. Great Britain's superb antiques are worthy of endless study and among minor pieces the beginner-collector may still acquire the gracious design and fine craftsmanship that give lasting satisfaction, but only the well-informed find 'bargains'.

No attempt is made here to treat any subject exhaustively but much essential detail is included that is hard to find in other books. This is based on many years of day-to-day concern with antiques and with the Victorian near-antiques that are now more generally available. It is hoped that it will go everywhere, as a reliable companion in constant, ready-to-hand attendance, so that many now bewildered or disappointed may find confidence, success and lasting pleasure in this country's rich inheritance from earlier centuries.

CHAPTER ONE

Furniture

Collectors of furniture assess the age of their specimens by material, form and finish. They recognise that value depends not only on age but on condition and to some extent must be related to the original quality standard required of a maker. It is particularly difficult to classify really old furniture; some Elizabethan oak chests, stools and tables remain, but far more oak furniture dates to enthusiastic revivals, especially in the 19th century, now sufficiently weathered to have acquired a pleasant patina, but often betrayed by an improbable wealth of poor-spirited carving, much of it produced by mechanical means.

Many pieces can only be accepted as part of an endless tradition; the plain-turned, three-legged stool, round or square topped, was equally at home in the Victorian kitchen and the Elizabethan. The simple spindle-and-socket work of the turner is particularly difficult to date and should be chosen for condition and intrinsic usefulness.

Other really early furniture has survived because extremely strongly made by the joiner. Here the collector looks for panels set into a frame of rails and stiles that are held together by tenon-and-mortice joints (Fig. 21), secured by dowel pins where later, from the second half of the 17th century, glue was preferred. Screws, unpointed, were not introduced until the late 17th century. Where end-grain meets end-grain, the collector notes the simple through dovetail that preceded the stopped or lapped dovetail of the late 17th century onwards required under veneers (Fig. 13). He looks for wrought iron hinges, sometimes elaborate and including the scrolling cock's head, and iron handles shaped as narrow loops (Fig. 4) or moulded drops. A variety of wood may be noted—elm, pear, yew, birch, beech as well as oak and Elizabethan walnut. Ornament is limited to colour, vigorous carving (Fig. 8) and inlay in simple patterns in contrasting wood, ivory or bone. In early Stuart furniture one finds a continuation of Elizabethan styles, but less flamboyant, much of the carving, for example, reduced to repetitive borders in low relief and, around the mid-century, an acceptance of ornament unrelated to construction, such as glued-on spindles and bosses and heavily projecting panels with elaborate glued-on mouldings mitred at the corners (Fig. 8).

In furniture of the late 17th century and onwards the collector finds a change of surface treatment from panels and carving to the wholly construction-masking veneer, the furniture carcase being hidden under thin layers of finer wood, $\frac{1}{16}$ to $\frac{1}{8}$-in. thick, often cut to display the grain in a way impossible in solid wood. The ultimate development of this was the assembly of small shapes in veneer fitted together to make a pattern (*see* Parquetry and Marquetry ornament). Walnut, plain or in veneer, is noted in use throughout the first three-quarters of the 18th century, and was popular again among Victorians. Split caning on walnut chairs dates from the late 17th century onwards, also some colourful japanned furniture showing Eastern designs in opaque paint mixed with hard lacquer varnishes, although this has rarely survived in good condition. Mounts from the 17th century may be of brass.

Mahogany furniture was introduced early in the 18th century, the early wood being dark, tough and heavy, excellent for the period's reversion to naturalistic carving of shells, eagles' heads, lions' masks and the like (Fig. 9). The splendid patterns of mahogany veneers are associated with the second half of the century. Chippendale's *Gentleman and Cabinet-*

8

1. Regency and early Victorian furniture. TOP: chiffonier with shelves and cupboard; games table with chess board over tric-trac recess and end compartments for games materials; Davenport. BOTTOM: what-not; sofa table; canterbury music stand.

Maker's Director was issued 1754, 1755, 1762, but there has been a tendency to give a Chippendale label to all the vigorous, sharply carved and fret-cut furniture of early and mid-Georgian manufacture, including 'Gothic' and 'Chinese' forms (Fig. 17). This pre-dated in style the change to plainer outlines and pseudo-classic ornament approved by Robert Adam that became widely popular in the 1760s.

Hepplewhite's name is associated with the gracious, un-ambitious furniture of the 1770s and 1780s, finely proportioned, often with bow or serpentine outline and elegant tapering legs (Fig. 18), but none of his own work is known. The light and colour in satinwood and other exotics was supplemented during the last quarter of the century by painted surfaces and ornamental detail.

Sheraton's designs reflect something of the disturbed mood of the 18th century's end, associated with more squarely angular chair and cabinet work (Fig. 18). The collector may find specimens of so-called Regency furniture made between about 1800 and the 1830s, emphasising long lines and glossy surfaces, with brief excursions into Egyptian ornament and more enduring interest in Greek and Roman antiquities. This was less extreme in England than in the French 'Empire' style of about 1800, with its exact copies of Roman Empire furnishings and Roman representations of Greek design. Egyptian ornament offers little beyond sphinx and lion motifs and figures with hands and feet in full relief introduced as pillars and corner pilasters (Fig. 10). Animal legs, paws and hooves abound in furniture legs, especially the lion monopodium, with head and leg carved in full relief, also the lion's head and ring handles (Figs. 6 and 9).

Heavy furniture rests on solid plinths rather than bracket feet. Much that survives is of superb workmanship. One notes delight in exotic woods such as burr amboyna, zebra wood and the like, and especially the rich grain and lustre of rosewood veneer. Narrow light and dark bandings take the place of elaborate marquetry and inlay. The glossy surface known as French polishing is not found on English furniture dating earlier than the 1820s. There is much use of marble and a delight in brass ornament, including brass inlay (Fig. 12); caning re-appears in light chairs on back and arms.

The period is associated with some attractive smaller furniture, including shapely games tables (Fig. 1), work boxes and other boxes such as teapoys upon pillar legs (Fig. 2), the sofa table (Fig. 1) with end-flaps and side drawer to accompany the period's scroll-ended sofa, and some furniture such as chairs and tables shaped and painted to suggest bamboo.

Late Georgian furniture is associated with a heavy-handed revival of the rococo and thereafter revivals overruled origi-

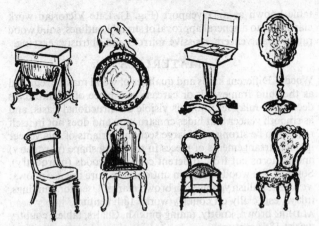

2. Regency and early Victorian furniture. TOP: pouch work-table with hinged flaps and lyre supports; convex mirror with eagle mount; teapoy; papier-mâché tip-up table. BOTTOM: chair of about 1830 with 'Greek' legs; two chairs of papier-mâché with cane seats; balloon-back chair with carved frame and buttoned upholstery.

nality in 'Gothic', 'Elizabethan', 'Louis XIV' and the rest, with a profusion of deep carving, often with story themes. Victorian developments include much seat furniture that appears today to be disproportionately long in the back and short in the legs, massive furniture for dining room and library and charmingly gay shell encrustations. Some wood furniture is encrusted with pearl shell, but this treatment is more especially associated with glossy papier mâché (Fig. 2) and was patented in 1825. This is only one of the period's delights in substitute materials. Furniture noted by the collector includes the space-saving Sutherland table, narrow topped and with deep falling flaps and the square little drawer-filled writing

11

table known as a Davenport (Fig. 1). Late Victorian work clarified into a general approval of straight outlines, solid wood rather than veneers, massive mirrors and obtrusive carving.

MATERIALS

Woods. Different kinds and qualities of wood may be required as the solid framework or carcase of a piece of furniture, as decorative inlay let into this visible constructional basis, and as smooth veneer that hides construction and does not in itself require to be strong or of large section; variants of this veneer include arrangements of pieces in matching shape (parquetry) and patterns cut from different coloured woods (marquetry). Some of the woods noted in antique furniture are as follows:

ACACIA: dullish yellow with brown marks. Used for bandings, inlays, especially on country work; 18th century.

ALDER: brown, knotty, fading pinkish. Chairs, tables, country work; 18th century.

AMBOYNA: warm light brown with a speckled, knotty, lively grain. Veneers on cabinet work; 18th century.

APPLE: warm light brown; hard. Inlays, carvings, veneers in late 17th century. Country furniture; 19th century.

ASH: white with light brown markings suggesting oak; straight grain. Tough and used for chairs, bedroom furniture, etc.; 17th, 18th and 19th centuries.

BAMBOO: creamy-yellow round stems with conspicuous joints. Sometimes painted; sometimes imitated in painted beech. Late 18th and early 19th centuries.

BEECH: pinkish-brown to grey, rather soft; it may be split to show small flecked markings somewhat like oak; frequently stained black or painted. Country furniture from the mid-17th century; mahogany imitations in 18th century; black chairs, etc., end of 18th century.

BENT WOOD: term for furniture such as chairs and tables usually of cheap native wood, turned and bent by the use of

12

heat, moisture and pressure, so that it retains the required shape. Extremely popular second half of 19th century.

BIRCH: pale golden with wavy grain, somewhat like satin-wood and used as substitute in 18th century.

BOG OAK: black because obtained from old peat bogs. Inlay and glued-on ornament, 16th, 17th centuries. Small cabinet work in romantic revival, 19th century.

BOX: pale yellow to brown, silky. Inlay and marquetry; 16th, 17th and late 18th centuries.

BURR WOODS: especially elm, walnut, maple, veneers chosen for their dense marbled patterns cut from malformations of trunk or root.

CEDAR: warm light brown, dry, aromatic, insect repellent. Drawer, box and blanket chest linings from late 17th century.

CHERRY: reddish, close-grained, sometimes stained to replace mahogany. Mostly turned legs of chairs and tables; 17th and 18th centuries.

CHESTNUT: horse chestnut is yellowish, soft-textured; Spanish or sweet chestnut is whiter. Both used as poor substi-tutes for satinwood in solid and veneer, inlay, carving. Late 18th century.

EBONY: black, very heavy, close-textured, brittle, smooth-surfaced. Other woods might be 'ebonised'. Cases for long-case clocks, etc. Late 17th century.

ELM: light brown, open grain. Tough but liable to warp and subject to worm. Wych elm generally used for good figure; burr elm for veneers. Country chair seats, etc. 18th century.

HAREWOOD: known in 18th century as silverwood or grey-wood. Sycamore or maple stained greenish-grey with oxide of iron. Cabinet work, late 18th century; Tunbridge ware.

HOLLY: very white, hard, slightly flecked, sometimes stained. Used in inlay, sometimes under ivory, and marquetry. Late 17th and 18th centuries.

KINGWOOD: one of the rosewood group, known in 18th century as princes wood. Dark brown, purplish, with vivid dark markings; hard and close-grained. Parquetry, late 17th century. Bandings, veneers, etc., late 18th century onward.

LABURNUM: yellowish with brown streaks. Oyster veneer; late 17th century.

LARCH: yellowish or reddish brown; subject to warping. Carcase work, where it may be mistaken for yellow deal (pine). Late 18th century.

LIGNUM VITAE: brown with black streaks. Very hard and durable. For factory processes and a little for veneer. 17th and 18th centuries.

LIME: whitish yellow, close-grained, fine for carving. Late 17th century.

MAHOGANY: Spanish, from San Domingo, dark, straight grain, little figure, wide for table tops, etc., and strong for fretwork, etc.; Cuban, easier to work, some with fine grain patterns; baywood, from Honduras, lighter in colour and weight with more open grain. Mahogany veneers were chiefly in Cuban, Jamaican and Honduras wood, mainly in second half of 18th century. Ousted from the drawing room about 1770 by satinwood, etc., but continued in great use to end of collector's period.

MAPLE: white, with veinings. Some stained, for marquetry, etc., 17th and 18th centuries. Bird's eye maple, from American sugar maple, golden, with fine figure and lustre; 19th century.

MULBERRY: golden brown with dark streaks. Tough. Veneers, etc.; early 18th century.

OAK: whitish to brown, showing silver grain when riven along radiating medullary rays. Clapboard and wainscot were imported oak, softer and whiter. Carcase work from early times and continued for country furniture and under veneer and japanning (protected from warping) throughout collector's period.

OLIVE: greenish-yellow, close-grained, hard. Parquetry and other veneers. Late 17th, 18th and early 19th centuries.

OYSTER VENEERS: usually walnut or laburnum saplings, but could be olive, kingwood, fruitwoods, cut in polygonal pieces applied as a parquetry, each piece marked with the concentric growth rings suggesting an oyster shell.

PADOUK: brown, red or crimson. Noted in copies of English furniture exported from Burma, Andaman Islands, etc. Occasionally used for English chairs; 18th century.

PARTRIDGE: brown and red with streaks like birds' feathers, close, heavy. Inlays, veneers, parquetry. Late 17th and late 18th centuries.

PEAR: pinkish-grey to yellowish-white, with fine, smooth grain. May be stained black to represent ebony as on clock-case veneers.

PINE: white to pale yellow, soft, known as yellow deal. Carcase work under veneers, etc. Red deal generally preferred from the late 18th century onwards.

ROSEWOOD: dark brown with darker brown, almost black, stripes and figurings. Some used for 17th-century inlay and 18th-century veneer, but especially popular in Regency and early Victorian days.

SATINWOOD: yellow, fine lustre. West Indian, used from the 1760s and on Regency chairs. East Indian, pale with dark streaks, used abundantly in the late 18th century.

SILVERWOOD: *see* Harewood.

SNAKEWOOD: red-brown with mottled veins and spots. Inlay, a little, in 17th century; veneers in late 18th and 19th centuries.

SYCAMORE: white, turning yellow, sometimes with ripple markings. Solid and veneers to imitate satinwood, 1760s to 1790s. *See* Harewood.

TULIP: yellowish to pinkish or rose colour, striped. Veneers: especially cross-banded borders. Late 18th century.

WALNUT: golden brown with rich markings. Solid wood used from second half of 16th century onwards; also veneers from second half of 17th century. Black walnut, deeper brown with veinings, imported from Virginia when France stopped exporting walnut in 1720.

WILLOW: dyed black to imitate ebony. Inlay and applied ornament; 17th century.

ZEBRA: light brown with wide bands of darker brown. Veneers, especially cross-banded borders. Late 18th and early 19th centuries.

Papier Mâché. Glossy, vividly colourful papier mâché furniture is now accepted as essential Victoriana, and certainly demand continued into the second half of the 19th century. The earliest of this imitation lacquer work furniture, however, was Henry Clay's 'paper ware' patented in 1772, which included expensive painted tables and screens as well as trays. Paper ware furniture of the Regency includes small tables, screens and teapoys (Fig 2). This early ware may be distinguished from the far less expensive pressed papier mâché made from 1836 by Richard Brindley; it is more perfectly smooth, without the least trace of texture, and lighter in weight and is less subject to the blemishes of wear than more brittle papier mâché. Frequently wood strengthens the work.

It is still possible to find some good quality specimens of Victorian papier mâché, such as much-curved chairs, stools, work-tables, their quality and durability depending largely on the prolonged and repeated stove dryings that set the colour of the background and the several coats of glossy varnish before the final wearisome hand polishing. Ornament on early work is in oil paints in gold borders, such as sporting subjects and patterns of flowers and butterflies. When carried out in bronze powders of various colours it dates mainly from the 1820s, being patented in 1812, and includes many Oriental motifs, sometimes worked partly in low relief.

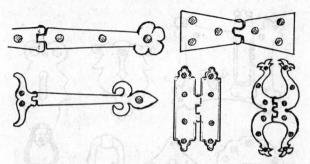

3. Metal mounts: iron. LEFT: strap hinges were used on heavy chests from the 12th century, contributing to their strength. TOP RIGHT: on early cupboards the butterfly was usual. In the 16th century, and more especially in the 17th, great use was made of H hinges, frequently improved from late in the 16th century by chamfering the edges. BOTTOM RIGHT: the most popular 17th century alternative was the cock's head in many designs, thinner towards its ends.

Fadeless black backgrounds became popular in the 1830s and prompted increased use of pictorial ornament in oil paints. Pearl ornament was patented and issued by Jennens and Bettridge in 1825. This had extremely thin and delicate shell stuck on—encrusted rather than inlaid. Thicker shell more coarsely cut was used by imitators of the patentee; still more substantial shell ornament dates from the 1840s (see also p. 73).

Metal Mounts. Mounts are important to the collector, although they are often replacements; a repaired piece of furniture may bear mounts of an earlier or a later date, and old styles have been reproduced. Mounts were of iron, attached by nails and with their holes not countersunk, until brass was developed for them late in the 17th century. Cast brass was used in England until after the mid-18th century, when gilded bronze (ormolu) appeared on some high quality

17

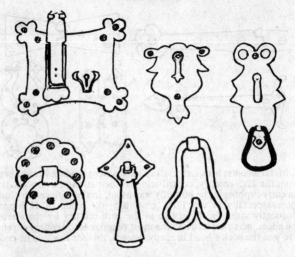

4. Metal mounts: iron. TOP: lock plates include the square style of the 14th century onwards, the flush face plate acquiring decorative corners in the 15th century and the hasp fitting between two up-rights as protection against being prised up. More ornamental key escutcheons were developed late in Elizabethan days acquiring more or less a shield outline. A 16th–17th century design often noted on cupboards consists of keyhole escutcheon with a ring handle on the same plate (right). BOTTOM: iron handles include rings, drops and heart-shaped loops.

furniture. Brass mounts from the late 1770s may be stamped with patterns in relief instead of cast, but heavy cast handles are associated with the Regency, when brass was used most conspicuously. Some revival of iron mounts is noted on early Victorian furniture in romantic mood.

HINGES. It will be noted from the accompanying sketches (Fig. 3) that early hinges on chests were frequently

18

strengthening iron straps. On cabinet furniture they tended to follow butterfly shapes, giving place to the Elizabethan butt hinges and the more familiar cock's head of the late 16th and 17th centuries—thinned towards the points. The contemporaneous H style is noted still in use on simple mahogany furniture when fashion had reverted to butt hinges but accepted the superficially handsome hinges matching corner and angle plates on japanned cabinets. Table hinges illustrated include the rule hinge used, for example, on late 17th-century folding tables, and the rule joints used with the hinging flaps of 18th-century gate tables (Fig. 21).

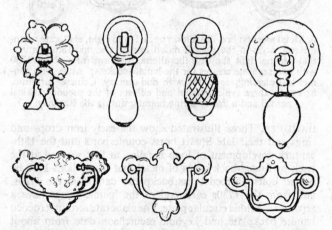

5. Metal mounts: brass handles. TOP: cast brass drop handles, those to left and right in late 17th- and early 18th-century styles; the two to the centre of early 18th-century design. BOTTOM: early 18th-century loop, thin and with tangs on loops to hold the handle; early 18th century, showing improved method with cast knobs to receive the handle ends; this design elaborated after about 1720 with the centre of the backplate cut away.

6. Metal mounts: brass handles. TOP: left and right, elaborate asymmetrical style in the rococo mood around the mid-18th century, that on the right showing the alternative form from about 1750 with two separate centres for the handle sockets; centre, with geometrical piercing associated with mid-century 'Chinese' furniture. BOTTOM: three typical circles and ellipses of the pseudo-classical revival and a lion-and-ring popular during the Regency.

HANDLES. Those illustrated show the early iron drops and rings and their late Stuart brass counterparts and the 18th-century development of loop handles, at first secured at the back by folded-back strips of metal, but from about 1700 by nutted bolts. Pierced brass backplates date from the 1720s, and from the 1730s each end of the handle might have a separate moulded circular plate. The elaborate scrolling rococo handle backplate and keyhole escutcheon date from about 1750.

The next major change dates to the 1760s and pseudo-classic design which is met by round and elliptical backplates and handles. Relief stamping, instead of casting to achieve the pattern, dates from the 1770s. Heavier handles are associated with the close of the century, including many lions' heads holding rings in their mouths, but also flowers and other motifs.

CASTORS. These were in minor use by the 1700s, of hardwood held in swivel jaws. Low leather discs were used on early Georgian work and by the 1770s brass rollers were conspicuous, attached by peg-and-plate or tapering sockets. Tall wheel castors are noted on some furniture around 1800 and broader brass castors on horizontal sockets are noted on the 19th century's heavy pillar dining tables.

METAL ORNAMENT. Metal applied purely for ornament on English furniture includes the door decoration on japanned cabinets, the brass or ormolu mounts on mid-18th-century drawing room furniture in the 'French' manner, the conventional classic motifs and lines set into the surface of Regency furniture, and the various small galleries and grilles of this period. Mid-19th-century romanticism is sometimes expressed in metal ornament.

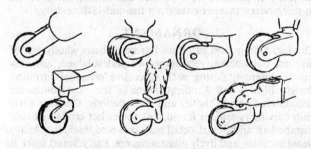

7. Castors. TOP: hard wooden wheel and axle, late 17th century; roller formed of leather discs held in brass arms, from 1740s; brass disc roller with low horizontal arms, from 1770s; wheel castor with socket to fit over leg, late 18th century. BOTTOM: brass, early 19th century: horizontal socket for pillar table; decorative socket; lion's paw socket-base.

8. Ornament. Carved cup-and-cover pillar motifs, Elizabethan and early Stuart; arch panel motif with guilloche pattern; mid-17th century applied motifs—split turnings, and mitred mouldings to produce effect of projecting panel.

It may be noted that machine-made nails date only from 1790. Screws, as introduced to some extent on furniture from the late 17th century, are unpointed and hand finished. Points in the modern manner date from the mid-19th century.

ORNAMENT

Carving. Carving on furniture has never been wholly out of fashion, but alternatively aggressive and subdued, and distinctly different, during each successive phase of furniture design. Figs. 8 and 9 indicate some of the most commonly encountered carved motifs and their periods. Genuine early chip carving is seldom found, but somewhat crude vigorous Elizabethan and Stuart detail may be noted, including heavy panel arcading and lively pilaster figures. Early Stuart work is associated with repetitive borders and much use of such detail as lunettes and guilloche patterns (Fig. 8).

Later Stuart furniture made greater use of the finer-grained walnut more suitable for delicate carving, and shows a wealth of carved crestings, on clocks, mirrors, cabinets, chair backs;

even a walnut chair's deep front stretcher may bear cherubs and crown and the chair seat frame small flower details. Flamboyant gilded and silvered work in baroque style began to appear on chest stands and console tables, continuing into the 18th century. The use of veneer checked the carver at the turn of the century, but the early 18th century is associated with much unexciting carving, particularly of shells and acanthus leaves, on cabriole leg knees.

Early Georgian mahogany offered splendid scope once again to the naturalistic carver and the period is associated with chairs and table legs showing vigorous lions' heads and paws, eagles' heads and claws, ball and claw—or dragon and pearl—feet and delicate asymmetrical bracket work in the gay rococo mood. The pierced carving on mid-century mahogany chairs is often conspicuously fine, such as the ribband back designs (Fig. 17). Lattice work is found, especially on 'Chinese' furniture of the mid-century, including chair legs and brackets (Fig. 17) and some cut-card work where the lattice is cut in relief, but not pierced right through the wood. It will be noted that pierced crestings and galleries on cabinet furniture and side tables are built up of three thicknesses of wood glued together in different ways of the grain.

From the 1760s carving returned mainly to low relief effects and one notes the paterae (Fig. 10) and the like of pseudo-classicism. Early 19th-century carving tends to be heavy and elaborately detailed, but of better quality than much that followed when machines were employed for much repetitive work, shallow and lacking the sharp clarity of undercut detail. Early Victorian work tends to be elaborately realistic, with delight in figure subjects, and considerable attempt at 16th-century imitation. Much of the amateur carving that remains on 19th-century furniture dates from an Edwardian craze.

Gesso. Another method of achieving relief effects, used notably in the late 17th century, was with a chalk and size com-

23

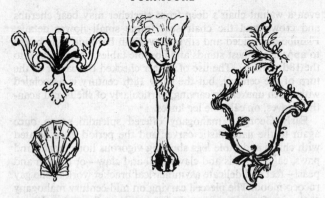

9. Ornament. Two versions of early 18th-century escallop shell motif; early Georgian leg with lion's head knee and ball-and-claw foot; mid-century asymmetrical rococo carving.

10. Ornament. Typical 'Chinese' railing and, below, late 18th century stringing; pseudo-classic patera and bell flower; honeysuckle motif, as found variously carved, painted and inlaid; 'Egyptian' pilaster of the 1800s.

position, brush shaped into arabesques and other all-over patterns covered with gold or silver leaf over suitably tinted colour and preserved by varnish. Small tables and stools may be noted. Some relief work such as details in Oriental scenes was built up in a similar way under japanning.

Paint. Flat ornament was first introduced as washes of colour. An occasional piece shows traces of this earliest opaque tempera sometimes emphasising rough carving. By the early 17th century some attempt was made to imitate Oriental lacquer and this developed into a craze in the late 17th century, continued through the early 18th century, on massive rectangular cabinet furniture intended to compete with genuine Oriental lacquer cabinets and the specimens shaped and assembled in England from Oriental lacquer boards. Some of this, executed on mild imported oak, adequately framed to avoid warping, is found in good condition. For many years long-case clocks were given japanned cases in similar mood. But poor quality japanning on soft woods, some of it amateur work, has worn badly. Much was intended only for minor rooms, such as mirror stands and frames and dressing cabinets.

On furniture of the mid-18th century, despite a resurgence of Oriental furnishing in lesser apartments, even the varnish paints that sought to suggest the glow of Oriental lacquer are largely replaced by ordinary painting.

Painted furniture of the 1770s and 1780s—chairs, tables, cabinets and so on—shows a new lightness and gaiety with pseudo-classical motifs, urns, ribbons, flower garlands, colouring the period's golden satinwood and more silvery harewood or the cheaper substitutes wholly painted over in the approved pale tones. Elaborate medallions may show figure groups in the Angelica Kauffmann style, but rarely in fact by her hand. Sometimes painted copper panels are inserted, and collectors highly prize panels not painted but made of the ceramic known as jasper ware, by Wedgwood or one of his imitators.

25

A late phase of painting is seen in chairs and settees in black painted beechwood with coloured ornament. This return to black backgrounds is a feature of the early 19th century's minor enthusiasm for Oriental lacquer, and of the early Victorian painted furniture, both wood and papier mâché. Work of the 1840s is distinguished by a restless determination to cover the ground with pattern, often naturalistic flowers including the extraordinarily popular blue convolvulus or morning glory.

Inlay. Inlay or set work constitutes a more lasting but difficult form of ornament used sparingly in the 16th century and in much of the 17th century, often as little more than chequer borders with small, shaped pieces of light wood about $\frac{1}{8}$-in. thick sunk into the solid oak or walnut. Bone and mother of pearl may be noted as well as holly and box wood, and holly was used to back and thus emphasise the colour contrast of inlaid ivory.

Inlay is suited to panelled furniture where marquetry cannot be applied. Through the later years of the 18th century it was applied to solid wood in the same limited range of patterns that appear in marquetry on veneered surfaces. On furniture of the early 19th century the inlay is more often in brass, reduced to a simple process by a patent of 1818 and applied lavishly to tables, chair backs and desk furniture. Pearl 'inlay' was an early Victorian delight, used on wood and papier mâché (q.v.).

Parquetry. Parquetry is comparable with inlay in that the result consists of patterns in contrasting pieces of wood appearing level with the surface of the furniture. But whereas inlay is set in hollows cut in the solid wood, parquetry is cut and applied to the surface of the carcase wood as a veneer that entirely hides this underlying surface. Like plain veneer it requires flat or smoothly rounded surfaces, but offers opportunities to display kinds and colours and grains of woods that lack the strength or size required for constructional work. Typically polygonal shapes are fitted together wholly covering the carcase, each shape with its own pronounced natural grain pattern contributing to a perfectly balanced whole. Slanting cuts from saplings, such as laburnum, produce the most familiar oyster parquetry (Fig. 11), the irregular concentric markings of the tree or branch growth suggesting oyster shells. Parquetry is associated with walnut veneers of Stuart days, but was revived in the last quarter of the 18th century and continued into the Regency when cube patterns were popular.

Marquetry. In this more elaborate development of veneer extremely intricate scrolling effects may be achieved by cutting patterns and backgrounds in contrasting colours of veneer to precisely matching outlines. Early work of the late 17th cen-

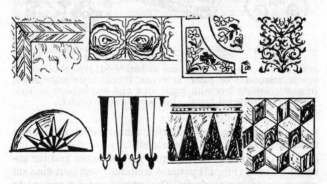

11. Ornament, flat-surfaced. TOP: feather or herringbone banding in walnut veneer to suggest panel outlines; oyster veneer; early flower marquetry; later seaweed marquetry. BOTTOM: star motif in contrasting woods; detail from late 17th-century backgammon board and adaptation of the motif to later Tunbridge ware parquetry; cube parquetry, flat surfaced, composed of different coloured woods.

12. Ornament, flat-surfaced. TOP: marquetry shell motif; satinwood fan and flower motifs, the shading lines sand-burnt and the edging lunettes in contrasting wood such as harewood; typical design for urn in marquetry or paint. BOTTOM: typical brass inlay motif, Regency; writing box with castle view and leaf borders in Tunbridge wood mosaic; two wood mosaic borders.

tury is naturalistic and colourful, much probably imported from Holland (Fig. 11). Intricate effects in simpler colouring are noted at the end of the century. Arabesques and the so-called seaweed (Fig. 11) patterns continued well into the 18th century on long-case clocks. The process was not applied to mahogany, but was revived in the pseudo-classic style of the late 18th century, ornamenting tables, etc. with classic motifs such as urns, swags and husks (Fig. 12). It was rivalled by inlay and cheaper paint. The usual late 18th-century application consists of a conventional border surrounding a panel of fine

28

veneer, or a central motif such as a stylised fan or flower shape, supplied to the cabinet maker by specialist marquetry men. Stringing in marquetry and inlay consists of chequer lines in contrasting colours to suggest twisted rope.

Marquetry at its most elaborate is found in Tunbridge Ware. Early examples, created mainly with undyed local woods, show parquetry patterns such as shaded cubes and deep van-dykes (Fig. 11), popular during the Regency. The most elaborate work is the mosaic, often showing pictorial motifs such as local views and castles, great houses, etc., with a souvenir appeal (Fig. 12), set within repetitive flower or geometrical borders. It is created in extremely small squares of differently coloured woods, the effect suggesting the squared design of early Victorian cross-stitch embroidery. The pattern was elaborately assembled by hand from strips of the differently coloured woods, but a single picture or strip of border would then be cut into a number of thin sheets, all with identical patterns, to be applied like veneer to desks, boxes, games tables and small souvenirs.

CABINET FURNITURE

Cabinets, bureaux and similar furniture went through recognisable phases. A few may be noted in oak, with projecting panels and glued-on ornament associated with Cromwellian furniture (Fig. 8), or bone or ivory inlay in the Spanish manner. These are on tall stands with corresponding turned legs and stretchers. The more frequent specimen of the late 17th century (Fig. 14) still suggests the period's chest-on-stand with a heavy straight cornice and swelling frieze (Fig. 13), often containing a drawer. The whole front consists of two vertical doors or a fall-front hinged at the bottom, opening to give access to small drawers and pigeon holes. Mirror-fronted specimens display the wide-bevelled glass in use from the late 17th century until the 1740s. The tall stand supporting this

29

13. Cabinet furniture. TOP: late 17th-century swelling frieze; early 18th-century rounded pediment; early Georgian broken pediment; detail of dentil moulding. CENTRE: pierced and carved swan-neck pediment; late 18th-century urn-topped pediment; honeysuckle detail on early 19th-century pediment; detail of arcaded or pear-drop moulding. BOTTOM: drawers. Through and lapped dovetails; drawer front, mid-17th-century oak with mitred mouldings; 1690s–1710s, walnut with reeded surround and feather banding; 1710s–1730s, with projecting drawer face; 1730s onwards, mahogany, cockbead.

structure may contain a drawer, and its legs follow the styles of its period. Alternatively a chest of drawers may replace the stand.

A bureau of the late 17th century and onwards may have a less extensive slanting fall-front with a book or curio cupboard above and drawers below. Looking glass or clear glazing may cover the upper portion. A later 18th-century specimen may have a drawer with a fall-front instead of a sloping desk lid. The changing styles of the pediment are indicated (Fig. 13), reflecting current architectural moods and the change from the smooth-surfaced veneers around the turn of the century to the heavy baroque and subsequent lighter rococo carving of early Georgian mahogany. Further changes indicated range from the 18th-century 'Chinese' and 'Gothic' novelties to the suave lines of pseudo-classicism and the heavier archaeological approach of the 1800s.

CHAIRS AND STOOLS

Chairs. The earliest chairs of interest to collectors are mainly the heavy oak specimens suggesting derivation from the chest with their solid panel and frame construction in the joiner's technique. These continued to be made in the 17th century, the alternatives including equally traditional turner-made

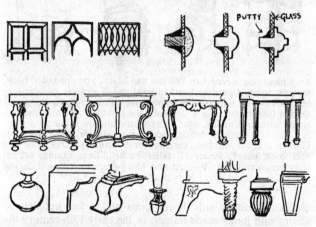

14. Cabinet furniture. TOP: changing patterns of glazing bars, early and later 18th century, and Regency brass grille; three cross-sections showing the changing outlines of the glazing bars on walnut cabinets. CENTRE: cabinet legs. Late 17th century; around 1700; early Georgian; later 18th century. BOTTOM: cabinet feet from the late 17th century ball and bracket through the 18th century to the Regency period.

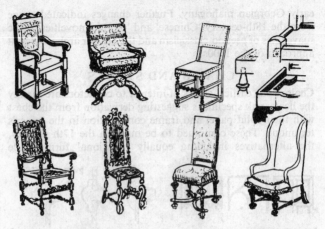

15. Chairs: early Stuart to William and Mary. TOP: panelled back, straight joiner's construction; upholstered X design; mid-century leather-covered with some ornamental turning; three chair seat details (dished seat for a cushion, the change from mortise-and-tenon joint to let-in leg, later 17th century, and the rail arrangement for the 18th-century drop-in seat with cabriole leg). BOTTOM: Charles II chair with twist turning, carved front stretcher, cane seat and back panel; James II, taller backed, finer caning, arched stretcher, scroll legs: William and Mary trumpet legs and curved stretchers; early overstuffed wing chair.

chairs assembled with dowel joints and a few upholstered chairs with joiner-made frames. In the early 17th century the joined chair back is still a solid panel framed between uprights which are continuations of the back legs, but there is a change in the top rail, often carved, which is extended across the tops of the uprights instead of tenóned between them. The front legs are turned and carved; stretchers are still low and broad, but in the mid-century, when serving less essentially as foot rests, these show more decoration, with two stretchers at each side for strength and one at the front set higher and often turned. (Figs. 15 to 20 indicate the changes in the outlines of chair backs and legs.) Arms gradually tend to slope more steeply, no longer framing panels, and single chairs are to be noted, too.

Chairs of the late 17th century show a far greater range of styles and even upholstered chairs express the tendency to break away from the solid back, whether with shorter panels of wood or upholstery open below, or with open cross rails. In work from the mid-century onwards the seat boards are frequently framed in instead of fixed over the rails (Fig. 15), the better to hold a flattish cushion; and there is much display of repetitive ball-and-bobbin turnery on uprights, legs and stretchers. Some plain, short-backed chairs have slung leather seats and backs, and there is considerable use of woollen pile known as turkey work.

Twist turning was developed in England after the Restoration (1660) on chairs of walnut and cheaper beech; the fashion lasted longer on tables. In fine work late in the period the simple barley sugar twist is developed into the more delicate open twist. In early Restoration chairs one looks for back uprights set at a considerable rake, but still each shaped in one with the corresponding back leg. The top rail is set plainly between the uprights, the arms are flat and outwardly bowed. Caning for back panel and seat was introduced at this period, coarse at first, and the flattish carving on the back rails and on a broadened front stretcher was sometimes arched late in the century.

In association with such detail one looks, in work of the 1660s, for somewhat dipped arms, often scrolled over their supports in outward curves, and also perhaps lightly carved, and for frequent use of S-scroll shaping for these supports and for the front legs instead of the twist turning, which in any

16. Chairs. TOP: early cabriole legs still with stretchers; early, with carved splat back; George I–George II armchair and wing chair. BOTTOM: mid-18th-century armchair with knurl feet; 'French' armchair; corner chair; details of three legs to show changing styles of 1690s, 1720s, 1750s.

case soon gave place to more restrained baluster turning. The swelling-knee, trumpet shapes of the century's end, and the development of diagonal stretchers in the Dutch style of William III are indicated (Fig. 15). Late 17th-century chairs show very tall, narrow backs, heavily carved and crested, placed between turned uprights. Chair seats may show a change of construction, the rails bored to rest upon the tops of the front legs instead of being tenoned into them (Fig. 15).

The change to the cabriole leg, soon free of restrictive stretchers, at the beginning of the 18th century is associated with a general delight in curves—hooped back, serpentine seat framing and shaped seat apron. The back rails, flat instead of turned, support an arched cresting and a flat panel replaces caning or upholstery between cresting and bottom rail. This may be carved and pierced or smoothly veneered, but the most notable feature is the fact that it is shaped to fit the sitter's back. The transition may be considered complete when the back side rails and cresting have become a smooth continuous curve and the arms, also unbroken curves, are set back from the front of the chair instead of being supported by continuations of the front legs.

The cabriole legs (Fig. 16) may show shell carving on the knees. Hoof feet appear occasionally. The more usual pad or club feet date from about 1705 onwards and the decorative ball-and-claw, which was an occasional 16th- and 17th-century feature, offers frequent evidence of its popularity from about 1720 to 1760. Where the seat rails have been made thinner at the top, to hold the period's newly-favoured drop-in seat, there may be triangular blocks to strengthen the joints (Fig. 15). This period is associated with much richly coloured home needlework for furniture, in tent stitch, cross stitch, Florentine stitch, etc., including covers for wholly upholstered chairs and settees.

Mahogany chairs became established in the 1740s, but walnut long remained popular. Early mahogany specimens show the period's delight in vigorous carving, the extremely hard wood acquiring wonderfully sharp detail. Figs. 16 and 17 show the typical early Georgian cupid's bow cresting and carved splat and a few of the mid-century's main variants in 'Chinese' and 'Gothic' styles and elaborate ribband carving, possible only with the immensely strong mahogany.

Legs towards the mid-century show lighter versions of the cabriole and delightful knurl and scroll toes (Fig. 16). Simpler mahogany chairs may show dainty versions of the countryman's ladder back, the legs straight but attractively wave-moulded on their outer sides (Fig. 17). Smooth-seated hall chairs may be found, and the delightful informal corner chair

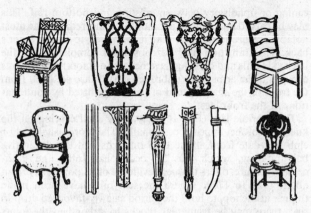

17. Chairs: mid- and late-Georgian. TOP: mid-18th-century mahogany. 'Chinese' style, fret cut with cane seat and cut-card legs; carved and pierced back in 'Gothic' style; carved and pierced back in ribband design; pierced cross rails in a good quality ladder-back. BOTTOM: 1750s–1770s. Armchair with 'French' legs, scroll feet; five examples of legs (mid-century wave-moulded and 'Chinese' card-cut, late-18th-century tapering, Regency beechwood); hall chair with saddle seat.

with a low back, short arm rests and notably decorative leg to the centre front (Fig. 16); also the horseman's chair, sometimes called a cockfighting chair, used with the 'back' as front arm-rest and convenient for those who valued their embroidered coat tails.

Chairs of the pseudo-classic years, dominated in England by Robert Adam design, date from the 1760s. These are often small, with low backs and straight, tapering, often fluted, legs; those of the 1770s onwards usually show the back wholly separate from the seat rail. Oval backs and the shields, then known as vase-shapes, are associated with the 1780s. Caning

36

is seen again, and ornament from the limited range of classic motifs (Fig. 12) in low relief carving, inlay, marquetry or paint. In the last years of the century more rectangular chairs came in, showing much use of horizontal lines, low backed, very light in weight and often with greater use of turned members.

The late 18th century is a notable period for painted chairs —mahogany picked out in gilt for the drawing room and painted beechwood with caned seats and backs for less formal use.

Chairs from the turn of the century may show scrolled-over cresting and curved cross rails, flat or in rope-twist turning. There is use of brass scroll-and-line inlay ornament, at its

18. Chairs: mid and late Georgian. TOP: 1770s–90s. Oval back, curved legs; vase-shaped (shield) back, serpentine seat, tapering legs; squarer style of the 1790s with its splat in urn outline; upholstered bergère. BOTTOM: end of 18th century. Two examples of the 1790s; two of the 1800s, one with a caned seat, the other dipped.

37

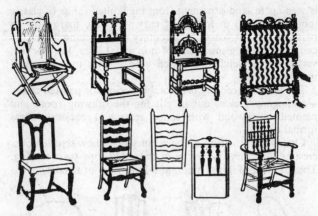

19. Regional and country chairs. TOP: 17th century. Folding, so-called Glastonbury, early; two so-called Yorkshire-Derbyshire types, the seats sunk for cushions, mid-century; back of Carolean armchair with flat splats shaped to resemble twist turning. BOTTOM: 18th century. Country modification of Queen Anne curved-back cabriole-legged single chair; country ladder back and spindle back, with rush seats and prominent front stretchers, showing also alternative back designs.

best on the period's rosewood (Fig. 12). Arms may be straight, scrolling over concave supports, or may be shaped in S-scrolls down to the dipping seat. Reeded legs sweep forward and backward in uninterrupted concave curves. Some chairs attempted to reproduce classical form as well as ornament with a general liking for scrolling curves and animal supports. Some are of bamboo and others shaped and painted to resemble it.

Less ambitious chairs for simpler homes may show plainer versions of fashion trends expressed in cheaper local woods, but a few styles may be recognised as distinctive designs that never attained to high fashion. Most popular is the Windsor (Fig. 20), probably originating in the early 18th century and still in considerable production, its members suiting the simplest style of mass production from local woods and escaping the restrictions of the joiner's mortise and tenon construction.

Typically, the saddle-shaped seat of elm or ash is the basic unit, receiving taper-tenoned back and arm verticals above and legs below. Back and arms of turned spindles may be enclosed in bent work of yew and the legs may be of turned beech. The chair parts could thus be assembled in bulk with a primitive pole lathe where the wood was felled. By the beginning of the 19th century various styles of these stick-back

20. Regional and country chairs. TOP: Windsor types. Two early comb-backs; the hoop-back at its simplest with central splat; detail of a typical late 'wheel' splat; plain hoop-back with saddle seat and stretchers to the cabriole legs. BOTTOM: ornate splat hoop-back with hooped 'crinoline' front stretcher; late so-called Lancashire Windsor with heavy turned supports; child's chair with movable footboard; so-called Suffolk version.

chairs were being made in many regions; the notably heavy, so-called Lancashire specimens have ornamental turned baluster legs and supports to the flattened arms.

Collectors consider the earliest Windsor is the comb-back (Fig. 20). This may have, for extra strengthening, spindles from the crest rail to a central tail behind the seat. More common today is the hoop-back. Sometimes the back has a central splat, either plain or, somewhat later, ornamented with piercing. Wheel splats (Fig. 20) date back to the late 18th century and later. Around the mid-18th century some Windsors were still given cabriole legs, often encumbered with stretchers which may include the in-curving cow's horn or crinoline stretcher. Later legs are turned and tapering, some in quite elaborate baluster shapes.

Other country chairs include the so-called Lancashire ladder backs, some with rush seats, introduced from the Netherlands and popular during the 18th century. Early specimens have low backs with two or three horizontal splats, but later ones may have five or more, some in decreasing width, and top rail and splats may follow a shaped outline (Fig. 19). Leg construction may show heavy ball feet on turned front legs, which have a turned stretcher between them, heavily knobbed.

Another design, perhaps introduced in the 17th century, but too narrowly credited to Derbyshire and Yorkshire, has an open back, usually with two carved, arching crescent-shaped rails and a sunk wooden seat (Fig. 19). Legs and front stretcher are turned. The Yorkshire spindle-back chair typically has two rows of turned spindles in the back; less usually, one, with three rows on armchairs, all decoratively turned (Fig. 19). There may be a shell carved in the cresting rail, and this rail appears wider and deeper in late specimens. The Norfolk and Suffolk chairs, with saddle seats, have elaborate backs of spindles and cross rails, sometimes including a row of small balls (Fig. 20).

Stools. An Elizabethan joiner-made stool may have plainly turned legs left square for the tenon-and-mortise joints (Fig. 21) of the seat rail and stretchers, and splayed forward and backward for greater steadiness. The top is plain, but the seat rail may be carved or at least show a shaped outline. Shallow arcaded patterns in the carving here may distinguish early 17th-century stools, which may have ball feet on turned legs, either plain or in ball or baluster outline. Similar stools have been noted in beechwood painted and gilded beneath upholstered seats.

Post-Restoration stools of quality are usually caned or upholstered, the framework of softwood, gilded or japanned, or of solid walnut. The legs, feet and stretchers follow the sequence observed in chairs (Figs. 15 to 18), including the ornamental carved stretchers across front and back, which continued until the last years of the 17th century. Early 18th-century stools introducing cabriole legs and scrolled feet continued with stretchers, plainly turned, across the ends and centrally linked.

Specimens dating from about 1710 may show the legs carried up to form part of the seat rail, and these more solid legs, often hipped at the corners of the frame, require no stretchers. Knee carving may be found, such as shells and foliage or the more lively lion masks of early Georgian days. Upholstered drop-in seats may be supported by triangular blocks of wood between seat rails and legs. Some upholstered stools in gilded gesso were patterned in low relief, but more from the first half of the 18th century are in walnut. Early Georgian mahogany stools may be carved on the knee and foot with the period's lion and eagle motifs, and the seat rails may be carved to match or more boldly carved with masks.

Some mid-Georgian stools were concave seated for the dining room or in so-called French style for the drawing room, with lightly curving legs on scroll or knurl feet (Fig. 16). Brief mid-century fashions are noted in straight legs in the 'Gothic' cluster-column style or the 'Chinese' square or L-shaped leg carved or fret-cut to match the seat rail and the corner brackets linking rails and legs (Fig. 17). Later 18th-century stools include double stools with six legs, plainly tapering, and window stools curving upwards at the ends, sometimes caned instead of upholstered and bearing the period's typical ornament such as husks and paterae (Fig. 10). Satinwood stools may be found as well as gold-touched mahogany and painted softwood.

Early 19th-century specimens show the period's outward curving legs, or the bamboo style with X stretchers or the never-outmoded cabriole. Heavy pseudo-classical styles include scroll-ended stools on X frames and the fluted tapering 'Greek' leg (Fig. 2). Some rosewood is noted, but more softwood. Bronzing dates from 1818 onwards.

CHESTS

At their simplest for storage and travelling these include rough boarded boxes, their sides horizontal planks, often elm, hammered on to vertical end-pieces, and frequently bound or cornered with iron. Simple construction is no proof of age. From as early as the 15th century the corner uprights—stiles—might be grooved to receive tongued horizontal side planks. Some simply-constructed chests are close-nailed in cow-hide or rain-resistant cloth woven with horsehair. Cloth-covered chests studded with rosettes of brass may date from as late as the 19th century. The rounded top, least harmed by rain, is associated with the travelling trunk, but noted too in some 18th-century blanket chests.

The joiner's chest was unsuited for close covering, being constructed with a framework of rails and stiles, mortise-and-tenon jointed (Fig. 21) around loose panels that could thus respond to atmospheric changes without damage. Heavy panel effects might be achieved in the 17th century merely with glued-on ornament (Fig. 8). By then the chest was often fitted with a small tray or till near the lid; a frequent development from about the mid-century was the inclusion of a drawer below the main chest. Chests of this period may be raised on short legs—frequently extensions of the end framing. Some rest on footed stands.

Chests of 18th century date may be found in early mahogany. Some richly japanned round-topped blanket chests, too, date to the early 18th century, ranging from genuine Oriental lacquer assembled in England to English amateur japanning work. Occasional examples remain, too, of 18th-century gilded gesso chests of highly ornamental outline. It must be remembered, however, that the great majority of chests found today are of 19th and 20th century origin.

Ornament ranges through the sequence of styles described on pages 22 to 29—arcaded Gothic, rich Elizabethan and flatly repetitive early Stuart carving, mid-17th-century applied mouldings, late Stuart veneers, simple marquetry and japanning, and straightforward handling of Georgian mahogany, all the styles overlapping and occasionally becoming confused with 19th-century attempts to reproduce earlier carved and panelled work.

Small chests of the 1750s onwards are often known as Welsh Bible boxes. Such a box has two small drawers beneath the chest portion and is usually made of oak or elm, sometimes inlaid with holly. This is comparable with the rare 16th- and 17th-century writing box, plain or carved on all sides, used on a table, its lid only slightly sloping at first when it was hinged at the top. The later 17th- and 18th-century designs are steeper and hinged at the bottom, opening out for writing with access to small drawers and pigeon holes or more elaborate fittings.

The most elaborate compendiums date to the 19th century,

fitted for writing, art and needlework. Some with heavy metal mounts were intended to suggest medieval workmanship. Many are splendid little pieces of cabinet-making in exotic woods finely mounted. Specimens are to be found too in straw-work, papier mâché and the elaborate marquetries known as cube and mosaic Tunbridge Ware (Fig. 12).

The writing box developed into the bureau, a favourite collector's piece that has many modern counterparts. The late 17th-century gate-legged stand (Fig. 22) to receive the fall-front might be replaced in the 1680s by a chest of drawers. Drawer mouldings are shown in Fig. 13. An early specimen may have a projecting plinth to balance the projecting base of the writing box section and stands on bun feet. The moulding between desk and drawers and the interior well are omitted on early Georgian bureaux and the flap opens onto oak bearers.

CHESTS OF DRAWERS

In the 17th-century work one notes a tendency to hide the drawers behind wide doors. Framework follows the construction methods developed for oak furniture with loose panels held in grooved frames mortise-and-tenon jointed (Fig. 21). The drawer sides fit together with the early 'through' dove-tailing (Fig. 13) and are grooved to fit fillets of wood projecting from the sides of the chest. Handles are usually knobs, turned or carved. By the third quarter of the 17th century chests of drawers in the accepted design were in production, oak gradually being usurped by walnut, the drawers fitted with runners and brass acorn and pear handles (Fig. 5), and feet reduced to conventional brackets (Fig. 14). A typical chest of drawers of the century's end is straight-fronted, five-drawered and about forty inches high. Wide concave moulding may edge the top and appear inverted around the plinth.

The plinth is omitted in the more sweeping styles after about

1760. Panel construction has given place to smooth surfaces of veneer and the handles are drop loops, their design being made stronger in about 1700 (Fig. 5). Subsequent styles in chests of drawers may be found down to the present day, the chief changes being in the surface ornament (Fig. 11), handles (Fig. 6), feet (Fig. 14) and treatment of drawer edges (Fig. 13).

This piece of furniture, too, may be mounted on a stand (Fig. 14) and, in the early 18th century, upon a second chest of drawers and treated architecturally with pediment and deeply concave or convex moulding (Fig. 13). Mahogany chests of drawers were straight-fronted until the 1760s, then sometimes serpentine and later often bowed. Drawing room commodes may have their drawer fronts shaped into swelling bombé silhouette or covered by doors in the mid-18th-century style. The change to modern construction of the drawer base dates to about 1770, when a central bearer was introduced to hold up half-width panels.

Canted corners, often fluted, are an early Georgian feature. These might be given architectural capitals in the mid-18th century. At the end of the century there was a liking for reeded quarter-columns to flank the drawers, above turned feet.

CORNER CUPBOARDS

Complete movable cupboards, as distinct from built-in corner buffets, date mainly from the early 18th century onwards. Some are two-tiered on bracket feet and retain much of the architectural style of the buffet, often with hooded cornice, or gabled or swan-neck pediment. Early wide-bevelled mirrors on the front gave place to glazing of the single or double doors flanked by broad chamfers often ornamented with fluted pilasters. (Fig. 14 shows the development from heavy glazing bars to the lighter treatment developed with mahogany.) In late 18th-century specimens, veneers and panels of marquetry frequently replace the glass and as a result the interior loses such details as the half-dome top and waved shelf outlines. There may be drawers in the lower section. A few were made bow-fronted, but by about 1810 the demand for such two-tiered cupboards was over.

Corner cupboards hanging on nails through holes in their back boards had developed meanwhile into delightful pieces of furniture now inevitably widely imitated. These date from the late 17th century onwards, at first often japanned or with the front in walnut, the doors showing the characteristic H hinges long associated with provincial work (Fig. 3), and with lines of herringboning (Fig. 11) to suggest panel outlines in the smooth veneer. At the beginning of the 18th century the fashion for arching outlines led to the introduction of hooded cornice and door or doors headed in particularly delightful cupid's bow outline. Sometimes a sheet of mirror glass follows the arching outline of the door. Many of the most attractive are in early Georgian mahogany, imitated in cheaper native woods.

The mid-18th-century cupboard is a charming piece, often with elaborate cresting in fretted design above the straight cornice or a swan-neck pediment, and with its doors divided into small panes of clear glass by a pattern of delicate mouldings (Fig. 14). The great majority of antique corner cupboards, however, date to the second half of the 18th century. These are comparatively plain with panelled double doors and unambitious cornice mouldings, such as peardrop arcading (Fig. 13). Some are of oak with bandings of more fashionable mahogany. One notes somewhat countrified handling of inlaid shelf motifs and checker border stringing (Fig. 10). Some of the most effective are plainly veneered in mahogany, but given the distinction of a bow-fronted outline. When double doors are used the central join may be masked by a length of plain moulding, often semicircular; reeding was more usual at the end of the 18th century and in work of the Regency years this detail may be brass.

TABLES

Dining tables are difficult to date because the Elizabethan refectory type have never lost their appeal. Designs of the 16th century show the boards cross-framed at the ends and dowelled to the underframing—a wide frieze tenoned into the square tops of the legs. Early stretchers may be T-shaped in section. Ornamental carving and inlay have been described (*see* pp. 22 to 29). Many late 16th-century dining tables are of the more elaborate design with two extensions on slanting bearers concealed under the central portion of the top.

Gate-leg tables. Towards the middle of the 17th century this design for dining tended to give place to the gate-leg table (Fig. 22). This has a rectangular frame on four legs as the rigid centre and has gate-legs to let into this, pivoting on the main framing, to support hinged table flaps. The rule joint for the flat edge was a late 17th-century introduction (Fig. 21), when screws took the place of nails to attach the rough iron hinges. These may be distinguished from later replacements. In the

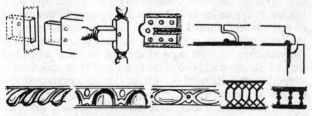

21. Tables: joints and rim ornament. TOP: mortise and tenon joint to be secured with wooden pins: section of turned table leg left square for mortise and tenon joint with stretcher; rule hinge for folding-over table top; two views of rule joint with table top open and closed. BOTTOM: rim ornament. Gadroon moulding; two specimens of egg-and-tongue or egg-and-dart moulding; fret-cut gallery; gallery composed of small turned spindles.

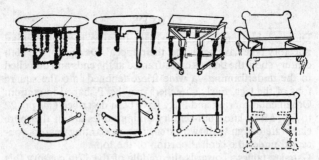

22. Folding tables. TOP: gate-leg; gate; early card; card with a concertina movement. BOTTOM: diagrams of tables above showing the fixed legs and framing dark and moving legs light.

18th century the top was screwed instead of fixed with wooden dowel pins.

Other small gate-leg tables may be noted with the flap folding back over the rigid portion, and this design was developed in the early 18th-century card table. The basic change from gate-leg table to gate table resulted from the use of cabriole legs without stretchers. Thus the whole of one of the table's four legs could swing out, complete with part of the underframing, and support the flap. In some tables half the underframing and two of the four legs may be pulled out to support the top. Heavier, well-carved cabriole legs and rounded corners to the underframing suggest early Georgian work.

For dining, from before the mid-18th century, the four-legged gate table was used. This has two hinged legs diagonally opposite each other, each supporting a flap which is a single piece of mahogany. A semi-circular table may be added at each end if required.

Various extending tables remain from the late 18th century, most frequently with underframing that could be pulled out for loose leaves to be inserted. By the early 19th century there was a liking for round tables again, with pillar and claw construction, but with four feet rather than three.

Pier tables, etc. Pier or side tables were never more handsome than at the beginning of the 18th century; console tables, equally decorative, are designed for attaching at the top to the wall, the legs—often elaborate pieces of full relief carving—being shaped inwards like brackets. Tops may be of gilded gesso composition or marble or its imitations. Flamboyant rococo ornament gave place to pseudo-classic grace in the 1760s.

Early Georgian occasional tables and heavier sidetables are more accommodating. They are noted in superb quality in mahogany, some with trellis rim ornament in the mid-18th century; others were painted. Satinwood and painted imitations date from late in the 18th century onwards with pseudo-classic ornament (Fig. 9). Even card tables follow the classic mood, shaped as semi-circles opening to the full circle for play. The Pembroke table dates from the 1760s onwards and more

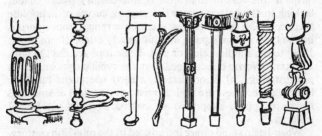

23. Legs. Early 17th century with T-shaped low stretcher; trumpet of about 1700; modified cabriole, about 1715; 'French' with gadroon ornament, about 1760; cluster column, about 1760; square tapering, about 1775; heavy turned tapering about 1790s (two); specimens of feet—pad or club, Spanish, scroll, gutta.

especially to the end of the century, the extensions at the ends consisting of two small rounded flaps resting on fly brackets. So-called Sheraton sofa tables often have legs in the cheval style (Fig. 1) also associated with firescreens and Regency mirrors.

PILLAR AND CLAW FURNITURE

The pillar and claw or tripod construction may be found in tables, often, from the 1740s, with the tops hinged to stand vertically and, from the 1750s, removable. Other claw furniture includes firescreens (Fig. 25) and the stands for wash-basins, kettles, candles, urns. The changes in general outline are indicated opposite from the late 17th to the early 19th century, in walnut, japanned woods and especially in sharply carved mahogany.

The latter lent itself to many decorative variants of the swelling pillar and ball-and-claw foot, and it is easy to differentiate a high quality specimen from the more mediocre work turned out in great quantity throughout the second half of the 18th century and on into Victorian days. There is a springy 'grip' to the feet of high quality mid-century pieces that is lacking in the flatter, somewhat sagging curves of many late specimens. Carving of the feet themselves ranges from vigorous ball-and-claw, lion's paw, dolphin head designs (from about 1750) to the simplest club or pad. Table tops around the mid-18th century may be scalloped or in the cyma curves known as piecrust (Fig. 24), hand-shaped in early specimens but later lathe-shaped. These are slightly raised at the edge; other raised rims are spindle-supported or consist of hand-cut fretted galleries.

Wash-basin stands were introduced in the mid-18th century, but soon lost the attractive tall pillar and arching tripod foot.

Pillar and claw firescreens appeared in walnut early in the 18th century, continuing until the 1760s, long after mahogany had become more fashionable. The turned, vase-shaped unit supported on a tripod foot resembles the table pillar and claw in its changing styles, and is topped by a thin pole supporting the firescreen panel. Some more elaborately shaped in attractive openwork scrolls break away from the constructional restrictions imposed upon the turner. The rectangular screen itself is frequently a piece of embroidery in a moulded, carved or plain narrow frame. Smaller screens with oval, square, or vase-shaped (shield) panels are noted in pseudo-classic designs from the 1760s, in mahogany or satinwood, or in japanned,

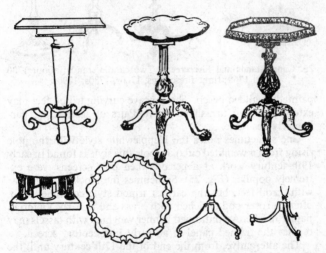

24. Pillar and claw or tripod furniture. TOP: early table, late 17th century; mid-18th century, with scalloped top and ball and claw feet; cabinet-maker's version with pierced carved gallery, pierced stem, heavily carved scrolling 'claws'. BOTTOM: 'bird-cage' under table top with removable central flat 'pin' that allows the top to lift off; top with piecrust rim; two late 18th-century versions of the claw.

51

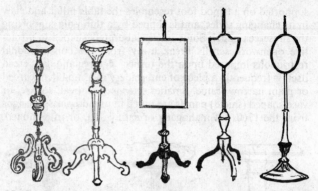

25. Candlestands and Firescreens. Two candle stands, about 1700 and 1760; three firescreens, 1760s, 1780s, 1790s.

painted or gilded beech. The concave curving tripod feet may extend from an urn-shaped unit. Pairs of screens are particularly desirable.

One sometimes notes the Hepplewhite style with the pole rising from a weighted circular foot; this style is found in early 19th-century work at a period when pole screens were extremely popular (Fig. 25). Sometimes the block is triangular with scroll feet, but the earliest tripod style continued, too, often in rosewood enriched with brass and in early Victorian papier mâché. An unframed banner weighted with tassels may replace the framed panel of an early 19th-century screen.

The alternative, from the end of the 17th century until the end of the collector's period, was the ornate cheval screen. The treatment of the framing indicates the date—provided the collector appreciates the early Victorian popularity of walnut as well as rosewood and mahogany, of heavy frames, and the closely worked tent stitch embroidery that was only gradually ousted towards the mid-century by heavier cross stitch.

FURNITURE SUMMARY

French monarchy	English monarchy	Period's usual name	Characteristics of English Furniture
Henri IV 1584–1610	Elizabeth 1558–1603	Late Tudor or Elizabethan	Oak the most important wood, carved and painted and inlaid. Notable beds, tables, buffets with carved bulbous turnings. Heavily carved arcaded panels and caryatid pilasters. Iron mounts. Few upholstered X chairs.
Louis XIII 1610–43	James I 1603–25 Charles I 1625–49	Early Stuart, sometimes Jacobean	Oak still most important, though greater development of solid walnut. Carving more shallow and repetitive; inlay. More and lighter chairs, some upholstered; gate-leg tables.
Louis XIV 1643–1715	Commonwealth 1649–53 Protectorate 1653–60	Cromwellian, but many features continued long after 1660	Some chairs with leather-slung backs and seats. Much use of repetitive ball and bobbin turning on simple, squarish chairs. Heavily projecting panels on chest furniture, including glued-on mitred mouldings and bosses. More use of drawers.
	Charles II 1660–85 James II 1685–89	sometimes called Carolean	Development of walnut, carved and veneered. Marquetry still mostly imported. Development of occasional furniture and of mirrors; caning; long case clocks. Brass mounts.
	William III 1689–1702 and Mary 1689–94	} Late Stuart	Veneers, marquetry, japanning, gesso. Caning on chairs and day-beds becoming finer. More overstuffed chairs and development of home embroideries for them as well as more bed hangings. Early bureaux; tables with fold-over tops, with swelling knees and straight tapering legs.
	Anne 1702–14		Continuation of above. Development of more curved effects, on cabinet furniture pediments, mirrors, chair backs. Great use of cabriole legs. Delight in card tables, cabinets, console tables, chests of drawers.
Regency (French) 1715–23 Louis XV 1715–74	George I 1714–27 George II 1727–60	Early Georgian	Palladian revival among the wealthy associated with William Kent. Development of vigorous carving. Much straight-topped chamfered cabinet furniture. Gradual change of interest from walnut to mahogany, used in the solid. From the 1730s onwards development of rococo mood

FURNITURE SUMMARY—continued

French monarchy	English monarchy	Period's usual name	Characteristics of English Furniture
Louis XVI 1774–92	George III 1760–1820	Mid-Georgian usually taken to cover the years 1750 to about 1790	expressed in flowing lines, asymmetrical scrolls in mounts, brackets, mirror frames. Mid-century 'Chinese' and 'Gothic' styles in chairs, bookcases, etc. Chippendale's *Director* first published in 1754.

Mahogany in rich veneers. Development of pseudo-classicism sponsored by Robert Adam. Sideboards introduced. Much use of light woods and painted ornament. Inlay and marquetry borders and classic motifs. |
		'Adam' or pseudo-classic period from about 1760	Widespread use of pillar-and-claw furniture, and shapely cabinet furniture often serpentine fronted; tapering legs to tables and chairs. Hepplewhite's name is associated with styles of the 1780s including oval and shield-back chairs. Sheraton's name is associated with somewhat squarer chairs of the 1790s. Legs still mainly straight and tapering, but round in section (turned) rather than square (thermed).
Republic 1793–94 Directorate 1794–99 Empire 1799–1815	Regency 1811–20	Regency style 1795–1830s	Archeological classicism. Egyptian, Roman and Greco-Roman ornament and attempts at actual furniture. Much brass ornament, such as inlay. Pleasant small furniture such as sofas, sofa tables. Some Oriental interest.
	George IV 1820–30 William IV 1830–37	Late Georgian	Regency styles merging into heavy-handed revival of rococo.
Louis XVIII 1815–23	Victoria 1837–1901	Early Victorian usually to 1860 including period of Great Exhibition 1851	Revivals of many styles including 'Gothic' and 'Elizabethan'. Heavy furniture including disproportionately long-backed, short-legged chairs. Round pillar tables. Much elaborate story-telling carving, but much carved ornament shaped by machine. Papier mâché furniture. Ornament included carving, shell-encrustation, painted japanning. Silk, bead and wool embroideries.

54

CHAPTER TWO

Long Case Clocks

Long case or grandfather clocks were made in England from the 1660s. In such a summary it is impossible to detail the changes in clock mechanism, but unless the clock itself is a replacement it is generally possible to date a specimen with some precision from details of case and face, their design, materials, and treatment. Slender and graceful, about six or seven feet in height, the early case was evolved as a grouping of three units: a hood, protecting the movement and dial; a long, narrow trunk for the passage of the weights and the swing of the pendulum; a squarish plinth into which the weights descended.

Early clock cases were made from ebony or ebonized pine, woods used until early in the 18th century. Handsomely figured veneers of walnut, yew, olive, laburnum, sycamore and fruit woods covering carcases of oak date from the 1680s onwards; colourful veneer wood marquetries were introduced from the Continent in the 1680s and might decorate doors and plinths in naturalistic flower designs framed in round-ended panels or in the more sophisticated arabesques or seaweed patterns. These continued on clock cases until the 1720s.

The quieter richness of walnut veneers continued fashionable only until the 1730s, for the lofty rooms of early Georgian splendour were unsuited to long case clocks. When such clocks were chosen it was for more homely apartments, gay with lacquer or its European imitation known as japanning. A conspicuous minor vogue of the early 18th century—and revived from time to time—was the case vividly japanned, its background of black, red, green, blue, yellow or cream being

26. Long case clocks. (1) 1670s–80s. Ebonised wood; gabled pediment; plain columns. (2) 1680s–90s. Walnut veneer or simple marquetry; carved cresting; twist-turn columns; body window to observe pendulum bob (bob glass). (3) 1700s–10s. Walnut veneer; seaweed marquetry or possibly lacquer; very tall pediment, slightly domed. (4) 1720s–30s. Walnut veneer or laquer; broken pediment above arched dial; dial window opening independent of side columns; no body window.

decorated in the oriental manner, including patterns in relief. This work is seldom found in good condition, but may be grouped into three distinct styles in and out of fashion for a century from the 1690s, all dates being only approximate:

1. Dutch style, 1695–1715, easily recognised by their solitary designs;

2. Oriental importations, 1715–45, covered with highly raised ornament;

3. English, 1720s–90s, but more especially 1730–60, in designs copying the oriental but much flatter.

Mahogany was most widely used for long case clocks during the second half of the 18th century and is associated with the somewhat broad, ponderous clocks ornamented with carving or applied frets and sometimes known as 'provincial Chippendale'. Some fine examples are associated with north country clock makers, including late 18th-century inlay ornament in satinwood or ivory. Oak was a favourite with provincial clock case makers, but is seldom found in association with fine quality movements.

An act of parliament in 1698 required every clock dial to be signed with the maker's 'Name and Place of Abode or Freedom'. At first the name appeared along the base of the dial plate below the hour circle. By 1700 it was introduced on either side of the numeral VI or engraved immediately below the centre of the dial, and from about 1720 often on a domed name plate in or below the arch. On an enamelled or painted dial it appeared below the numeral XII. *Watchmakers and Clockmakers of the World* by G. H. Baillie (1951, 27s. 6d.) lists 35,000 names with dates and localities.

Sheraton, writing in 1803, recorded that long case clocks were then 'almost obsolete in fashionable London', but they continued to be made until early Victorian days by country craftsmen in a hotch potch of Georgian designs.

CASES

The hood rested upon a seat board to which the mechanism was secured. It was removable to give access to the movement. At first it could be lifted upward: after about 1700 the majority could be drawn forward but by then hood doors had been introduced permitting quick access to hands and winding holes. The hood originally was plain, usually with a square top, but sometimes gabled in the Dutch manner. From the

57

27. Long case clocks. (1) 1760s–80s and later. Mahogany veneer; heavy scrolled and carved pediment; brass-capped pillars flanking dial and body doors; carved base with clipped-corner panel on small bracket feet; so-called Lancashire type. (2) 1770s–90s and later. Mahogany veneer; hollow dome pediment; body door matching dial outline; base panel. (3) 1780s–90s and later. Mahogany veneer with marquetry panels and bands of stringing instead of raised panel on base; cluster columns flanking 'Gothic' arched body door; small bracket feet, popular in North. (4) 1800s and later. Mahogany veneer; serpentine pediment and top to body door; no columns; heavy base with projecting panel.

mid-1680s it might be brought into harmony with other furniture by a narrow cresting elaborately carved. By the mid-1690s the hood was becoming taller, frequently topped by three finials, usually urns, the centre one placed higher than the others. This fashion persisted in the domed or bell-top hood enriched with gilded spire finials. A conspicuous change in hood design dates to about 1720 when the dial, previously square, was given an arched top, low at first, and the whole hood was made taller and gradually assumed a more rounded outline in harmony. For tall rooms the hood was elaborately tiered. The broken pediment hood, usually with a central ornament between the scrolls, was fashionable throughout the third quarter of the 18th century, and offered considerable scope for carving: an extremely popular alternative to the end of the century was the solid pediment with concave shaping to its slanting sides.

The columns that ornamented hood corners were usually twist-turned until about 1700, although plain columns with turned caps and bases had been used from the early 1680s. Later columns were usually in doric or corinthian shape with brass caps and bases.

The door in the body or trunk of the case was square headed until about 1720, and edged with small half-round moulding. A green bottle-glass bull's eye window showed the pendulum movement. Until about 1705 the moulding at the top of the trunk might differ from that at its base: thereafter both mouldings were usually concave. The slender proportions of the long case clock were abandoned from about 1720 in favour of a wider and shorter trunk and a shorter plinth. The bull's eye was omitted from the door which was given a break arch top harmonizing with the arched dial. The plinth was decorated with a raised panel. The edges of the trunk might be splayed and their surface either reeded or decorated with fret-cut ornaments. Columns, capped and based in brass, were sometimes introduced late in the century.

London-made long case clocks of the late 18th century were of fine workmanship, in beautiful veneers of curl mahogany, or even of exotic woods such as satinwood, with various marquetry devices in so-called Hepplewhite or Sheraton style.

Towards 1800, however, the majority of these clocks were of provincial manufacture, the grandeur of heavy mahogany, carved or inlaid with stringing, being contrasted with many extremely simple clock cases in oak and mahogany. When these have brass dials instead of the more usual white enamel there may be a slight risk of ante-dating, for often the dial itself is square, and the hood has a gabled pediment resting on pedestal columns. But the 12-inch dial and mahogany casing quickly dispel the illusion. The serpentine arched top to the hood is a feature of this period, continuing well into the 19th century, as an alternative to square or circular shaping.

DIALS

Dials form a special study. Until the 1770s and even later they were cut from latten plates (*see* p. 249), not cast and planished as so frequently stated. Until about 1705 they were square, the usual size being 10 inches square, although examples as small as $7\frac{1}{2}$ inches and as large as 11 inches are recorded. During the early years of the 18th century they became standardised at 12 inches. In about 1720 the arched dial was introduced, low at first, early specimens often showing the maker's name here. Animated pictures appeared in the space by about 1730, such as a moon on a bed of clouds with the mechanism timed to show the phases of the real moon. From the 1740s small moving figures were popular, such as ships rocking up and down in rhythm with the swing of the long pendulum, on blue seas of enamels. Alternatively, a seconds dial and hand might be placed in the arch, or a 'strike or silent' hand. A calendar automatically showing the day of the month through a small square aperture cut above the VI appeared in the dial in the 1690s and continued throughout the period of long case clocks.

Latten dials in long case clocks, almost from the beginning, were matted within the hour ring, the matt-textured surface showing up the hands. This decoration is usually described as pinched, but this is incorrect. To avoid marking the matted surface by careless insertion of the winding key, the winding holes were finished with bright, grooved rings after about 1690. From the mid-1680s a heraldic rose might be engraved in the centre of the dial, and the hours engraved upon a detach-

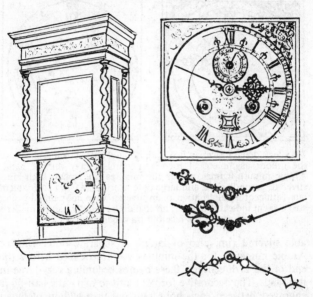

28. Long case clocks. LEFT: early style of lift-off hood. TOP RIGHT: early square dial, about 1690s. Simple cherub-head spandrels; heavy hour hand; bright rings round winding holes; half-hour and quarter-hour divisions marked between Roman numerals; minutes in Arabic numerals around the outer ring; seconds dial and date aperture as well as surface ornament on the matted area inside the hour rings. BOTTOM RIGHT: specimen hour and minute hands. Late 17th century; early Georgian; late 18th century.

61

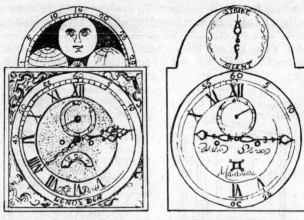

29. Clock dials. LEFT: arched dial, about 1760s showing phases of the moon; asymmetrical rococo spandrels; wavy minute hand; Arabic minute figures outside the minutes ring; plain hour ring, silvered; seconds hand and large date aperture. RIGHT: a frequent late-18th-century alternative, plain silvered when not painted white; strike-silent indicator in arch; no spandrels; spindly hands; maker's name across the face but no ornamental detail.

able silvered rim, also of latten. A separate outer ring of Arabic numerals for the minutes was introduced before the end of the 17th century, these figures becoming very large in the 1730s. The decorative formal motif to mark the half-hour engraved between each hour numeral was seldom included after the 1740s and even the quarter-hour divisions were omitted.

Rich engraving on the latten dial within the silvered hour ring became briefly fashionable early in the 18th century, but this was found confusing on a dial already enriched by the wide winding rings, date aperture, seconds dial and increas-ingly ornamental hour and minute hands. By the 1750s there was considerable use of a dial consisting of a single latten plate without a separate hour ring, but the change was not complete until the 1770s. Some were silvered. Cast brass dial plates were introduced in the mid-1770s, always without hour rings.

By then, however, the most familiar enamelled copper plate dial was in use, introduced in the 1740s. Early examples had a creamy hue, but from the 1780s the enamel was pure white. Painted iron and wood were used from the 1790s during a period of copper shortage.

SPANDRELS

The dial of costly latten was ornamented on the four corners, outside the hour circle, with spandrels cast in princes metal and fixed with small screws or rivets. The period of a dial may be confirmed by the spandrel design. On some 17th-century dials the spandrels were engraved on the plate itself, a feature still noted on some Georgian clocks. The earliest cast spandrels were small and carefully chased. Until about 1700 the design was commonly a cherub's head with wings, gradually elaborated, or replaced by a pair of amorini supporting a crown among elaborations of scroll work. In the 1750s the crown might be accompanied by crossed sceptres. By then, however, the various masks and scrolls of early Georgian work had developed into irregular rococo designs of little meaning. An urn of flowers was often included in the design from about 1740.

Brass castings processed to appear richly golden were used from about 1770 (*see* p. 250). On costly clocks the spandrels continued in princes metal and might be engraved after chasing. The number of patterns was limited—no more than about sixty between 1690 and 1790, suggesting that they were the specialist work of casters in princes metal. The corners of painted dials were usually enriched with decorative motifs in full colours.

HANDS

Until about 1680 the long case clock movement operated one hand only, yet this allowed accurate reading of the minutes before and after the hour indicated. When minute hands were introduced, one-hand clocks continued to be made and were common throughout the 18th century, the simple movement being cheaper than one with a minute hand. Hour hands during the 1680s and 1690s were generally of the broad loop pattern. Later they were of the spade-headed type, pierced and carved by cut-steel workers. Examples cut from latten are known. From about 1730 length was increased.

The minute hand was comparatively simple in design, longer than the hour hand so that it reached precisely to the minute divisions on the hour ring. The early S-scrolls only slightly resembled the hour hand elaborations but by the mid-18th century the long straight finger tended to be replaced by elongated versions of the hour hand patterns, both appearing less solidly substantial than formerly. After about 1790 clock hands were stamped from thin steel in designs necessarily conventional, plain and solid.

The lead weights in fine clocks were cased in latten or brass and might weigh as much as 28 lb. A bag of sand was kept in the bottom of the plinth as a precaution against damage if the gut line broke.

CHAPTER THREE

Barometers

Mural barometers for domestic use were English inventions of the early 1660s, four types being evolved: the stick, cistern or Torricellian; the dial and siphon; the diagonal; the portable. The name 'barometer' was first used in 1665 when the *Philosophical Transactions* recorded that 'a Barometer or Baroscope was first made publick by the Noble Searcher of Nature, Mr. Boyle.'

Stick barometer. This type was evolved by Sir Samuel Morland, Master of Mechanics to Charles II. A 34-inch glass tube, emptied of air, was placed with its open end immersed in a small cistern of mercury. Atmospheric pressure upon the mercury forced it part of the way up the airless tube so that register plates alongside indicated the intensity of the pressure and hence acted as a considerable guide to weather conditions. This tube and cistern were fitted into a wooden frame. John Smith in 1688 recommended 'the choicest such as Ebony, Walnut or Olive-Wood. The Shape may vary, but the Size must always be such that the Length may admit a Glass Tube of at least three Foot and its Breadth sufficient to affix thereon the Register Plates. In the middle is a half round Channel sufficiently deep to secure the Tube from being Broken by Accident. Near the Bottom of the Frame is Affixed the Cistern-Box and cover as may admit a Glass Cistern of about Three Inches Diameter and One Inch in Height. Lastly upon the upper part of the Frame are fixed two Register Plates.'

Narrow stick barometers, about 40 inches overall, were in production until mid-Victorian days. Their frames were the work of cabinet makers specialising in clock cases. Flat,

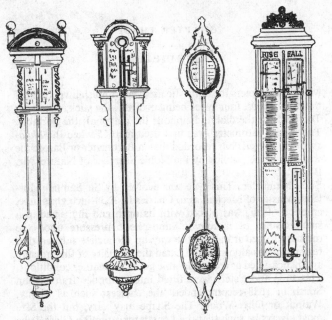

30. Stick or cistern barometers. (1) Veneered in burr walnut with swash-turned pillars, about 1700. (2) Mahogany, of George II's reign. (3) With the oval face and patera cistern-cover of the 1770s–80s. (4) **Admiral Fitzroy's barometer,** including two columns of his 'remarks' on weather interpretation and below these a coloured diagram about the atmosphere, sometimes including a storm glass, and a thermometer. The pointers are adjusted by knobs in the framing.

finely grained panels bordered by raised and carved rims, sometimes gilded, were a fashion: the flat surface might be enriched with colourful marquetry. One may note cornice and

superstructure designed as miniatures of those decorating long case clocks, the earliest flanking pillars showing barley-twist turning, followed by fluted columns, and, later, turned Doric columns. At first the superstructure was placed above the register plates: in some instances this consists of the owner's coat of arms carved in the round and coloured.

Register plates by 1690 were usually framed within the hood in the same way as clock dials, and similarly enriched with ormolu mounts. Metal-work on all barometers was heavily gilded to avoid the polishing essential with other metals as this might shake the column of mercury and incorporate air bubbles: hence the necessity of fixing to the wall. At the lower end of the frame was fitted a cistern cover, plainly turned and hollowed, with a downward pointing finial. Immediately above the cistern was a pair of scrollwork wings, either carved or fretted: this feature is rare on barometers made later than about 1710, but otherwise one notes little variation in barometer design until the 1740s. Frames from this period are found in mahogany, fine examples being wide and lavishly carved in the rococo manner.

Barometer cases. These follow the changing moods of furniture. The majority, however, are severely plain, broadened at head and base and with a broken cornice pediment. In a specimen of the 1770s or 1780s a carved oval patera cover may conceal the cistern, and the register plates may be framed in matching carving within a similar oval. Cases made from about 1800 tend to be narrower, with the mercury tube concealed beneath a convex mahogany cover. Glazing covers the register plates, which may be of printed paper. The cistern is no longer open and, although stick barometers are not to be regarded as portable, this design can be moved gently without hazard to the mercury. By 1810 a flattish hinged box tended to supersede the turned cistern cover.

Fitzroy's barometer. The first inexpensive barometer, produced by mass production methods, is Admiral Fitzroy's mercury barometer. These are commonly believed to have been made early in Victoria's reign but the design was not registered at the patent office until 8th August 1881, more than twenty years after the admiral's death. Examples made during the early 1880s bear the diamond-shaped registration mark showing that three years' protection against industrial piracy had been granted. The flat, glazed case is machine made from light imported oak and the mercury tube with its cistern is fully visible. A thermometer and a storm glass containing crystals in a solution occupy one-quarter of the frame. Some examples bear a shield marked W H PATENT M.

The dial or wheel barometer. Developed from the siphon barometer with recurved open tube instead of cistern. An indicator on a dial is operated by a float rising and falling on the surface of the mercury. An attached thread passes over a pulley and is almost balanced by a counterpoise at the other end. A series of dial barometers made between 1720 and 1760 were devised by John Hallifax (1694–1750) of Barnsley. This design resembles a miniature long case clock with the long mercury tube concealed in the narrow trunk of the case. The square dial with ornamental corner spandrels is flanked by a pair of turned pillars and superimposed by a broken pediment cornice, its arch containing a circular convex plate engraved 'J. Hallifax, Barnsley, Inv. & Fecit.' Other makers of these barometers during the 1740s and 1750s were John Whitehurst, F.R.S. of Derby and London, and Rice Williams and John Bird, both of London.

The dial barometer became fashionable in the early 1760s, with the mercury tube set in a case of handsomely figured wood, chiefly mahogany with satinwood inlay in shell or star designs and edged with the stringing characteristic of the late 18th century. The most familiar form is the so-called banjo shape. The upper part of the case is fitted with a thermometer.

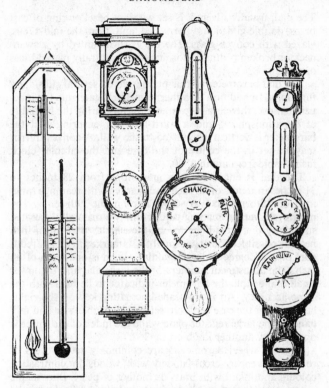

31. Siphon and dial barometers. (1) Early siphon design, with thermometer, George I's reign. (2) Pediment type in walnut by John Hallifax of Barnsley, with hygrometer, 1726. (3) Most familiar banjo type, with thermometer and hygrometer. (4) Later version of banjo with hygrometer, thermometer, clock, and at the bottom, spirit level, about 1800.

The dial, usually silvered, is set within a bezel or ring of cast brass, double gilded and burnished, and, from the mid-1780s, glazed with convex glass. The top is surmounted by a swan-neck or broken pediment cornice with a centrally placed brass ornament.

The dial barometer of this period served several subsidiary functions. In addition to a thermometer, detachable for independent use, there is a hygrometer for measuring the humidity of the atmosphere, and a spirit-level for ensuring that the barometer is vertical when fixed to the wall. A convex mirror may be set in the centre of the case and the circular clock fashionable from about 1800.

The dial is engraved with gradations from 28 inches to 31 inches in tenths of an inch and marked with readings ranging from 'Stormy' to 'Very Dry'. Early in the 19th century, by means of a vernier reading taken from two manually operated subsidiary dials, readings to one-thousandth part of an inch became possible The upper small dial is marked to a hundredth part of one degree of the large dial, which is one-tenth of an inch. The adjustment pointers of the large dial and the lower small dial enable the barometer indicator to be read with the same accuracy. An ivory-headed actuating key on the right-hand side of the case serves to set the adjustable 'rise and fall' hand of the large register plate while the index of the lower is operated by another knob on the left.

Regency wheel barometers are commonly set in cases of rosewood veneer, cross-banded with woods in contrasting colours and inlaid with brass or mother of pearl. Burr maple is sometimes noted, rubbed with a dark stain to enhance the figuring of the grain. Glazing is more highly convex than in earlier specimens. The cistern is provided with a visible ivory float for indicating zero level, and the thermometer may be sunk into the case and surrounded by intricate satinwood inlay, the pattern being repeated below the dial.

The diagonal barometer. The most accurate of domestic barometers was the diagonal, known also as the 'sign post' or 'yard arm', devised in 1670 by Sir Samuel Morland. The slightest variation in air pressure causes a considerable move-

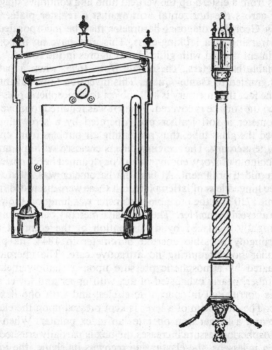

32. Diagonal and portable barometers. LEFT: diagonal barometer with hygrometer and thermometer, sometimes flanking a mirror, 1750s. RIGHT: portable barometer, walnut with silvered metal dials and gilt-metal feet, end of 17th century.

ment along the slanting arm. These barometers reached their peak of popularity between 1720 and the 1740s. The wooden frame is composed of two 30-inch sections: one vertical, the other extending horizontally from the top. The mercury tube rises from a cistern up the vertical limb and continues diagonally across the horizontal arm against a register plate. The early Georgian diagonal barometer may be incorporated in the framing of a looking-glass. This may have an imposing pediment decked with gilded brass figures in the round.

Portable barometers. These date from 1695, when a patent was granted to Daniel Quare. This invention took advantage of the fact that mercury is still subject to atmospheric pressure when the surface is covered. When it was required to move the barometer a soft leather pad, operated by a screwed rod, sealed the glass tube, thus preventing air bubbles from entering the mercury. The mercury tube is enclosed within a tapering column of ivory, ebony, walnut or japanned beech enriched with gilded ornament. At first the barometer was fitted with three hinged legs of latten plate, but these were discarded from about 1710 and the portable barometer was hung on the wall.

The aneroid barometer. The expensive mercury barometer was eventually displaced by the invention of the compact and thoroughly portable aneroid barometer in 1844, its plain circular body requiring no attractive case. The aneroid is actuated by atmospheric pressure upon a shallow metallic chamber, nearly exhausted of air, with upper and lower surfaces corrugated in concentric circles, and with one flexible side. The short arm of a lever is kept pressed upon the elastic side and a longer arm operates an index pointer. When the atmospheric pressure increases the box is partially crushed in; when it lessens, the elastic side recovers its shape, the index pointer moving in the opposite direction. The actual movement is very slight, but the pointer shows it multiplied 657 times. In 1847 such barometers were advertised at £3 each.

CHAPTER FOUR

Papier Mâché

Papier mâché is a tough material, heat and moisture resistant, that was made from sheets of paper so prepared and assembled that it could be japanned to acquire a surface lustre suggesting oriental lacquer. It was developed by Henry Clay of Birmingham in 1772, but little more than trays and panels was made until 1816, when Clay's successors, Jennens and Bettridge, produced an endless variety of small wares.

Collectors look for work boxes, tea caddies, portable desks, standishes, bellows, cigar and card cases and, later products, even chairs, cabinets, tip-tables and other light furniture mentioned on page 16. Dates of manufacture can be approximated by decoration techniques. Oil painting of course was used throughout the period particularly on trays. In addition to landscapes, sporting and coaching scenes, trays dating from the 1780s until 1820 may be painted with colourful flower heads and foliage, all extending to the edges of the wide flat rims. Those made in the early 19th century until 1820 may have background masses of bamboo, palm, pampas grass and butterflies.

Flower decoration. This experienced passing vogues. The change from conventional designs to gay, realistic flower studies dates from the early 1830s. At this time black japan backgrounds began to be used: formerly backgrounds had usually been in pale shades. By 1850 flower painting had become coarsely flamboyant, the blossoms overblown. Fern leaf sprays, fashionable between the early 1830s and 1850, are noted, painted in vivid green against backgrounds of white, yellow and grey. The peacocks found among flowers on much papier mâché were the work of Frederick Newman from about 1840. Sea shells date from about 1845.

Gilding became fashionable for pictorial work early in the 19th century in allegorical, oriental and sporting scenes and, from the mid-1820s, in all-over decorative effects of flowers, butterflies and insects. A single piece of papier mâché dating to 1840 or later may display gold in several hues, the metal being alloyed with copper, zinc or brass.

Bronzes. Glittering metallic powders, known as bronzes, date from about 1815 onwards. Eighteen colours were used, made from finely ground brass, copper, zinc, Dutch metal and other coloured alloys; some were chemically stained. Trees, for instance, are seen in green bronze, their shadows darkened with black lead. These bronzes prompted the development of oriental motifs, then fashionable on table services, many being carried out in various tones of gold and copper. In specimens from about 1825 this decoration may show more elaborate treatment, with temples, towers, pagodas and junks, mandarins and willow trees, outlined in relief gesso tinted with coloured bronzes.

From 1825 pearl ornament may be noted for trees and the like in conjunction with gold tracery: palm trees with alternate fronds in pearl and gold were much favoured. A method of bronzing that produced attractive atmospheric effects of contrasting sun and shadow was evolved in about 1845 and became known as the Wolverhampton style. Fascinating light effects are found, particularly in outdoor scenes with brilliant sunshine and ruined buildings showing brightly against sombre masses of trees. Pillared church interiors appear bathed in golden light streaming from coloured Gothic windows. The rare silvery bronze made from aluminium appears on moonlight studies and cloud edgings from about 1860.

Decorations restricted to bronzing were followed by nearly twenty years of varied ornament dominated by pearl inlay.

Pearl shell motifs introduced before about 1840 consist mainly of large, sturdy flakes of shell, thicker than those applied later: their outer edges may be concealed beneath gold or bronze. Pearl shell is found in many ingenious effects such as a lake scene by moonlight or a view of sunlight glinting upon a waterfall. One blotter cover, made in many thousands, carries a view of the Crystal Palace, its myriad pearl windows lit by a declining sun. Flowers from 1840 were often depicted by slabs of pearl brushed over with transparent colours, little attempt being made to paint in details.

Gem inlay. This dates from 1847 and consists of gem stones, river pearls, enamels, ivory, tortoiseshell and cut-glass backed with tin foil cemented to the under surface of a glass panel diapered with gold. The papier mâché background is painted in a contrasting colour.

During the 1850s there was a vogue for papier mâché painted to imitate malachite, blue john, coloured marbles and agates. These imitations are difficult to detect except by touch. This must be differentiated from the mounting of thin slices of the actual stones upon papier mâché. It was the forerunner of imitation woods for trays and other articles subject to hard use too severe for the handsome veneers such as the favourite walnut realistically reproduced on the stove-hardened, laboriously polished papier mâché.

CHAPTER FIVE

Tea-trunks, Chests and Caddies

England first tasted tea in the early years of the Stuart regime but not until the 1660s were its pleasures appreciated in the home. Tea-leaves were so costly that the mistress of the house guarded them under lock and key, in tea-trunks, tea-chests and tea-caddies.

The domestic store of tea was kept originally in a tightly closed vessel of tin or tutenag, approaching the whiteness and lustre of silver when burnished to close the grain. These were quickly succeeded by wide-mouthed, short-necked rectangular jars of red stoneware or blue and white porcelain from China. By the end of the 17th century canisters of silver were fashionable in the same shape (pages 182–4).

From early in the 18th century a pair of tea-canisters in silver, pewter, japanned iron or porcelain would be protected in a handsome leather-covered box with an arched lid, shaped like a travelling trunk. This was known as a tea-trunk and stored two qualities of tea. It was usually in a soft wood and either veneered with walnut or amboyna or covered with scarlet or green morocco leather, or with the longer-wearing shagreen, and was enriched with silver lock mounts. By the 1740s the rims of box and cover were enclosed in silver, the visible surfaces engraved with intricate scrollwork. By the mid-18th century the tea-trunk had given way before the flat-topped rectangular tea-chest which also might be covered in shagreen. At this time a central canister was introduced as a sugar container.

Instead of silver, pewter or porcelain canisters the majority of tea-chests are found to contain snugly fitting tea-boxes of wood with hinged or sliding lids, sometimes bearing silver labels naming the quality of tea, such as green or bohea. These boxes, lined with tea-lead—a foil of hard pewter containing no lead—hold 1½ lb of tea, a weight equivalent to a Malayan kati: hence the term tea-caddy. Each compartment of the tea-chest and its lid is lined with velvet or flowered brocade edged with narrow braid.

Tea-chests of solid mahogany date from the late 1740s, lavishly carved with foliage, scrollwork, shells, pendant husks and so on. Chippendale in his *Director*, a pattern book published in 1754, advocates tea-chests in the form of miniature bombé commodes: these he illustrates in rectangular and serpentine shape on scroll or rococo corner feet. In each example the lid is shown hollow so that the canisters or boxes rise an inch above the rim of the chest, just sufficient for easy withdrawal. The receding concave lid made space for the finials ornamenting many canister lids. These tea-chests are decorated with lock escutcheons either carved in solid wood or in the form of heavy applied castings, and with ormolu foliage handles on their lids. Alternatively heavy ormolu mounts are noted.

Lighter, more colourful tea-chests became fashionable from the early 1770s. Panels of veneered satinwood, harewood, burr walnut, cocoa-wood and fruitwoods were cleverly quartered to obtain handsome grain effects. Carcases for the finer examples are usually in carefully seasoned red deal.

Hepplewhite's *Guide*, 1788, reflecting the fashion of the previous decade, illustrates five tea-chests elaborately inlaid with all-over designs of scrollwork and urns: four stand flat upon the table and one has short bracket feet. Corners may be canted and decorated with vertical lines of stringing in contrasting colours between cross-banded columns. Each of the four faces of the chest may display an oval medallion in holly wood worked by the hot sand process. Satinwood may be inlaid with ovals of attractively grained burr walnut and narrow bands of ebony. Handles are less cumbrous and much reduced in size. Ornate ormolu was superseded by a plain D-shaped handle hinging at the ends in a pair of collared sockets inserted into the lid and immovably fixed by means of thin, square nuts and washers below. This style was succeeded by the fixed upright loop handle rising from a short collared stem. In others the loop is hinged from a flat plate following that of the chest outline.

Tea-chests of the Sheraton period around the end of the 18th century continued to be veneered, satinwood and rose-wood being favoured. Inlay appears less intricate than for-merly although checker patterns may frame marquetry motifs in polychrome or monochrome, such as medallions of shells, scrollwork, lozenges, wreaths and flower sprays. Some dating to the 1790s are trimmed with little brass ball feet matching the silver balls on silver teapots and are fitted with brass ring handles at the ends. Solid keyhole escutcheons are featured, engraved with crest or monogram. The lid interior may be set with a panel of satinwood or other exotic wood.

Tea-chests of mahogany dating from about 1790 are usually ornamented with stringing or varieties of plaited inlay, the lids of the enclosed caddies similarly decorated. One may note also neat modifications of fluting suggestive of linen-fold carving together with fan, shield and urn-shaped ornaments. The key-hole escutcheon is frequently shaped as a heart of ivory set in a diamond of ebony, or of ebony set within mother of pearl.

The commode shapes of the mid-Georgian period returned in about 1810, but these are heavier and clumsier versions in dark mahogany, amboyna, rosewood or maple. The lid interior is fitted with a bevelled mirror or, less expensively, covered with lightly embossed red or green paper.

Tea-boxes of mahogany, often sold in matching pairs, came into use during the 1770s and single boxes could be bought by those who preferred unblended teas. These eventually became known as caddies to distinguish them from tea-chests. Oval caddies filled with tea were considered handsome gifts in the late 18th century, constructed 'of the most curious English and Foreign Woods' enriched with colourful all-over designs in inlay. In red beech they may be found vividly painted with conventional flowers and allegorical scenes, festoons, medallions or coats of arms in full colour.

Octagonal caddies, that is, rectangular with broadly clipped corners, date from the early 1770s. These are usually enriched with inlay on each face. The front may display a shield-shaped silver plate engraved with crest, monogram or inscription.

A passing vogue is remembered in urn-shaped caddies on stemmed feet. Others are veneered in mother of pearl, ivory, tortoiseshell and ebony, often engraved with floral or scenic designs or inlaid with a contrasting veneer.

Some attractive tea-caddies are found in sycamore, burr beech, masar birch and various fruitwoods in forms resembling fruit such as melons, pears, apples and figs, the upper portion opening on a hinge. The melon shape is divided into longitudinal inlay. Some later examples are fitted at the 'stalk' with wide hand-grips of silver. In the 19th century such caddies were made in box-wood and lignum vitae. The tea known as gunpowder, a costly tea made from tender green leaves, was presented in a caddy resembling a gunpowder flask.

The names tea-chest and caddy distinguished the two types as late as the Great Exhibition, 1851, when the tea-chest lid might hold a box for wax vestas and a brass striking plate to light the spirit lamp beneath the silver kettle.

CHAPTER SIX

Ceramics

China collectors are faced with a bewildering array of pottery
and porcelain techniques, each producing a different type of
ceramic. A connoisseur will always look first at the paste or
body and then at the glaze—the glassy composition thinly
covering the paste. To him the technical details are infinitely
more important in attributing origin and period than the
presence of factory trademarks, which may be forged. Definitions are given here from which thirty common English pastes
or bodies may be recognised. When in addition the collector
has a working knowledge of the dates when major inventions
and improvements were introduced and of the numerous
methods of decoration (p. 91), he can attribute specimens
within well-defined limits.

A LIST OF WARES

Agate ware: earthenware intended to imitate agate stone by
wedging tinted clays together so that the colours extend
through the body.

Basaltes: a black vitreous stoneware characterised by its fine
grain, dense, uniform texture, and smooth, rich surface. It is
so hard as to be practically impervious to water and requires
no glaze. Developed by Josiah Wedgwood in the 1760s.
(*See* Stoneware, Egyptian black.)

Biscuit for figures: a soft-paste porcelain evolved at Derby
during the early 1770s and known to contemporaneous potters
as 'sculpture body'. Figures and groups came from the moulds
cleaner and more distinct than anything formerly known. It
was close-textured and semi-transparent with a light ivory

tint. From the early 1790s its surface was smear-glazed, making it velvety to the touch.

Bone china: a non-frit porcelaneous paste intermediate between hard porcelain and artificial or frit soft porcelain. Made from china stone and china clay, with a large proportion of calcined bone added to give it a milky-white translucency. Evolved by Josiah Spode in the early 1790s.

Bristol stoneware: double slip glazed—i.e., the upper part of the vessel was dipped into a liquid glaze that matured to a rich creamy or brown colour, and the lower part was dipped into a different glaze which fired to a creamy yellow. Dates from 1835.

Cane ware: tan-coloured, fine-grained stoneware introduced by Josiah Wedgwood in 1770. Known as bamboo ware when shaped into vessels resembling short lengths of bamboo fastened together with cane.

33. Agate ware. Solid agate ware can, thrown and turned, of Wedgwood-Whieldon make, 1756. Teapot, about 1740. RIGHT: **Basaltes** can by Wedgwood, entirely black, with a straw-work pattern in relief.

34. Bone china. Three examples of the delicate encrusted wares produced in this fine but strong ceramic: Coalport covered bowl; cottage pastille burner; Coalport candlestick.

Chalk body: a white earthenware of a powdery texture made in the late 18th century by adding chalk to the ingredients of a cream-coloured body.

Crazing: a network of thin irregular cracks occurring in the glaze of earthenware. Surface crazing was usual, but in some instances the cracks were so deep that food penetrated to the ceramic causing discolourations impossible to remove. Crazing was caused by perpetual changes in atmospheric conditions, the body and covering glaze contracting and expanding in response to these changes at differing stresses. Not until the mid-1880s was this defect overcome.

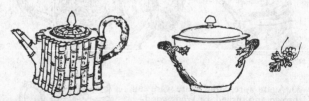

35. Cane ware and cream-coloured earthenware. Teapot in caneware, glazed only inside, made to resemble lengths of bamboo, Spode, 1790s. Cream-coloured sugar bowl with the typical Leeds twisted handle and a detail of a Leeds handle showing the pad moulded in relief.

Cream-coloured earthenware: evolved by the Staffordshire potters in the mid-18th century by cleansing local clay and mixing it with clays from Devonshire and Dorset, plus a proportion of calcined flint. This was fired to a deep cream colour. Josiah Wedgwood in about 1760 lightened its tint. In 1775, by using Cornish clay and china stone in his formula, he made an earthenware stronger and lighter in weight than any that had preceded it. The formula was made available to competing potters. Progressive improvements in quality were made during the 19th century.

Delft ware: *see* Tin-enamelled earthenware.

Dry bodies: non-porous stoneware requiring no glaze. Colouring oxides or ochreous earths were added to give the desired hue. They include basaltes, jasper, and red, cane, buff, drab, chocolate and olive stonewares.

Duck egg porcelain: a fine soft-paste porcelain with a clear green translucency when held to the light. Made at Swansea from the autumn of 1816 to the spring of 1817.

Earthenware: opaque ware, porous after the first firing and needing to be glazed before being taken into domestic use. It is made from clay selected for its plasticity, hardening qualities and fusibility.

Egg shell porcelain: fine china finished in the lathe until of Bristol board thickness. This fashionable emulation of Chinese porcelain was made from about 1850 by Coalport, Minton and several other Staffordshire potters.

Felspar porcelain: one of the most translucent ceramics ever made in England, produced by adding pure felspar to the bone china formula, with an equal reduction in the china stone. Harder, tougher, whiter, free from surface flaws and less liable to fracture than soft-paste porcelain or bone china; evolved by Josiah Spode II in 1805.

Felspathic wares: moderately hard fine earthenwares made in the 19th century. Their white bodies possess a slightly yellow-

36. Granite ware. Illustrated by a sturdy frog mug, the frog placed on the near side to remain invisible to the drinker until he had swallowed his murky liquor. Side view of the mug shows a typical 'Sailor's Farewell' scene and verses.

ish tinge and often slightly translucent. Known also under the trade names of semi-porcelain, opaque porcelain, opaque china, demi-porcelain and flint ware.

Granite ware: a cheap, white stone china with an even surface and durable glaze and extremely hard. Two types were made —pure white and light in weight for the home trade; faintly bluish and heavy for export. Dates from the mid-1840s.

Ironstone china: a hard white earthenware, slightly transparent but of great strength, compactness and density of texture and durability, and possessed of some porcelain characteristics. It has a clear ringing tone when struck. Patented in 1813 by Charles Mason. At first it was clumsily modelled and thick of section; such ware bears a mark in which the name Mason is included. In the 1840s various improved ironstone chinas came into production, thin of section, pure white, and most of them imprinted with a mark including the name 'ironstone'.

Jasper: a dense white vitrified stoneware of nearly the same properties as porcelain, developed in 1774 by Josiah Wedgwood and still in production. Its smooth surface was never glazed and when thin in section the ware is translucent. This extremely hard body contained carbonate or sulphate of baryta and could be coloured throughout its texture by the

37. Wedgwood jasper ware cup and saucer in white and lilac dip.
Ironstone china. Mason jug with vivid pattern and snake handle.

addition of metallic oxides. When solid stained it was called
solid jasper; when the white body was dipped in a solution of
coloured jasper it was known as dipped jasper. Until the 1820s
texture was fine and uniform of grain and never chalky in
appearance. Jasper made by Josiah Wedgwood between 1780
and 1795 feels almost like satin and is known to collectors as
waxen jasper.

Lava ware: a variegated stoneware used chiefly for cottage
table ware. It is stronger than granite ware and coloured with
oxides of iron, manganese and cobalt. Its hard, almost
indestructible glaze, consisting of flint and felspar, required
intense heat to fuse it. Popular from the 1850s to about 1880.

Parian statuary: a highly vitrified translucent porcelain containing a high proportion of felspar. It is silky to the touch and
notable for the delicacy of detail into which it could be
modelled. Early examples are ivory tinted; from the mid-
1850s, pure white. Invented 1842.

Parian ware: a non-frit porcelain used for elaborately moulded
vases and table ware, possessing a delicate smear-glazed surface. Evolved in the late 1840s.

Pearl ware: a hard, durable white earthenware body containing a greater percentage of flint and white clay than cream-

38. Parian ware and **pearl ware.** Parian ware jug patterned in low relief, partly coloured blue over a rough 'orange skin' surface; pearl ware puzzle jug with holes through the centre of the flattened body and around the neck, the liquor in the outer rim of the body being obtained through the nozzles, Spode, dated 1814.

coloured earthenware. It was used mainly for underglaze blue transfer-printing. Dates from 1780.

Porcelain: a translucent vitrified ceramic fired at a high temperature.

TRUE PORCELAIN OR HARD-PASTE PORCELAIN: a blend of two natural earths which fuse with the overlying glaze into an extremely hard vitreous white substance when fired at a very high temperature. This porcelain breaks with a clean, smooth fracture, disclosing a fine sparkling grain of compact texture. When lightly struck it rings with a clear sonorous note.

SOFT-PASTE PORCELAIN: contains a glassy frit in its composition. This frit porcelain displayed at its best a creamy or ivory white tint to which glazing gave a wax-like surface. Where chipped it feels roughish and granular. Three types were made with frits containing either bone ash, soapstone or flint-glass.

To distinguish between hard porcelain and the soft porcelains and bone china, one may scrape the glaze with a steel

86

blade. If it appears scratched, the ware is not hard porcelain, in which paste and glaze have been fired in a single operation. In hard porcelain the base of the foot is never glazed. If the glaze lacks gloss the porcelain is hard, upon which enamel decoration has a matt appearance and does not reflect light. Soft-paste porcelains and bone china are lead glazed and this is fired in a second operation. Enamels blend into this glaze and mature with a glossy surface. So soft was the lead glaze on early soft-paste porcelain that cups were scratched inside merely by the friction of spoons. (*See* Bone China *and* Soapstone Porcelain.)

Pottery: soft, lightly fired, opaque earthenware.

Queen's ware: an earthenware of an ivory or cream colour developed by Josiah Wedgwood in the early 1760s and improved 1775. (*See* Cream-coloured Earthenware.)

Red ware: a hard fine stoneware dating from the late 17th century; improved by the addition of calcined flint by Bell in about 1728; further refined by Josiah Wedgwood who named his fine-grained version *rosso antico*.

Slip: potters' clay in a liquid state of about cream consistency, used for casting and slip decoration.

Slipware: coarse reddish-burning clay which after shaping was

39. Parian ware. Entirely distinct from pearl ware is the mother-of-pearl glaze used, for example, by Belleek over parian porcelain from 1857 onwards. Illustrated are a shell fruit dish, an openwork basket with flower encrustations and a teapot partly coloured in enamels as well as the pearly glaze.

40. Porcelain and Queen's ware. An interesting but unsuccessful maker of exquisite porcelains was William Billingsley who also produced superb decorations including his most famous roses of which a typically unconventional example is illustrated (left), about 1814. The Wedgwood queen's ware pot is a Flaxman design.

41. Red stoneware unglazed tea-pot, 1760s; and **slipware cradle,** early 18th-century, both from Staffordshire. RIGHT: Wedgwood red **stoneware** punchpot.

decorated with slip and then glazed. In production until the second quarter of the 19th century.

Soapstone porcelain: a soft-paste porcelain containing steatite instead of china clay. Very soft and plastic, it vitrified at a comparatively low temperature, producing a porcelain denser and harder in texture than other soft porcelains, considerably heavier, with a less undulating surface. It could withstand contact with boiling water without cracking and seldom crazed.

Stone china: good quality glazed earthenware with a dense opaque body which emits a clear ring when lightly tapped. It is double the weight of ordinary earthenware and its smooth, unflawed surface is without undulations. Evolved by Josiah Spode II in 1805. Early examples had a delicate blue-grey tint; from the 1830s it was pure white.

Stoneware: ordinary earthenware fired at a temperature high enough partially to vitrify the ingredients and make the ware impervious to liquids.

Stoneware, brown salt-glazed: an almost vitrified pottery,

42. Soapstone porcelain. Two typical Worcester scale patterns used instead of plain colour for backgrounds. **Brown salt-glazed stoneware** in a figure cordial bottle (Lord Brougham by Doulton, 1832) and an 18th century greybeard bottle.

43. White salt-glazed stoneware. Sauce boat with a clear-cut self-colour trailing pattern in low relief, 1740s.

opaque, intensely hard and non-porous, displaying an almost glassy texture when fractured. The colours to which good quality clays usually burn range from a yellowish buff to dark brown, and to greyish and bluish tones. The salt-glazed surface until about 1850 resembled the granular texture of orange skin; afterwards the finish was more smoothly glazed.

Stoneware, Egyptian black: first made in about 1720 and stained with iron oxide until the mid-1760s. The texture was then improved, becoming uniformly dense and finely grained and stained with manganese dioxide, often mistaken for basaltes. Much of this was cast and finished in the lathe, thus giving a dull, dead black, unfired appearance. Manufacture continued to the 1890s.

Stoneware, white salt-glazed: England's first refined earthenware evolved in Staffordshire during the late 1720s and containing calcined flint in its composition. At first the body was dull cream, but had been whitened by the mid-1730s, thus displaying the translucency of the salt-glaze to its best advantage. Minute pinholes or granulations covered the surface until the 1750s, when a softer, thicker, smoother glaze was evolved. From the 1740s it could be made as thin, light and translucent as Chinese porcelain. Production continued until the 1780s.

44. Terra-cotta jug from a Wedgwood tea service of 1830.

45. Tin-enamelled earthenware (delft ware). A Lambeth dish of the late 17th century showing the rope effect known as 'blue dash'; and a puzzle jug with perforated neck and three nozzles, only one connected with the hollow handle to make a siphon.

Terra-cotta: unglazed red earthenware in colours ranging from lobster brilliance to the matt opacity of brick dust. Its hard, compact texture ensured a smooth, impervious surface, faintly glossy yet capable of holding decoration without glazing. Sharpness of detail distinguishes hard Victorian terra-cotta from earlier, softer qualities.

Tin-enamelled earthenware: earthenware coated with white opaque enamel to conceal fire cracks and other flaws and made lustrous with transparent lead glaze. The English ware is denser and more vitreous of texture, more durable and less costly than the Dutch variety known as delft ware. Crazing is frequent, a fault rarely associated with Dutch delft. Made throughout the 17th, 18th and early 19th centuries.

FORMS AND METHODS OF DECORATION

Aerograph: a process for applying ground colours evenly on inexpensive wares; invented 1890.

Banding: colour lines applied freehand, one finger being used as a guide to regulate the distance of the band from the edge

46. Carving and engine turning. Worcester teapot illustrating the carving technique with elaborate perforations in the central area of the double-thickness body; and Spode teapot in Egyptian black showing self-colour pattern in engine turning.

of the article. Since the early 19th century circular articles have been placed on a whirler, the loaded brush being applied to the rotating object; the hand steadied by an adjustable rest. These display no irregularity as in freehand banding.

Bianco-sopra-bianco: designs, usually border patterns, painted in slight relief with thick opaque glaze on tin-enamelled ware tinted greenish-white or greyish-blue.

Carving: decoration cut through the outer wall of double-walled vessels such as teapots and jugs.

Chrome green: a colour made from oxide of chromium, more opaque and yellowish than green made from copper oxide. Discovered in the mid-1790s.

Email ombrant: decoration on porcelain in which a monochrome picture in a variety of tones was obtained by impressing designs in deep relief and then flooding them with transparent coloured glaze (usually green) to level the surface. The cavities in the design appeared as deep green shadows of varying intensity, while the parts in the highest relief gave highlights to the picture. There was a great demand for tea services in this ware, which was developed in the mid-1860s.

Enamelling: carried out with low firing pigments derived chiefly from refined mineral oxides for painting over the glaze and given a separate firing in a decorating kiln. Until about 1750 unfired or cold colours were used; these were oil paints fixed by placing the piece in a warm oven. This decoration was short lived. Enamels in England date from about 1750. In designs composed of several colours each needed a separate firing. A muffle kiln invented in 1812 matured the colours to greater brilliance. In widespread use by the 1820s.

En camaieu: monochrome painting in several tones.

Engine turning: geometric, diced, fluted and other complicated incised decoration on fine dry stonewares. These were cut by means of a lathe equipped with an eccentric motion, causing the article to oscillate while rotating, the cutting tool remaining still. From the mid-1760s onwards.

Famille rose: a range of colours for decorating porcelain derived from the purple of cassius developed by the Chinese potters early in the 18th century. The bright rose colour decorated Bow, Chelsea and Worcester porcelain, and in the 19th century appeared on bone china, stone china, felspar porcelain, ironstone china. *Famille rose* colourings are valued because of the long range of rose tints obtainable as well as violet and purple. As the temperature of the enamelling oven

47. Enamelling at its finest required separate oven firings for the different colours at progressively lower temperatures, as for these Chelsea exotic birds; in contrast is the simple 'flowering' with blue pigment introduced in incised lines on a 1750s mug.

increases the hue of the enamel changes, starting at red-brown, and passing through rose-purple, rose-violet, violet, pale violet, very pale violet, until at 1,000 degrees C. all trace of colour vanishes.

Famille verte: Chinese porcelain of the K'ang Hsi period (1662–1722), painted over the glaze with vivid green, red, yellow, aubergine-purple, black, violet-blue enamels, with green predominating. Gilding was sometimes added. These colourings were copied by English potters on bone china, felspar porcelain, stone china and so on.

Flowering: a style of decoration on earthenware contemporaneous with engraved flowering on flint-glass during the 18th century. Unfired earthenware thinly coated with slip was incised with flowers and foliage by means of a sharp pointed iron nail and afterwards glazed.

Gilding: chronological changes in gilding enable specimens to be placed into well-defined, dated groups. It would have been impossible, for instance, for mercury gilding, introduced in the late 1870s, to have been used at Chelsea or for brown-gold to have been applied earlier.

OIL GILDING was used until about 1800. Gold, cut to shape from the leaf, was fixed to the ware by means of a linseed oil preparation containing gum arabic and mastic. Oil gilding was impermanent and could not be burnished. Rarely used on fine productions after 1760.

UNDERGLAZE GILDING was in limited use between about 1760 and the 1820s. Unfired oil gilding was dipped into transparent lead glaze and fired. This protected the gilding from wear but reduced its brilliance considerably.

JAPANNED GILDING was in use by the 1720s and continued throughout the century. The gold leaf was fixed with japanner's size and fired at a low temperature. This could be burnished to a medium lustre, far below full brilliance.

HONEY GILDING: the first method of gilding with permanence,

was introduced in the mid-1750s and continued until the 1790s. Being costly, it was used only on fine quality wares. Gold leaf, ground with one-third its weight in honey and tempered with oil of lavender, was painted thickly upon the ware, raising it appreciably above the surface of the glaze. As the glazes were soft, very little flux was required to cause the gold to adhere. It was fixed by gentle firing. Honey gilding is hard with a characteristic rich dullness entirely different in appearance from any other gilding. Honey gilding was so thick on the ware that it could be further enriched by chasing.

MERCURY GILDING was introduced from Meissen in the late 1780s, but was in very limited use until the early 1790s and is still in use. Much less costly than honey gilding, producing a more brilliant, harder film of gold, but brassy in appearance. A high brilliance could be secured by burnishing.

TRANSFER GILDING was patented in 1835 and prepared transfers sold to the leading potters of the day. Examples are as brilliant as when made, having withstood burnishing after firing.

BROWN GOLD: applied in the form of a thin paste containing gold chloride, was invented in 1853, but little used until the 1860s. The fired gilding was dull, but burnishing and cleaning with vinegar produced a film of permanent gilding more richly brilliant than any other.

LIQUID GOLD was introduced to England in the early 1850s and used for decorating cheap ware. Although extremely brilliant without burnishing, it is not wear resistant.

ACID GILDING, resulting in a polished relief pattern against a dull matt gold background, was introduced in 1862. The design is printed on the ware with an acid resist. This is dipped in hydrochloric acid, causing the exposed glazed surface to be corroded to a required depth, and leaving the pattern in slight relief. The whole is then gilded, fired and burnished.

Green-glazed ware. A clear liquid green glaze developed by

48. Green-glazed ware. The teapot in two-colour cauliflower effect and the vine-leaf dessert service centre-piece entirely green.

Josiah Wedgwood in 1759. It enabled him to produce teapots and other domestic vessels in the form of cauliflowers and pineapples, their lower portions encircled with appropriate leaves rising from the base. The glaze was soon copied by other potters and has been in continual production ever since, particularly in the form of leaf plates and dessert services.

Ground laying. Covering borders and large surfaces with one colour. Until 1826 these were painted with a flat brush, most colours being difficult to apply on a smooth surface without showing brush marks. Yellow was less difficult to work than other colours and this appears more frequently among early ground patterns. Some colours, such as peach bloom, fawn, pale red were also much used because they could be laid evenly, being so thin as to be little more than stained oil.

A new method was introduced in 1826. Finely ground dry colours were dusted on a surface previously oiled; when fired a level glossy surface was produced. When great depth of colour was required the operation was repeated several times. The most usual colours were dark blue, apple green, deep yellow, canary yellow, turquoise, crimson, salmon, yellow-green, lavender and cane colour. The aerograph, by which coloured grounds could be applied evenly, dates from 1890, superseding ground laying on cheap wares.

High temperature colours. Metallic oxide colours capable of withstanding the heat of the glazing kiln and painted on the unfired surface of the biscuit ware which was then fired to set the colours and finally glazed. Among the colours a thick brownish yellow, orange ochre, pale yellow and greyish brown are common, with dull olive green, manganese purple and a dull blue. Ware so decorated is known to collectors under the generic name of Pratt Ware.

Inlay. Colourful mosaic designs in clays of various tints in the manner of Berlin woolwork were inlaid in earthenware, stoneware and terra-cotta from 1839 to the 1870s. Pictorial and figure inlay was patented in 1843 by Richard Boote, who licensed the process to others.

Japan patterns. A term applied indiscriminately to a wide range of oriental designs adapted by English porcelain decorators such as brocaded Imari and the distinctive asymmetrical style enamelled in turquoise, red, green, yellow, blue, *famille verte* and *famille rose*. The English enamels exceeded the oriental in brilliance. Chelsea used Japan patterns during the gold anchor period; and Worcester delighted in them from about 1760, cataloguing such decoration as 'old mosaick japan pattern' and 'fine old japan fan pattern'. They appeared on Spode's bone china and stone china early in the 19th cen-

49. Japan pattern on a Minton plate of the 1820s.

tury and were extensively used at Derby from about 1817; also used by Masons on their ironstone china and by several other bone china potters such as Thomas Minton and John Davenport.

Lithography. First used for pictorial effects on ceramics in 1839 in light blue under the glaze. Multicolour lithography dates from 1845 with pink, green, purple, grey and black composing a single picture. Lithography earlier than the late 1850s has a dull, uninteresting surface owing to economy of colour.

Lithophanes. Transparencies made from thin, glassy, hard porcelain. When placed before a light, the precise variations in the thickness of the material and its consequent opacity were transformed into vivid detailed pictures resembling mezzotint engravings in monochrome. They date from 1828, the patent rights being controlled by Grainger, Lee & Co. of Worcester. Several other potters made them from 1842 until the end of the century. Among the articles found are window and lantern panels, lampshades, night lights, and hand fire-screens. A tea cup apparently decorated in the ordinary way with enamels and gilding might surprise the tea-time visitor, revealing a picture in the bottom when it was tilted against the light.

Lustre ware. Made commercially from the early years of the 19th century. It is difficult to classify closely. Very few examples are marked and the collector is aided only by the times when various processes were introduced. The colour of the basic earthenware was found to have considerable effect upon the brilliance and colour of the lustre from the early 1820s. White, yellow and light grey clay mixtures were preferred for silver lustres. Reddish-brown clay, in a quality that could be finished with a smooth, mirror-like surface, gave depth and richness of tone to low carat gold and copper. In high quality productions the biscuit was given a coating of glaze stained purplish pink with purple of cassius; this made the lustre scintillate like shot silk. The basic principle consists of coating the smooth, opaque glazed surface of earthenware with a film of prepared metallic oxide.

SILVER LUSTRE was derived from platinum oxide; silver oxide could not be used because its lustre was dispelled on exposure to air. There is no record that silver lustre passed the experimental stage until 1805. It was introduced in delicate stencilled designs set off by the glazed ground. The patterns

50. Lustre. TOP: 'silver' lustre. Entirely silver-lustred in a silver-smith's design, probably by Davenport, early 19th century; and silver-resist lustre showing the pattern in white against a silver-lustred background. BOTTOM: copper lustre with a band of coloured flowers; and pink, blobby 'Sunderland' lustre around a transfer print.

were cut so skilfully that hairline details were of pen-and-ink-fineness. This costly work was succeeded by resist lustre.

Lustre ware, potted in shapes resembling fashionable silver plate and silver lustred all over, dates from the early 1820s. In early work the ware is of excellent quality with no relief ornament apart from fluting and beaded edges which reflected high lights. After 1845 the illusion of plate was abandoned; the ware was lined with white glaze and painted with gaudy flowers or banded in horizontal rings of blue, cream or pink. Silver lustring by an electro-deposit process was carried out between 1852 and the early 1860s, when it was abandoned as impermanent.

RESIST LUSTRE dates from about 1810. Until the late 1820s the ground colour was almost invariably in white or cream glaze, the exceptions being coloured grounds such as buff, pink, apricot, blue and canary yellow. Until the late 1820s these were hand-painted, distinguishable by a slightly uneven surface. In 1826 a method of making ground colours level and glossy was evolved. Designs include fruiting vine, geometric and scroll patterns, song birds, roses, strawberries, thistles, ivy, fuchsias, sporting scenes.

GOLD LUSTRE was produced from gold oxides in hues ranging from guinea gold to reddish and coppery gold and the not very durable ruby. Tint variations resulted from using several qualities of gold; the higher the copper content of the alloy, the darker and more bronze-like was the lustre. Examples dating earlier than 1815 are scarce. Until about 1820 the lustre had a distinctive guinea-yellow colour. These lustres were applied to glazed ware in styles similar to those of silver lustre.

COPPER LUSTRE, made from copper oxide, dates from about 1825 and was at first disfigured with specks, pinholes, pimples and bubbles. It is conspicuously heavier than the earlier gold lustre ware. Hollow-ware was usually lustred inside, while the

CERAMICS

exterior might be decorated with colourful motifs painted directly to the lustre, or upon glazed bands, some of which were ground coloured forming a background for relief moulding.

PURPLE LUSTRE, often termed pink lustre, derived from purple of cassius, thinly painted in design over white glaze, dates from about 1810 in a quality capable of retaining its brilliance. Marbled effects were obtained by mingling various tints. Irregular spots, splashes and waves form another and inexpensive variant.

REPRODUCTIONS of lustre ware are common. One potter, established in 1831, has continued making silver lustre and resist lustre ever since, using the original formulae, processes and shapes. Other potters make gold and silver lustres. Sixty years ago J. F. Blacker warned people against the lustre ware which the Staffordshire potters were even then 'distributing to the antique shops of the world'.

Majolica, imitation. A coarse, cane-coloured stoneware with relief ornament covered with a white glaze. This is decorated in glazes of various tints of green, yellow, blue, purple and red. Introduced in 1850 by Herbert Minton, whose successors continued manufacture until the end of the century. Wedgwood produced imitation majolica from 1860 in a white earthenware body, the relief ornament painted with transparent coloured glazes. Among other potters making this ware were Daniel Sutherland & Sons, Longton; George Jones, Stoke-upon-Trent; Moore Brothers, Longton; and James Woodward, Swadlincote.

Marbled ware. Surface ornament produced by working together coloured slips or enamels.

SLIP MARBLING dates from the 17th century and continued until the end of the 18th century, with a revival in the third quarter of the 19th century in recognised 'antique forms'. Thinly applied lines or splashes of light-coloured slips in two

51. Marbled ware. Slip marbled plate, around 1700; and painted marbling resembling combed paper marbling.

or more tints, such as red and white, buff and brown, light red and buff, dark red and brown.

GRANITE AND PORPHYRY MARBLING were fashionable during the late 18th century. Granite effects were achieved by spraying cream ware with grey or bluish mottled glaze. Porphyry effects were produced by sprinkling with green glaze.

PAINTED MARBLING decorated cream ware and pearl ware from about 1815 to the late 1850s. Streaks and curls in yellow, reddish brown and chocolate coloured enamels were applied in the manner of the freer type of paper marbling.

52. Mocha pottery jar and **sprigged ornament** on a teapot with crabstock handle and spout, about 1760.

Mocha pottery. A variety of dipped ware decorated with coloured bands of specially prepared slip and with moss agate effects introduced under the glaze. Because earthenware, decoration and glaze matured in the kiln with a single firing, and the labour costs of ornament were low, mocha pottery was very inexpensive. It was first made of cream ware in the 1780s, and in the 19th century of pearl ware and cane ware. It was designed chiefly for domestic use, for public house serving jugs and mugs for measures used to serve shrimps, winkles, nuts and so on.

Pâte-sur-pâte. Literally paste on paste, a technique developed at Sèvres in 1860 and introduced to England ten years later by M. L. Solon at Minton's. It consists of a stained parian paste painted with relief designs in white or tinted slip, supplemented by modelling with chasing tools. The reliefs, being translucent, allow the darker tones of the background to show through in varying degree, producing an effect of perspective and moulding. Made by Minton, Worcester, Derby, and elsewhere.

Pierced ornament. Resembles fret-work and was made by perforating unfired green ware or very soft biscuit porcelain

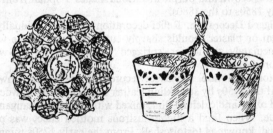

53. Pierced work. Staffordshire plate with pierced rim cartouches interspersed with basket work patterns in low relief; and Leeds twin salt cellars, about 1790.

or earthenware. Piercing was carried out in all-over symmetrical designs composed of lozenges, hearts, leaves, trefoils, pales and similar shapes. Common ware was cut with hollow steel punches, but intricate piercing was carried out with a series of sharp, fine-pointed knives or a fretsaw. Great skill was required and it was essential not to reduce the strength of the piece unduly or it would warp in the kiln. Wedgwood and Leeds were celebrated for fine piercing of hollow ware in the late 18th century; Slee of Leeds made similar ware in the late 19th century. The Staffordshire potters produced delicate border piercings, mostly pales, in bone china flat ware.

Powder blue. A powdered, sprinkled, ground-colour effect first used at Worcester. Dry, finely powdered smalt was blown through a tube, covered at one end with a piece of lawn, on to an oiled surface before glazing. It may be recognised by the resultant granular effect, the bright blue being mingled with pinpoints of the steely blue shade.

Sponging. A method of decorating inexpensive earthenware, usually granite ware, in bright colours applied over a thick glaze with a sponge impregnated with pigment. The colours used in monochrome or polychrome were blue, pink, green, yellow, brown and purple in various shades. Popular from the early 1850s to the 1880s.

Sprigged Decoration. Relief decoration shaped individually in metal or plaster moulds sharply cut in intaglio. These were immediately applied or 'sprigged' to the body of the ware before firing.

Tortoiseshell ware. An effect secured on cream earthenware until the 1750s by sprinkling leather hard clay with powdered lead oxide and calcined flint, mixed with a trace of manganese oxide. When fired a highly lustrous mottled effect was produced, known as tortoiseshell. From the early 1750s mingled colour glazes were made by dusting the surface of the biscuit with metallic oxides and then coating with liquid transparent

54. Tortoiseshell ware figure coloured with mingled glazes. Typical early **transfer-printing** from Spode's earliest willow pattern with one man on the bridge.

lead glaze. During firing these blended into a range of varie-gated tints. The limited palette consisted of green, yellow, slate blue, dark brown and mottled grey. The more usual colour combinations are mottled green and brownish grey; brown, green and slate blue; grey, green, slate blue and yellow.

Transfer printing. Engraved decorations transferred to cera-mic surfaces by means of tissue paper and prepared potter's ink. The process was evolved at the Battersea enamel works in 1753.

OVERGLAZE PRINTING was applied on the glaze of soft-paste porcelain at Bow and Worcester in 1756, continuing in use on porcelain until the 1790s. Designs were simple and printed with clear, sharp lines in black, brick red, dark purple or brown, and might be overpainted with washes of nearly transparent colour.

BLUE UNDERGLAZE, printed on fired biscuit before glazing, was developed during the late 1770s by Turner of Caughley and improved by Josiah Spode in 1781. The protective coating of glaze over the decoration gave it a lifetime of resistance to hard wear. Until about 1800 cross-hatching appeared slightly smudgy. Lines were then engraved more thinly and variation of tone became possible, thus introducing shadow and high lights. From 1810 line and stipple effects might be combined and finer tone variations appeared. The blue, obtained from cobalt oxide, was in various gradations of tint; in some early 19th-century examples dark and light blue transfers might decorate a single article. After 1830 quality deteriorated, the blue being lighter and the pattern for the most part less carefully engraved. Harsh, synthetic blues date from 1845. Among the two hundred or more Staffordshire potters who produced underglaze blue probably no more than twenty made fine quality ware sought for by collectors; most of this bears the makers' marks.

COLOUR UNDERGLAZE dates from 1828 when the discovery was made that the high temperature colours, green, red, yellow and black, when mixed with Barbados tar, could be used for transfer-printing without the hazard of distortion. Two or more colours might decorate a single piece, a separate firing being required for each colour. Examples are uncommon.

MULTI-COLOUR UNDERGLAZE PRINTING dates from 1848, when a patent was granted for transfers from which blue, red and yellow could be fixed by a single firing. Brown and green were added in 1852.

BAT-PRINTING was an overglaze process of transfer-printing on soft-paste porcelain dating from the early 1760s, but little used until the mid-1770s. It was widely used to decorate bone china from the 1820s until the 1870s. The patterns were stippled on copper with a fine point, short lines also being incorporated, subsidiary to the stippling. A bat of gelatine took the place of transfer tissue. Bat printing proves especially successful for small motifs such as flowers, foliage, fruit, shells and cartouches for coats of arms, crests and inscriptions.

FLOWN BLUE was a transfer-printed effect introduced in the

55. Vermicular pattern on a lustred jug. **Welsh ware** baking dish.

early 1820s by the Wedgwood firm. The blue patterns merged into the overlaid glaze with coloured halo effect, caused by adding a little volatile chloride to the saggar containing the glazed ware during firing. Brown and green transfers were used occasionally.

Vermicular ground. Continuous irregular meandering lines in gold or in colour over a coloured ground.

Welsh ware. Shallow, oval meat dishes of coarse earthenware decorated with slip combed and feathered in zig-zag patterns and streaked with yellow and brown glaze. Dates from the 18th century, but nearly all existing examples were made between about 1800 and the 1880s. Until about 1815 the slip was hand applied with a single pipe. Later the colour was distributed by a device containing a number of pipes, such ware being distinguished by more meticulous placement of patterns.

MARKS ON CERAMICS

Potters' marks of the 18th century are well known and rarely seen by the casual collector except on reproductions. These marks must necessarily be omitted here in favour of lesser known but more commonly found marks impressed or printed on fine quality ware. On the following pages are illustrated a few of the marks used by celebrated potters selected from the many

56. Ceramic marks. TOP: ship mark of W. A. Adderley, Longton, from about 1876; two eagle marks of William Adams, Stoke-upon-Trent, 1772–1829. BOTTOM: Edward Asbury, Prince of Wales Works, Longton, from about 1875; Belleek, Northern Ireland, founded 1857; two marks of Bishop and Stonier, Hanley, from 1890 (the caduceus sometimes without the contraction Bisto).

hundreds of master potters who operated during the 19th century.

Below are described the marks and their periods of use by ten potters whose output was tremendous.

Coalport: established by John Rose in 1796 and operated throughout the 19th century as makers of fine bone china and associated ceramics. His first productions had little trans-lucency and were flawed with multitudes of specks. By 1820 these defects had been overcome. There is no typical Coalport style of decoration and reproductions of Sèvres, Chelsea and Meissen were made.

Coalport bone china was unmarked until about 1815; from then until 1828 COALPORT was painted in blue script under the glaze. A very translucent porcelain was made from about 1816, at first backstamped J.R.F.S. Co printed in red. More usually the mark, printed in red, was a circle two inches in diameter inscribed COALPORT (IMPROVED) FELTSPAR PORCELAIN within a fruiting laurel wreath encircled 'PATRONISED BY the SOCIETY of ARTS. The GOLD MEDAL awarded May 30th, 1820.' For several years the central inscription might include the name J ROSE. The marks on bone china from 1828 until about 1850 included 'Coalport' in script letters not joined; JOHN ROSE & CO.; COLEBROOK DALE; C.D.; C. DALE; CBD; in various styles of blue script. The blue or gold monogram CBD was used from the late 1840s to the early 1860s. This was succeeded until 1875 by C combined with an S-scroll, forming three loops containing the letters

57. Ceramic marks. TOP: two marks of T. G. & F. Booth, Tunstall, from 1884, the crescent on earthenware imitating Worcester; T. & R. Boote, Burslem, from 1842; Bridgwood, Sampson & Son, Longton, late 19th century. CENTRE AND BOTTOM: typical marks used by Bow, 1750–70, including two early incised marks.

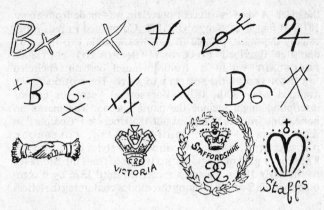

58. Ceramic marks. TOP: marks, incised and in blue, used by Bristol 1748–52, the third and fourth probably workmen's marks and the fifth used also by Cookworthy at Plymouth. CENTRE: marks used at Bristol under Champion, 1773–82. BOTTOM: Buckley, Heath and Co., Union Pottery, Burslem, about 1885–1900; Cartwright & Edwards Ltd., Longton, 1860–64; two marks of the Crown Staffordshire China Co., Fenton, from 1890 (previously M. Green & Co.).

CSN in gold, occasionally in red or blue. The mark COALPORT AD 1750 was used on biscuit taken from stock after 1865 and on current productions between 1875 and 1881. From then until 1892 this mark was accompanied by a crown; the word ENGLAND might then be added.

Crown Staffordshire Porcelain Co. Ltd.: this firm acquired a pottery at Fenton in 1890 and have made some astonishingly close reproductions of 18th-century English, Continental and Chinese porcelain. J. F. Blacker wrote of these reproductions in 1910: 'By long and careful experiment their chemists have discovered the exact shades of the marvellous enamels which the Chinese brought to perfection . . . powder blue on the

110

vases is the result of some thousands of trials extending over ten years. Each piece is what it professes to be, a copy, which is marked with a crown over "Staffs", or over "Staffordshire" surmounting two G's, one reversed, in a monogram. The flowers painted at Derby, Worcester, Nantgarw, Swansea and Coalport are among the schemes of decoration used.'

Derby Crown Porcelain Co.: established at Derby in 1877. J. F. Blacker in 1910 recorded that the firm 'manufactures immense quantities of tea, breakfast, dessert and dinner services and it specializes in japan patterns and in reproduc-

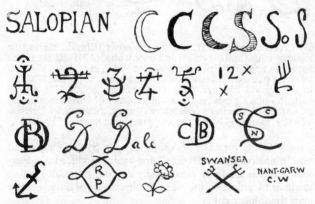

59. Ceramic marks. FIRST AND SECOND ROWS: marks of Caughley, Shropshire, 1750–1814, the name Salopian impressed also being found in lower case letters among early marks, and the marks on the second row dating from 1780 onwards, mainly disguised numerals. THIRD AND FOURTH ROWS: marks of Coalport or Coalbrookdale, Shropshire, about 1796–1958, the first three used about 1828–50, the fourth 1850–61, the fifth 1861–75. In the fourth row are Coalport adaptations of the marks of Chelsea and Sèvres, a rare mark of John or W. Rose, and marks from 'Swansea type' wares.

60. Ceramic marks. FIRST AND SECOND ROWS: Chelsea marks, the incised triangle and the crown and trident about 1745–50, the raised anchor in applied relief, latterly picked out in red, about 1749–52, and three painted red anchors, also found in blue or purple, 1752–56. In the second row are three gold anchors, about 1758–69, an imitation of a Chinese seal, two imitations of Meissen marks and an impressed repairer's (assembler's) mark. THIRD ROW. Chelsea-Derby marks, 1770–82, the N impressed on figures 1770–1800.

tions of Old Crown Derby designs . . . Dr. Syntax figures and the "Mansion House Dwarfs" are again produced . . . Eggshell china is made of wonderfully delicate porcelain, yet so tough as to withstand the highest temperature of liquids better than the thicker china.'

The mark until 1898 was a crown surmounting two crossed D's, one in reverse: the words 'Royal Crown Derby' were added to the mark in 1890 and from 1892 'made in England'. **Don Pottery, Yorkshire:** potted pearl ware, cream colour, brown-blue-and-green glazed, marbled, black-printed on glaze, blue-printed under glaze, painted and enamelled earthenware, and fine stoneware such as cane ware, Egyptian black and jasper.

From 1807 to 1833 under the proprietorship of Greens, Clark & Co. They published a catalogue illustrating 292 items, many of them inspired by Wedgwood, including pierced ware, tea and dessert services and vases. Some excellent decoration in full colour was carried out in landscapes, coats of arms, and

61. Ceramic marks. FIRST ROW: Derby marks: two of Duesbury period, 1780–95; Duesbury and Kean, about 1795; two of Bloor period 1815–48. SECOND ROW: Derby marks: Bloor period; Stevenson and Hancock, about 1860–70; Crown Derby Porcelain Co. from 1876, and two imitations of foreign marks—of Sèvres, Bloor period and later, and of Meissen about 1809. THIRD ROW: (impressed) Thomas Fell. Newcastle-on-Tyne 1817; two marks of Thomas Forester & Sons, Imperial Works, Longton, 1870; two marks of Hilditch & Sons, Longton, about 1815. FOURTH ROW: Two marks of John Dimmock, Hanley 1862–1904, who also used a mark with a lion; Fulham, John Dwight, 1740s; Green and Clay, Longton, about 1886–91.

specimen flower paintings with the name of the plant beneath. An uncommon production was pearl ware covered with buff engobe and decorated in black. The impressed marks were DON POTTERY and GREEN DON POTTERY; the printed mark in black or blue was a demi-lion rampant holding in his paws a pennon inscribed DON rising from a plinth inscribed POTTERY.

From 1833 to 1893 owned by Samuel Barker of Mexborough Old Pottery. The impressed mark was S.B. The printed mark was the demi-lion slightly modified in shape from formerly with the name BARKER or B above the pennon.

From 1851 to 1893 traded as Samuel Barker & Son, the manufactures now including ironstone china. The marks were blue-printed; a shield containing an eagle rising out of a ducal coronet which might have the name IRONSTONE above and S B & S below; and the demi-lion rampant holding in his paws the pennon enclosed within a garter and the initials S B & S beneath. A hitherto unrecorded mark is a castle chess piece with a coronet above, a demi-lion rampant below and the initials S B & S.

Meigh, Job and his successors: established at the Old Hall, Hanley, 1790 and continued until 1861, potting every type of English ware such as creamware, Egyptian ware, stone china, bone china, parian. Their fine stoneware differed from others from the 1830s, having a semi-matt finish by smear-glazing. More than 700 workmen were employed in the 1840s.

The early mark was MEIGH impressed. By 1820, blue-printed and other earthenware bore a blue-printed oval cartouche composed of small flowers and foliage enclosing the name of the pattern with J M & S below. Stoneware from 1830 might be printed in black with the royal arms above CHARLES MEIGH HANLEY. An imitation Chinese seal used between 1835 and 1847 incorporated the initial M among the complicated symbols. Other marks used from 1830 were INDIAN

STONE CHINA C M in a circle; ENAMEL PORCELAIN; OPAQUE PORCELAIN; IMPROVED STONE CHINA C M.

In 1861 the firm became a limited company, Old Hall Earthenware Co., and the mark, printed in red, was a castle with three turrets above OLD HALL with the date 1790 in a Staffordshire knot.

New Chelsea Porcelain Co., Ltd.: established at Longton in 1912, specialising in reproductions of Bristol, Plymouth, Bow, Lowestoft, Swansea, St Cloud, Sèvres, Dresden, Chinese of the K'ang Hsi period and other porcelains. The mark is N C P CO. An associated firm made bone china reproductions marked with a gold anchor and the name *New Chelsea* in script. Since leaving the factory some of these marks have been removed and bogus marks have been added.

Ridgway, Job and his successors: established in 1794 and moved to Cauldon Place Works, Shelton, in 1802. Made earthenware and bone china of fine quality in designs similar

62. Ceramic marks. TOP: two marks of Hicks, Meigh & Johnson, Shelton, 1822–36; two marks of E. Hughes & Co., Fenton, from 1883. BOTTOM: two marks of William Hudson and Middleton, Sutherland Pottery, Longton, 1889–1930; Case, Mort & Co., Liverpool, 1822–41 (from the city crest); Seth Pennington, Liverpool from 1780s; two rare marks of Longton Hall 1751–60.

to Copeland and Minton until 1855. The ground colours are of exceptional purity and the gilding has the appearance of solid metal. A translucent cane ware and stone china were made.

Some of the numerous marks were as follows. Until 1814 I. RIDGWAY or I R impressed, or the name over a potter's kiln, printed; 1814–30, under John and William Ridgway, J & W R painted or impressed; J W R in a shield containing the pattern name; J W R STONE CHINA; 1830–40, J R impressed or printed; 1841–55, J R & CO, and from 1842, JOHN RIDGWAY & CO, CAULDON PLACE, POTTERS to HER MAJESTY with the royal arms above and BY ROYAL APPOINTMENT below.

Rockingham: the brothers Brameld made fine bone china from 1820, displaying an advanced potting technique. Enamel colours were unrivalled and ground colours resplendent, including a notable smooth opaque apple-green. Rockingham yellow is considerably darker than that of Derby, with which it is liable to be confused on unmarked pieces. Gilding was lavishly applied and has often acquired a faintly coppery tinge.

Until 1826 finer pieces were marked with an oval medallion bearing BRAMELD surrounded by a wreath of floral emblems, all in relief. On less costly china BRAMELD was impressed or printed in red or purple. From 1826 marks were always printed. First came a griffin *passant* above ROCKINGHAM WORKS BRAMELD in copper plate script, printed in red, brown or purple. In 1830 the griffin was surmounted by a royal crown and the inscription MANUFACTURER TO THE KING below the factory name. In 1837 the word KING was altered to QUEEN. By 1840 royal references were discontinued. The royal crown surmounting the script legend ROYAL ROCK^m WORKS BRAMELD—without the griffin—marks some bone china made during the 1830s. From 1840 until the factory closed in 1842 the firm reverted to the griffin mark as used between 1826 and 1830.

John Wager Brameld, who decorated bone china in Bayswater, London, from 1844 to 1854, marked his ware with the griffin and the name BRAMELD.

Initials. Collectors find it difficult to attribute initials, often alone, sometimes contained in a cartouche enclosing the name of the pattern. The dates given below are those of the period during which the marks were in use, although this is not necessarily the potter's full period of production. The dates for the most part have been collated from examples sent to Country Life Ltd. for identification, and many have the confirmation of registration marks. The dates for Poole and Unwin,

63. Ceramic marks. TOP: Lowestoft marks, including imitations of Worcester and Meissen and ill-formed figures between 1 and 60. CENTRE: marks used by the Old Hall Pottery from 1790 (the firm founded by Job Meigh), and by their successors the Old Hall Earthenware Co., 1862–87 and the Old Hall Porcelain Works Co. Ltd., 1887–1902. BOTTOM: two marks of the Middlesbro' Pottery Co. (I. Wilson and Co.) Middlesbrough, 1834–87; impressed mark used by the firm of Neal and Co., Hanley, when worked by D. Wilson, 1801–17; James Pearson, Whittington Moor Potteries, Chesterfield, founded 1805, mark used after 1875.

for instance, are usually given as 1871–76; dates interpreted from registration marks extend this to 1869–80.

Many Staffordshire potters copied shapes and patterns from Continental makers of hard porcelains. Such a piece would be marked with a cartouche containing the firm's initials in minute type, and the name of the original such as Sèvres, Dresden or Limoges, and is liable to be mistaken for an 18th-century original by beginner collectors.

A & B SHELTON   Adams and Bromley. Earthenware, jasper, majolica, parian. 1873–94.

A & CO *often with Prince of Wales's Feathers*   Edward Asbury & Co., Ltd., Longton. Bone china. 1857–1925.

A B & CO   A. Bullock & Co., Hanley. Earthenware. 1880–
H   1915.

A S   A. Stanier, Burslem. Earthenware. 1895–1930s.
B

A S & CO   Ambrose Smith & Co., Burslem. Cream coloured ware and china glazed ware painted blue. 1780s.

B *incorporated with an anchor*   British Anchor Pottery Co. Ltd., Longton. Earthenware. 1865–.

B & B   Bates and Bennett, Cobridge. Earthenware. 1808–mid-1890s.

B & B   Bridgett & Bates, Longton. Bone china. 1883–1915.

B B   Barker Brothers, Longton. Cream coloured, enamelled, printed and sponged earthenware and bone china. 1876–early 1900s.

B B & I, *or* B B & CO.   Baker, Bevans & Irwin. Earthenware. 1814–39.

B & C   Bridgwood & Clarke, Burslem. Earthenware. 1858–74.

B C CO   Britannia China Co., Longton. Bone china. 1895–1906.

B & H   Blackhurst & Hulme, Longton. Bone china. 1870–
         1930s.

B & H   Bednall & Heath, Hanley. Earthenware and bone
         china. 1879–1901.

B & L   Burgess & Leigh, Burslem. Earthenware. 1851–.

B P CO   Brownhills Pottery Co., Brownhills, Burslem. Fine
         earthenware, creamware and stoneware.
         1871–96.

64. Ceramic marks. TOP ROW: Minton marks (Thomas and his son Herbert) Stoke, the mark used 1822–36 and the 'ermine' mark used on some wares to be painted from 1851; and two typical title marks with obscure initials, M in this position dating 1822–30, M & B (Minton and Boyle) 1836–41, M & CO, 1841–44, and M & H (Minton and Hollins) 1846–68. The firm was styled Minton & Co. again 1858–83 and from 1883 Mintons Ltd. SECOND TO SEVENTH ROWS: symbols used by the Minton firm, changed yearly.

119

65. Ceramic marks. TOP: five marks used by Pinxton, Derby, 1796–1813, two early and three later; three marks used at Plymouth 1768 to 1770 when William Cookworthy transferred to Bristol. BOTTOM: two marks of William Ratcliffe, Hanley, 1831–40 and, below, a lion mark of Thomas Poole, Longton, end of 19th century; the Registration mark used 1842–83 to protect a design from copying by rival firms, the IV at the top indicating the class of goods (ceramics) and the surrounding figures and letters indicating date of registration and location of the design at the Patent Office; mark of John Ridgway, Cauldon Place, 1834–40.

C B   Charles Bourne, Foley Pottery, Fenton. Bone china. 1818–30.

C B   Charles Birks, Lane End. Bone china. 1819–34.

C B   Collingwood Bros., Longton. Bone china. 1888–1903.
L

C & E   Cork & Edge, Burslem. Earthenware, Egyptian black, lustre ware, stone china. 1848–65.

C F monogram   Charles Ford, Shelton. Earthenware. 1858–1913.

C & G   Copeland & Garrett, Stoke. Earthenware, bone china, parian etc. 1833–47.

C M   Charles Meigh, Old Hall Works, Hanley. Every variety of earthenware, caneware, stone china, parian, Egyptian black. 1835–47.

C M S & P Charles Meigh, Son & Pankhurst, Hanley. Every variety of earthenware, caneware, stone china, parian, Egyptian ware. 1850–51.

C P C Crystal Porcelain Co., Longton. Bone china. 1880–
L 1920.

C & W K H Charles Harvey & Sons, Longton. Earthenware, gold lustre, granite ware, bone china. 1840–53.

D B & CO Davenport, Banks & Co., Hanley. Copies of antique earthenware, majolica, terra cotta, Egyptian black. 1860–73.

D B & CO *sometimes beneath a beehive* Dunn, Bennett & Co., Hanley. Earthenware. 1880–87.

D P G Dresden Porcelain Co., Longton. Bone china. 1896–1904.

E & C C E. & C. Chalinor, Fenton. White granite and printed earthenware. 1862–90s.

E J B E. J. Birch, Shelton. Fine stonewares, including black basaltes, jasper and cane ware. 1796–1813.

E K B Elkin, Knight & Bridgwood, Fenton. Cream coloured and blue printed earthenwares, bone china, Egyptian black. 1820–40.

G F B *in a Staffordshire knot* G. F. Bowers, Tunstall. Bone china and also from 1860 earthenware.
G J 1842–71.

G J & SONS George Jones & George Jones & Sons, Stoke. General pottery and parian. 1861–1952.

H & B *within a garter* Heath & Blackhurst, Hadderidge Pottery, Burslem. Earthenware. 1859–80s.

H & B, *sometimes on a pennon* Harrop & Burgess, Mount Pleasant Works, Hanley. Earthenware. 1895–1904.

121

...

H & G, *sometimes accompanied by* LATE HARVEY Holland &
Green, Longton. Earthenware and granite
ware. 1853–82.

H & M Hilditch & Martin, Lane End. Bone china. 1814–22.

H P CO Harvey Pottery Co., Burslem. Earthenware, bone
china, granite ware, lustre ware. 1822–53.

H & S *within a wreath and beneath a crown, or in a cartouche*
Hilditch & Son, Lane End, Bone china.
1822–67.

66A. Ceramic marks. FIRST ROW: Sampson Smith, from 1846 (the
reference to a registered number indicating a date after 1883 and
the inclusion of 'England' a date after 1891; Andrew Stevenson,
Cobridge, 1810–18 (also used eagle and draped urn as marks);
Wedgwood & Co, Tunstall, Staffs, founded about 1840, this mark
among others used 1892–1900 when 'Ltd' added, a firm not to be
confused with Josiah Wedgwood, Etruria. SECOND ROW: upper
and lower case Wedgwood marks used by the firm of Josiah Wedgwood, Etruria, from 1771; Wedgewood spelt with a middle e, a
mark used by William Smith & Co., Stockton-on-Tees from 1826.
THIRD ROW: confusing mark of F. Winkle & Co, Tunstall, 1891–
1932, having no connection with the famous potter Thomas
Whieldon; three marks of the New Chelsea China Co. Ltd, Longton, from the end of the 19th century, having no connection with
the famous 18th century Chelsea porcelain factory.

66B. Ceramic marks. FIRST ROW: eighteenth-century marks of Worcester, crescents and Ws, mainly in underglaze blue, 1751–83, and two imitations of Chinese seals. SECOND ROW: Worcester imitations of Oriental marks on Japan patterns, about 1760–75; Worcester imitations of Meissen and Sèvres marks (Furstenberg, Tournay and Chantilly were also imitated); Worcester under Barr, Flight and Barr, 1807–13 (followed by F.B.B. for Flight, Barr and Barr, 1813–40); the Worcester mark under Kerr and Binns, 1852–62; the Worcester Royal Porcelain Co., from 1862.

J B, *sometimes in a bell*   John Bell, Glasgow. Earthenware, pearl, granite, terra cotta, parian ware, bone china. 1842–50.

J D *in monogram*   John Dimmock & Co., Hanley. Good quality earthenware. 1842–1904.

J E & S   James Edwards & Sons, Dale Hall, Burslem. Earthenware, stone china, ironstone china, white granite. 1842–79.

J H *also in monogram on a circular pad*   Joseph Holdcroft, Longton. Parian, majolica, silver lustre ware. 1870–1906.

J & M P B & CO   J. & M. P. Bell & Co., Glasgow. Earthenware, pearl, granite, terra cotta, parian, bone china. 1850–90s.

67A. Rockingham marks.
Rockingham griffin and two
other Rockingham marks used
by the Bramelds from 1826.

J M & S   Job Meigh & Son, Old Hall Works, Hanley.
Earthenware, red stoneware, cane ware.
1812–35.

J M & S   J. Meir & Son, Tunstall. Bone china. 1812–36.

J R   J. Rogers, Longton. Blue-printed earthenware. 1814–36.

J R   John Ridgway, Shelton. General earthenware and bone
china. 1834–40.

J R & CO   John Ridgway & Co., Shelton. General earthenware and bone china. 1841–55.

J & R R   John & Richard Riley, Hill Works, Burslem. Bone
china from 1816, stone china figures,
cream coloured ware. 1802–30.

J T   John Tams, Longton. General earthenware, lustre,
printed wares, mocha ware, lustre ware.
1774–1903.

J T H, *sometimes with an anchor* John Thomas Hudden,
British Anchor Works, Longton. Printed
earthenware, granite ware. 1859–84.

J T LTD   John Tams Ltd., Longton. Earthenware. 1913–.

J T & S   John Tams & Son, Longton. Earthenware. 1903–12.

J W R *and* J & W R   John and William Ridgway, Shelton.
General earthenware, stone china and bone
china. 1814–33.

K & W   Keeling & Walker, Longton. Gold and silver lustre
figures. 1850s.

67B. Spode and Copeland marks. TOP: c. 1785–1810; 1800–24; 1833–47. BOTTOM: 1833–47; 1860–90; 1860–1910; 1894–1900.

M Minton & Co., Stoke. Earthenware and bone china. 1800–36 and 1878–84.

M & C Martin & Cope, Longton. Bone china and lustre ware. 1818–30s.

M & CO Minton & Co., Stoke. Earthenware, stone china, bone china. 1841–44 and 1847–76.

M E C Middlesbrough Earthenware Co., Middlesbrough. Opaque china, lustre, printed earthenware, cream coloured ware. 1844–52.

M & N Mayer & Newbold, Lane End. Earthenware and bone china. 1817–33.

M P CO Middlesbrough Pottery Co., Milldesbrough. Opaque china, lustre ware, cream coloured ware, printed earthenware. 1831–44.

M & S Charles Meigh & Son, Old Hall Works, Hanley. Earthenware, stone china, parian, bone china. 1851–60.

68. Ceramic marks. TOP: Don Pottery, mark used 1820s–34; Herculaneum Pottery, Liverpool, mark used 1822–41; three Minton marks, two early marks and the 'ermine' mark used from 1851, also six typical year symbols in the style introduced 1842: for 1842, 1850, 1853, 1862, 1867, 1875. CENTRE: Neale and Co., late 18th and early 19th centuries; New Chelsea Porcelain Co. Ltd, established 1912, Old Hall Earthenware Co. Ltd., marks of the Meigh firm from 1861, the date 1790 in the Staffordshire knot being that of Job Meigh's establishment at the Old Hall, Hanley; three arrow marks used by Pinxton to 1813. BOTTOM: two marks of John and William Ridgway, successors to Job Ridgway, at work 1814–59; two marks of Thomas Poole, early 20th century; Worcester mark used by Kerr and Binns 1852–62, the same mark but surmounted by a crown being used by the Worcester Royal Porcelain Co. Ltd. formed 1862.

M & S Mayer & Sherratt, Longton. Earthenware. 1907–.

N C P CO New Chelsea Porcelain Co., Longton. Porcelain reproductions. 1912–.

P & B Powell & Bishop, Hanley. Cream coloured and ordinary earthenware, enamelled and printed, granite ware, bone china. 1865–78.

126

P & B Price Brothers, Burslem. General earthenware. 1897–
B 1903.

P B & CO Pinder, Bourne & Co., Burslem. Bone china, earthenware, red ware, Egyptian black. 1862–83.

P B & H Pinder, Bourne & Hope, Burslem. Bone china, earthenware, red ware, stone china, Egyptian black. 1857–60.

P & D Poulson & Dale, Stoke. Bone china. 1816–20s.

P S & W Poole, Stanway & Wood, Stoke. Parian, bone china, terra cotta, stone china, cane ware. 1873–90.

P & U Poole & Unwin, Longton. Gold and silver lustre, majolica. 1869–80.

P W & CO Podmore, Walker & Co., Tunstall. Earthenware. 1834–55.

R H Ralph Hammersley, Shelton, earthenware; Tunstall, earthenware, enamelled and blue-printed, Egyptian black, red, Rockingham; Burslem, earthenware and stone jugs. 1822–82.

R H & S Ralph Hammersley & Sons, Tunstall and Burslem. General earthenware. 1882–1905.

R & L Robinson & Leadbeater, Stoke. Parian. 1865–86.

R S R *in the three loops of a Staffordshire knot.* Ridgway, Sparks & Ridgway, Hanley. Earthenware, stoneware, terra cotta, jasper, all of fine quality. 1872–79.

S A & CO *sometimes accompanied by a beehive* Samuel Alcock & Co., Hill Pottery, Burslem. Fine earthenware, semi-porcelain, bone china, bisque figures, parian. 1851–59.

S & G Shore & Goulding, Isleworth. Earthenware and slipware. 1760s–1830.

s s Sampson Smith, Longton. Gold and silver lustre, earthenware figures, groups and chimney ornaments. 1846–58.

s & s Daniel Sutherland & Sons, Longton. Majolica, parian and stone china. 1863–.

T B Thomas Baggeley, Lane Delph. Bone china. 1808–20s.

T B Thomas Birks, Longton. Bone china, gold and silver lustre, earthenware. 1850–80.

T B Thomas Bevington, Hanley. Bone china, including imitation Sèvres. 1869–92.

T & B G Thomas and Benjamin Godwin, Burslem. Queen's ware and blue-glazed earthenware. 1780s–1809.

T & R B Thomas and Richard Boote, Burslem. Parian, granite earthenware from 1750. 1850–90s.

T R & CO Thomas Rathbone & Co., Portobello, Scotland. Earthenware. 1810–45.

T T *in a Staffordshire knot* Thomas Twyford, Hanley. White
H granite and cane ware. 1849–80s.

T T Taylor, Tunnicliffe & Co., Hanley. Earthenware. 1868–75.

W B William Brownfield, Cobridge. General earthenware. 1850–70.

W B & S William Brownfield & Son, Cobridge. Earthenware and bone china. 1871–92.

W & C Wood & Caldwell, Burslem. Earthenware, cane ware, Egyptian black. 1790–1818.

W & E C W. & E. Corn, Burslem. Earthenware. 1864–1891.

W H & S William Hackwood & Son, Shelton. Earthenware and figures. 1818–53.

W N
L E William Nutt, Lane End. Bone china. 1816–20s.

W & R
  L   Wayte & Ridge, Longton. Earthenware, lustre ware, parian, bone china, figures. 1864–90s.

W S & CO   William Smith & Co., Stockton-on-Tees. Earthenware. 1826–47.

W S & T R   W. S. & T. Rathbone, Tunstall. Bone china. 1816–30s.

W W & CO   Wiltshaw, Wood & Co., Burslem. White granite. 1869–90.

Z B & S   Zachariah Boyle & Son, Hanley. Earthenware and bone china of fine quality. 1828–50.

CHAPTER SEVEN

Battersea and Bilston Enamels

One of the most delightful manufactures of artist-craftsmen
in Georgian England was the painted enamel of Battersea,
Bilston and Birmingham. Typically this takes the form of a
small box for snuff or for fragments of sponge soaked in
aromatic vinegar. One may find an etui 4 or 5 inches long
fitted with toilet accessories and occasionally also containing
a central spy-glass, or a rasp-fitted nutmeg holder or some
similar little essential elegance. Other enamels are more
ambitious—handsome caskets and tea-caddies, candlesticks,
scent-bottles and purely decorative plaques. They were produced by fusing what amounted to opacified glass on to wafer-
thin copper, their decoration being painted by hand, often
over a transfer-printed base. Lasting brilliance was obtained
by firing in a muffle stove at high temperature. Their edges
were rimmed with gilt-metal neatly hand-tooled, and their
whole assembly was so perfect that no box for carrying in the
pocket ever required a fastener.

For three years, from 1753 to 1756, a factory at Battersea,
London, produced painted enamels of notable quality, mainly
decorated with transfer printing, a process developed in this
factory. The application of transfer prints opened up the
whole field of porcelain printing and was in keeping with
England's reputation for mechanical inventive genius.
Battersea decoration was dominated by the graceful, slightly
effeminate engravings of Simon-François Ravenet, and
catered for a sophisticated enjoyment of daintily illustrated
classical lore and a knowledgeable appreciation of high quality
one-colour printing over lustrously white enamel.

For some years prior to 1753, however, and until the early years of the 19th century, South Staffordshire was by far the most important source of these delectable little 'toys'. Early collectors established the fame of the Battersea enamels, but only since the 1940s has there been a long-overdue revaluation of South Staffordshire enamels and acceptance of the fact that preference regarding the best examples in either style of treatment must be a matter of personal opinion.

The general changes in taste during the 18th century make it easy to distinguish comparatively early Bilston and Birmingham enamels from those of the middle, more ornate period, and to distinguish these in their turn from the mass-production trifles that end the story of English enamels. At first, in the Battersea style, the lids of enamelled boxes were usually covered entirely with pictures and the white sides with painted posies or transfer prints. Some elaborately mounted shell-shaped boxes may be regarded as transition pieces, brightly painted with figure scenes taken from contemporaneous engravings such as De Larmessin's 'L'Après Dîner' after Lancret, and Watteau subjects.

Colours. Three enamel colours may be associated especially with Battersea: a deep bright crimson, a clear bright blue and a warm reddish dark brown. Brown was also used for outlines requiring a warm undertone. Bilston enamels may be found with ground colours in several tints. These serve as aids in differentiating Bilston productions from those of Battersea: dark blue was first used in 1755; pea green, 1759; turquoise and claret, 1760; silver, yellow and golden reds from 1770. The peculiar pink or rose-coloured ground painted with small flowers and gilt borders was made in nearby Wednesbury. This colour originated at Sèvres in 1757, a year after the Battersea factory closed: it did not appear on enamels earlier than about 1784 when a chrome-tin pink was introduced in imitation. This was known on the Continent as 'English pink'.

A new technique was evolved in the early 1780s, a film of coloured enamel being sprayed over the basic white enamel.

A delightful detail of most middle period enamels is the background detail of scrolls and asymmetrical escutcheons in the rococo manner of their period, formed in raised white enamel covered with rich gilding. In enamels made after about 1770 one may note, too, the ground colours patterned with raised diapers of criss-crossed lines in white enamel interspersed with dots in one or more contrasting colours. The reserves may contain decorations copied or adapted from *The Ladies Amusement; or, Whole Art of Japanning Made Easy*, published by Sayer in about 1760.

Candlesticks. Following early Georgian silver, these were made at an early date: they were advertised in Dublin during 1762. The stick was constructed in three segments, the seams concealed beneath double-gilt mounts. Enamelling muffles were too small to accommodate lengthy pieces. A tall candlestick enamelled as a single entity may be dated later than about 1780. This tends to look clumsy, even when colours are good. Some are handsomely painted, but in general violent colour contrasts rather than subtle harmonies characterise such work.

Boxes, etc. Boxes of every shape may be collected, and tea canisters and sugar vessels, tobacco presses, cassolettes, counter trays, salts, mustard pots, cream jugs, hot-water jugs and standishes with their equipment for ink, shot, pounce and wafers. Some later enamels bear evidence of having been quickly dipped in liquid, milky enamel rather than coated in more viscid paste with a spatula: frequently, dipped pieces lack the metal mounts that rim all exposed edges on earlier pieces. Egg-shaped nutmeg holders fitted with graters for their customary use with wine, hand-made thimbles turned and drilled from the solid metal, bodkin cases, even games counters in the form of tiny enamelled playing cards may be noted among the very considerable output.

Bonbonnieres in animal form adapted from Meissen porcelain were popular novelties during the 1770s and 1780s. Boxes were modelled and painted in the shapes of human heads, birds, animals and fruit. Such a box has a hinged base serving as a lid and this too is a painted enamel, often a tiny picture associated with the model. In an associated style, from about 1780, some boxes, scent bottles, plaques and so on were embossed with designs in relief and appropriately painted to fit these shapings. A typical feature is the box lid embossed with a flower posy, the raised shape suggesting the general contour of the flowers, with surface painting to fill in the details of petal and leaf.

The boxes with steel reducing mirrors of the 1770s were succeeded by those with glass mirror fittings in the late 1780s. From about 1780 date many small articles such as buttons, studs, brooches, breast pins and end-pieces for curtain poles decorated simply with stippled transfer prints.

Unfortunately the final phase of this delightful manufacture was dominated by the urge to cut costs. By 1790 quality was being sacrificed disastrously: painting tended to be applied carelessly and the quality of transfer printing deteriorated. The market was flooded with innumerable tiny boxes not in any way comparable with the earlier enamels and the market for quality work was lost. Typical of this mass production were the little boxes in dullish colours, usually oval, less well-hinged and lacking base rims which nevertheless were so well constructed that they required no fasteners. Even at the time these were regarded largely as souvenirs to be sold or given away at fashionable watering-places and holiday resorts. Many are transfer-printed with local views and the words 'A Trifle from . . .' such as Cheltenham, Bath, Tunbridge Wells, and so on. Some, in addition, are painted with the names of the shops that presented them to favoured customers. The collector, however, must look beyond such unambitious mementoes if he is to appreciate the true worth of the English painted enamel's colourful contribution to 18th-century manufactures. **Copies.** Painted enamels have been reproduced extensively and these for the most part take the form of table snuff-boxes, some conveniently enlarged to cigarette size, patch boxes, wall plaques and candlesticks. Copies of Battersea originals were imported from France during the mid-Victorian period. Hinges on reproductions often have little projections in the middle and press tool marks are clearly visible. The faker's enamel tends to have a thin, high glaze with a wonderfully glossy surface during the first years of life. Its colours, especially the blues in sky and water, are too bright and the general tone lacks the creaminess of Battersea and the dead white of Bilston. Often these fakes are cleverly aged, deliberately cracked and stained. Any piece marked with a cross is an acknowledged reproduction made by Sampson of Paris.

CHAPTER EIGHT

Glass

ENGLISH TABLE GLASS

Collectors rarely seek English glass predating the incalculably important English development of flint-glass, introduced by George Ravenscroft in 1674 and associated in early work with heavy ponderous designs. Manufacturing improvements were made in the 18th century, most notably in about 1740 and 1780. The glass lost its early dark tinge and became tougher, clearer, and more brilliant although some hint of 'colour' remained until the beginning of the 19th century.

The technicalities associated with glass-making are an important study to the serious collector, but the terms explained below provide a working vocabulary.

Annealing: toughening of flint-glass by raising its temperature high and slowly lowering it again. Improvements in this process made in about 1740 and 1780 are reflected in the

69. Blown-moulded. Specimens of the blown-moulded technique. Two sweetmeat bowls and two feet, 18th century.

70. Moulded pillar flutes and three specimens of **pinched** work—two
decanter stoppers and a foot.

development of surface ornament from the 1740s and the
delight in deep cutting at the century's end.

Blown or free-blown vessels: shaped by hand tools while the
molten glass is expanded into an air-filled bubble on the end of
a blowing iron. 18th-century glassmen often shaped their
vessels by blowing the glass into a small mould to give it the
required shape; they then expanded it by further blowing.
Pattern on the outside is marked by slight surface ripples
inside the vessel.

BLOWN-MOULDED glass was used for bottles, etc., in the 18th
century but more fully developed in the early 19th century
when the old one-piece mould was superseded by full-size
moulds, the two-piece (1802) and three-piece (1820). These
open-and-shut moulds permitted elaborate ornament on the
glass surface, detectable by the fact that the surface indentations are repeated inside the vessel and because slight marks
in the glass show the joints of the mould. These are not to be
confused with the sharp hair-line mould marks associated
with pressed glass.

PRESSED GLASS: a process, dating from the 1830s, by which
the molten glass was forced into the surface-patterned mould
by a plunger. Such vessels show no corresponding patterns
on the interior and no pontil marks.

FIRE POLISHING on blown-moulded and pressed glass largely obliterated tool and mould marks and left clean smooth edges suggestive of cut glass.

PINCHING was another method of shaping glass, used for making solid units such as decanter stoppers and parts of candlesticks, using hand-operated pinchers. Men specialising in the work became known as pinchers.

Decoration. CUTTING consists of grinding depressions into the glass surface with revolving wheels. These may have convex, pointed V-shape or flat rims to produce hollow, mitred

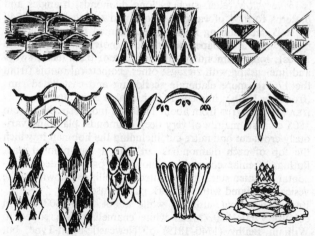

71. Cutting. Shallow early cutting of the 18th century. TOP: shallow rounded-hexagonal facets and large diamonds. CENTRE: scalloped rim and three examples of sprigs. BOTTOM: three stem facets—diamonds, hexagons, scales—fluting, and a shallow-cut foot with scalloped edge.

137

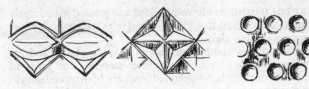

72. Cutting. Late 18th and early 19th-century motifs, swags, heavy diamonds, printies.

or flat panel cutting. On pre-1740 glass edge-cutting and shallow blunt-edged scallops may be noted. Surface faceting is in very low relief, such as long diamonds, triangles and patterns formed of various scoops and slicings. From 1740 to 1805 such cutting might be augmented by sprig motifs; fluting with a V-shaped cutting tool (notched from the late 1760s); long diamonds double cut (from the 1750s); swag-and-line cutting with zigzags; other geometrical motifs (from the 1760s); more elaborate scalloping and castellated rims (from the 1770s); immensely fashionable stem faceting.

HEAVY CUTTING from about 1790 and more especially from 1805 consists mainly of very deep diamonds, plain and variously cross-cut and mitre-cut, including the hob-nail in which the top of each diamond is cut with a four-pointed star; fluting; circular concavities known as printies; deep horizontal prisms; stars, the pointed-end ellipse known as the vesica associated with the Cork glass houses.

Enamel ornament: used in white about 1720–1800 and in colours 1760–1820. Much white enamelling is credited to William Beilby (1740–1819) of Newcastle-upon-Tyne, but faking is common.

ENAMEL GLASS is opaque white glass, made from the 1750s onwards, often decorated like porcelain.

Engraving: hand engraving with a diamond or graver dates

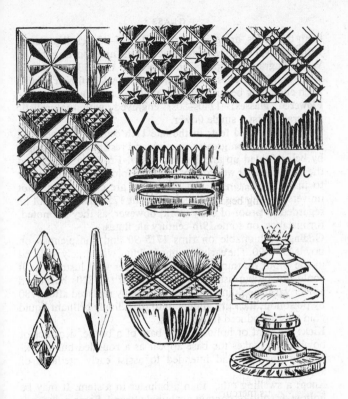

73. Cutting. Examples of late, heavy cutting. TOP: typical deep cutting including hobnail and cross-cut diamonds. CENTRE: strawberry diamond cutting; the three cutting outlines—mitre, hollow and panel—and below them part of a water jug showing vertical and horizontal prismatic cutting; blazes and fan cutting. BOTTOM: two views of an early pendant lustre; the later style of lustre; bowl showing elaborate early 19th century cutting; two cut feet—hollowed facets above plinth and circular with star cutting.

from the 1720s, armorial work; and 1725–40, scroll patterns, with a revival in early Victorian coaching and sporting scenes. Wheel engraving appears on rims from the 1730s to 1800s, scroll and leaf arabesques giving place to wider flower motifs. Such engraving began to appear polished in about 1740.

Flowered glasses: 1740s–80s, engraved with naturalistic flowers, at first a single flower.

Folded and welted feet: in the late 17th century a wine glass foot rim was given greater strength and resistance to chipping by being folded up and back on itself. From this developed the more familiar welted foot, the edge folded down and under to make a substantial rim. Such feet are common but not universal on glasses made before about 1750. They cannot be regarded as proof of early work, however, as they are noted, for instance, on some 19th-century ale flutes.

Gilding: fashionable on rims 1715–90 and conspicuous on bowls 1760–90. The early japanned gilding was largely replaced in the 1750s by thin honey gilding, never very lustrous as it could not be burnished. From the 1760s to 1820s burnished amber varnish gilding was used, gradually replaced after 1780 by poisonous mercury gilding until sparklingly brilliant liquid gold was introduced in the 1850s.

Kick: the dent or hollow in the base of a bottle, decanter or bowl which makes the base appear as a rounded hummock. Mainly pre-1760 and intended to assist early methods of annealing.

Knop: a swelling other than a baluster in a stem. It may be hollow or solid or contain air bubble 'tears'. Some names are self-explanatory such as acorn, ball and the smaller bullet, cylinder, drop, mushroom, quatrefoil. In addition, the angular knop is a flattened cushion shape with rounded edges introduced horizontally; the annulated is flattened and sandwiched between two, four or six other knops thinner and in decreasing sizes; the bladed is flattened with sharp edges; the cushion, an only slightly flattened sphere; merese, sharp-edged flattened button connecting bowl and stem or stem and foot; multiple, several of the same shape composing a stem; swelling, slight protruberance containing a tear.

Pontil or ponty or punty: long iron rod used to hold the glass vessel usually by the base—the hot glass being adhesive—so that it can be removed from the blow pipe for finishing.

Pontil mark: the hot glass adheres to the end of the rod and has to be broken off. The scar thus left was usually ground away and the surface polished into a smooth depression after about 1750, but on cheap glass may be noted even on mid-19th-century specimens such as rummers and dram-glasses.

Prunt: glass seal applied to the stem or bowl of a drinking glass, sometimes plain but often tooled and known as a strawberry prunt.

Straw-shank: stem drawn from the drinking glass bowl as a single entity. The alternative is the STUCK-SHANK where bowl and stem are made separately and joined, making, with the foot, a THREE-PIECE GLASS.

Tear: air bubble enclosed in solid glass as decoration, at first in the stem, but about 1715–60 used in clusters in bowl base, knop and finial.

Trailing: threads and bands of glass applied in wavy patterns on the surface of the glass.

DRINKING GLASSES

Most collectors begin with the forms most conveniently and widely classed as wine glasses. Bowl, stem and foot are considered separately below for ease of identification. For a few purposes, however, special styles of vessel were developed, such as the rummer, and these are considered separately.

In basic construction a wine glass may be a three-piece glass or have a straw-shank as detailed above. The **bowl** is thinner

GLASS

in work of the 1740s onwards, but a little thicker again when subject to the deep-cut ornament of the 1790s onwards. By bowl form alone it is impossible to date a glass: the dates here are offered as a guide to periods of conspicuous use. Thus the most obvious shape known as OGEE and the two-tiered DOUBLE-OGEE are noted in shallow expansive form on early 18th-century glasses and smaller and more shapely from 1750; FUNNEL bowls were never out of fashion, but the BELL that developed from the funnel, a deep bowl waisted and wide-mouthed, is associated with the period 1715–1800. In the associated THISTLE, dating from 1715 onwards, the lower part is a glass sphere, solid or hollow. In the TRUMPET, 1730s onwards, the bell-mouthed bowl merges into the drawn stem in an unbroken curve. The BUCKET, 1730–70, has horizontal base and almost vertical sides, sometimes waisted, and sometimes with a lipped rim. The plain OVOID is noted on late 18th-century glasses.

Stems. The DRAWN stem formed directly from the base of the bowl was introduced in the 17th century; 1720–45, used with waisted, thick-based bowls; from 1735, usually with trumpet bowls, and from the 1770s mainly in poor quality glasses. Drawn stems containing tears may be found 1700–60, the tears becoming long threads of air from the 1720s. Drawn stems are often ornamented with particularly attractive facet-cutting from the late 1740s to 1800s, the facets cut at first across the stem and not down and shaped as long diamonds or as long hexagons (1755–80) or scale pattern (1760–75). The central cusped knop dates from about 1760 onwards. Facets were cut more deeply from about 1770 and in the 1790s such stems tended to be shorter. Incised twists on drawn stems date 1780–1800. Vertical flutes cut from bowl to foot date to the 1790s; they may be notched, sliced or horizontally grooved.

Plain STRAIGHT stems are found on many three-piece glasses from 1725 onwards, somewhat thinner in the second

74. Chronological sequence of drinking glasses. FIRST ROW: knopped and silesian stems and drawn stem with tear. SECOND ROW: drawn stem; straight stems, plain, incised twists, air twists. THIRD ROW: four more elaborate twists and three facet-cut stems. FOURTH ROW: strong ale flute; surfeit water flute; rummer; firing glass; toasting glass; dry sweetmeat glass; jelly glass.

half of the 18th century. Hollow cylindrical stems date from the 1760s to 1780s, occasionally knopped. Incised spiral ornament may be found on such stems, 1740–80, the stem narrowing very slightly towards the centre in early examples and the incisions less regular. (*See* Twist ornament below.)

Swelling stems. (a) The simple curve known as a BALUSTER (1685–1760) is usually heavy in specimens pre-dating about 1725 and occasionally bears incised spiral ornament; thereafter it is lighter. One finds also such variants as inverted baluster and double baluster. (b) Stems composed of KNOPS include the single simple knop of the early 18th century and more elaborate groupings of knops and of knops and balusters, heavy until about 1740 and lighter 1740–55. (c) The SILESIAN or moulded pedestal has the swell as a pronounced 'shoulder'. It is noted on high quality glass of about 1705–30, the four-sided moulded stem like an inverted pyramid, never collared at the foot in early specimens. From the 1720s the stem was pinched into deep vertical flutes or reedings. Six-sided and eight-sided designs appeared about 1725–35 and 1730–50, followed by thin, coarse-ribbed versions, 1750–80. Some of better quality, four-sided and six-sided, date from the 1760s to 1780s with attractive cut ornament.

Twist ornament. Many stems, drawn, cylindrical and knopped, are ornamented with spiral patterns within the thickness of the glass. Ribs tooled in the surface of the stem, 1680–1720, were followed by incised spirals, 1740–1800, already mentioned, but the earliest twists inside the stem are the air-twists (1735–60)—usually somewhat flawed in pre-1750 work. In so-called MERCURY TWISTS (1740–60) high quality glass gives particular brilliance to the thick corkscrew air spirals. OPAQUE WHITE TWISTS (mid-1740s–80s) appear in the stuck-stems of three-piece glasses and compound arrangements of two spiralling threads of white enamel are restricted to unknopped stems. COLOUR TWISTS (1760–80) are found, some in mixed colours, or colours and white but rarely colour with air twists.

Feet. Until about 1750 feet were often but not invariably folded or welted, the early fold being very narrow. Except on sweetmeat glasses the pre-1750 foot is notably expansive. The blown foot, in trumpet shape with the end opened out to form a flat rim, folded for greater strength, is found on very early flint-glass and without the folded rim from the late 1740s into the 19th century. The early alternative is the domed foot, often surface moulded; some domes are tooled into terrace effects. The plain conical foot, rare before 1740, is almost flat underneath. It acquired a more concave lower surface from 1735 but this decreased again 1750–80. The solid square foot dates from 1770 onwards, sometimes domed or stepped.

Flutes: these are drinking glasses associated with light-coloured sparkling wines, especially with the potent drink known as strong ale, with cider and, throughout much of the collector's period, with champagne. They have deep conical bowls to retain undisturbed the slight sediment long expected in these liquors. Long flutes, 10 to 14 inches tall, were made only in light soda glass until about 1800, but short flutes in flint-glass date from the 1680s onwards. The typical flute of the 1740s has a deep, narrow, round-based bowl, its rim slightly everted, on plain, silesian, twist or facet-cut stem. From the 1770s the bowl might be a straight-sided cone vertically fluted from the base, resting on one or two knops or directly upon the foot—often square, hollow-based, from about 1780. Barrel and bucket-shaped bowls also served for strong ale late in the 18th century.

From the 1740s engraving, enamelling or gilding on the bowl may distinguish the strong ale flute (hop and barley) from the cider flute (fruiting apple tree and associated motifs), but by 1760 bucket-bowl glasses might be used for cider. Some were engraved with the cider-maker's NO EXCISE

75. 'Yard of ale' trick glass.

propaganda against threatened duties, which were imposed, nevertheless, in 1763. In the last years of the century deep flutes with twisted stems were used for cider.

Champagne was served in flutes until 1715 and again from the 1730s to the 1830s. The tall, long-stemmed champagne flute holding a gill of liquor dates from about 1745, often engraved or enamelled in white or colour with fruiting vine motifs; fluting on the lower part of the bowl might serve to obscure the sediment. Champagne glasses other than flutes consist of the almost hemispherical TAZZA, usually on a silesian stem, from about 1715 to the 1730s; and the tall-stemmed, wide-brimmed hemispherical COUPE of 1830 onwards, lavishly cut or engraved. YARD-OF-ALE FLUTES for beer may be found, the 18th-century specimen ending in a ball knop and highly domed welted foot. The 19th-century

76A. Jacobite glasses. Symbolic ornament. Star of hope and thistle, on air-twist stem; butterfly and rosebud; jay bird and jacob's ladder plant; seven-petal rose, on airtwist corkscrew stem.

76B. Jacobite glasses. TOP: with inscriptions. *Fiat* (password of the Cycle Club) with rose; *Fiat* with oak leaf; *Redeat* with star of hope; *Revirescit* with burgeoning of smitten tree (Oak Society). BOTTOM: with portraits of the Young Pretender. In tartan with Garter ribbon and inscription *audentior ibo*; in tartan between rose and thistle; in laurel wreath; with crown above and inscription *Ab obice major* below.

specimen lacks the knop and has a flat foot. The trick form, popular in the 1830s and 1840s, has a hollow bulb at the base of the flute.

Cordial glasses: small-bowled, since 18th-century cordials were fifty per cent alcohol. Until about 1740 the glass had a small, thick-walled funnel or bell bowl on a baluster or knop

stem, or a drawn trumpet bowl. Specimens of the second half
of the century are often extremely ornamental with twist or
facet-cut stems and bell, bucket or trumpet bowls engraved or
lightly cut. Some are long, very narrow tapering flutes, with
equally long drawn stems and feet twice the bowl diameter;
these are now sometimes called RATAFIA GLASSES, but were
more probably intended as distinctive vessels for the brandy
cordial known as surfeit water (Fig. 74).

Dram glasses: small sturdy vessels for spirits. The early 18th-
century bowl might be cup-shaped or conical on a knop or
baluster stem or, from 1710 to 1750, with the stem omitted
or reduced to a brief, plain stump above the heavy foot which
was always wider than the bowl rim. Another design in use
1720–1850 has trumpet bowl and short drawn stem. Ovoid,
hemispherical and thistle bowls belong to the 19th century,
and also tumbler designs with ribbed bases.

Firing glasses: a type of dram glass used for banging on the
table as a form of acclamation. They mostly date from the
1760s onwards, and are stumpy glasses on thick short stems
and heavy flat disc feet. They may be confused with SHIPS'
GLASSES, short-stemmed and with thick spreading feet designed for stability afloat (Fig. 74).

Jacobite glasses: these are particularly liable to be spurious
since their distinction depends only on the engraved ornament, more or less cryptic and associated with the Old and
Young Pretenders, such as the formalised Jacobite rose, oak
leaf, bee, stricken and burgeoning oak tree, certain Latin
phrases, etc. (Fig. 76).

Williamite glasses: with Williamite decanters, these are associated with William III and frequently dated erroneously by
collectors. The most usual ornament is an equestrian portrait
of William surrounded by a ribbon inscribed THE GLORIOUS
MEMORY. It has now been established that the majority of
these glasses were engraved no earlier than the founding of

the Orange Institution, established in Ireland in 1780 and in Manchester 1795. For technical reasons engravers after about 1805 sometimes preferred to use old glasses annealed in a manner that suited their technique, because contemporaneous glass was prepared for deep cutting. In shape and fabric, therefore, a certain number of Williamite glasses belong to the mid-18th century, although even such details as a drawn bowl

77. Williamite or orange glasses. TOP LEFT AND RIGHT: medallion heads, with classic wreath and with contemporary wig, and with *Immortal Memory* inscriptions. Tear in right stem. **CENTRE:** Williamite decanter. **BOTTOM LEFT:** fruiting vine and *Glorious Memory* inscription. **BOTTOM RIGHT:** orange plant and *Ever Flourishing* inscription.

149

78. Williamite or orange glasses. LEFT: with inscription *The Glorious Memory of King William* and equestrian portrait resembling that on the warrants used by the Grand Lodges of the Orange Institution signed by the Duke of Cumberland. CENTRE: Williamite rummer of the 1790s or later. RIGHT: typical top glass from a sweetmeat salver, often confusingly called an orange glass.

and domed or welted foot appear on a considerable amount of 19th-century glass produced by minor glassmen.

The purpose of the Orange Institution was to insist on a male descent for the British crown and so retain the united monarchy of Britain and Hanover. Engraving on Williamite glasses is comparable with the portraits and inscriptions on lodge warrants and membership certificates. Glasses engraved with copies of the Van Nost statue of William III appear to date from 1822 when the Duke of York became grand master.

Another term for these glasses is ORANGE GLASSES, but this name is better reserved for the orange or top glass on the dessert table pyramid of salvers, a tall, heavy version of the dry-sweetmeat glass, 7–11 inches high on a small foot.

Rummers: short-stemmed goblets used from the 1750s onwards for long drinks such as rum and water. The early design has an ovoid bowl and short drawn stem on a small foot. Fluting low on the bowl dates from the 1770s, hand cut and, from about 1805, blown-moulded. Other rummers have ovoid bowls, short spool-shaped stems on thick feet. Square feet date from about 1790 onwards.

The larger TODDY RUMMER, intended for preparing hot toddy, dates from the late 1780s onwards; of thick glass with ovoid bowl at first and thick square foot. Bucket and barrel bowls date from about 1800 onwards and with deep relief cutting from about 1805. The toddy would be served with a glass pipette known as a TODDY LIFTER and these too are collected.

Toastmaster glasses: from the 1740s these have tall stems and thick bowls almost wholly solid glass. For similar deception tavern keepers used short thick-walled SHAM-DRAMS, 1775–1850. These are not to be confused with TOASTING GLASSES, delicate flutes with slender stems easily snapped after an important toast. Remaining specimens date from the mid-18th century onwards.

Coolers: for individual wine glasses, these date from about 1750 to 1860 and may be confused with FINGER BOWLS (1760 onwards), but the rim of the cooler should contain one or two lips. In blue glass they date from about 1780 onwards and in ruby or green from the 1820s (Fig. 92).

79. Rummers. Serving rummer about 8 inches tall; two drinking rummers, about 6 inches; toddy lifter for serving rum toddy on the pipette principle; sugar crusher.

80. Sweetmeat glasses. TOP: two lidded sweetmeats and two for dry cuckets with openwork rim and toothed rim. BOTTOM: four sustard glasses, first and second mid-18th century, third, 1780s, fourth, Regency period.

Sweetmeat or dessert glasses. Dry sweetmeats or suckets lifted with the fingers appeared on the dessert table in wide-mouthed, tall-stemmed glasses with highly domed feet made markedly small to allow for close grouping on a glass salver. Scalloped rims date from about 1720 and the arch-and-point outline from about 1725, with more elaborate alternatives from the 1730s such as openwork loops of trailed glass. Plain rimmed glasses for dry sweetmeats are recognised by their thick rims and small feet. Almost hemispherical bowls on short stems are associated especially with the 1750s.

JELLY GLASSES of the early 18th century have waisted trumpet bowls, straight stems, plain, small, welted feet and paired double-loop handles, but those of the 1720s onwards have lost handles and stem. A knop between bowl and foot was introduced in about 1725, but fell out of favour after about 1750.

Bell-shaped bowls date from about 1740 onwards. Engraving and shallow cutting date from the 1750s onwards and deep cutting and square feet from the 1790s (Fig. 74).

SYLLABUB GLASSES, also for dessert, are twice the capacity of jelly glasses to hold the frothy whipped syllabub sweetmeat introduced by the Hanoverians. The vessel has a notably wide mouth to a double-ogee bowl which suggests in outline a saucer above a cup. Demand continued into Victoria's reign.

CUSTARDS also appeared among the wet sweetmeats of Georgian dessert tables. Early custard cups are like small tea-cups, 1½ inches tall and 2½ inches across the rim, the loop of the single handle rising a little above the rim and ending at the base in a curl. Some are shallow cut or, of the 19th century, cut deeply with diamond patterns, late specimens being a little larger and including covered and footed examples.

81. Sweetmeat glasses. TOP: two syllabub glasses, stemmed and stemless (left) and two jelly glasses (right). BOTTOM: typical salver and an indication of how a pyramid was set up; top or orange glass, about seven inches tall; detail of 'dog tooth' rim to dry sweetmeat glass.

ICE CREAM GLASSES ever since the 17th century have been straight-sided conical vessels, thick and wide-rimmed, on disc feet or on short, knopped stems and conical feet.

Collectors look too for glass SALVERS that displayed the sweetmeat glasses on the dessert tables. The general design is a flat plate on a central footed stem. Three or four salvers could be placed on top of each other and loaded with small-footed sweetmeat glasses, with a top glass—a tall-stemmed dry sweetmeat glass—for the centrepiece. The typical salver has a silesian stem and a vertical rim to the plate; in the second quarter of the 18th century the rim might project downwards too. The glass EPERGNE developed from the pyramid of salvers in the 1760s, with curved branches extending from silver or gilded brass fittings on a tapering facet-cut stem.

BOTTLES

Early English wine bottles were blown with rounded bases and protected with osier; these may be found made as late as the mid-18th century and mis-identified when the wicker is missing. They are of medium green glass, thinly blown and showing streaks and whirls both on the surface and within the glass (known as cords and striae) due to ill-heated glass. There is an applied string rim at the mouth, vertically ridged, but no base pontil mark.

The other main types of bottle are of thicker, tougher, very dark green or olive-amber glass. (a) The rounded, tall-necked shaft-and-globe was made by blowing and tooling. (b) The short-necked, cylindrical bottle appears slightly dappled from contact with the metal in which it was blown-moulded and bulges a trifle at the base, a defect remedied in the 1790s. Dated seals may help identification.

The shaft-and-globe with a knife-edge string ring was long-necked pre-1650; more boldly shouldered and incurving at the

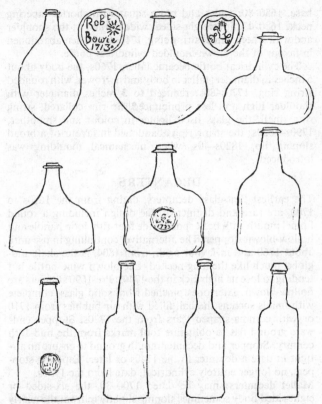

82. Bottles. TOP: wanded bottle as made to the end of the 18th century, without its osier covering; 1650–80; 1680–1715; two typical seals found on bottles. CENTRE: around 1715; 1740s; 1760s. BOTTOM: 1770; 1780s; 1800s; 1820s. All dates are approximate, with considerable overlapping.

155

base, 1650–80; wider and more squat with shorter tapering neck, 1680–1715; straight-sided, wide-necked at the shoulder and with a high, small string ring, 1715–50s, when abandoned in favour of the blown-moulded cylindrical bottle.

The cylindrical bottle became taller, 1760s, the body about 5 inches in diameter; taller in body and narrower, with rounded string ring, 1770s–80s; reduced to 3 inches diameter with shoulder high and less pronounced, lip rim collared, string ring small, the glass itself lighter in colour and smoother, 1790s–1820s; the string ring abandoned in favour of a broad sloping lip, 1820s–40s, when mechanical moulding was introduced.

DECANTERS

The earliest flint-glass decanters, dating from the 1670s to 1700, are rare and distinctive, the design including a round funnel mouth with beak spout, wide foot-rim, loop handle and hollow-blown stopper. The alternative, continuing in use until about 1760 and in favour again from 1804, is the shaft-and-globe, much like the long-necked, free-blown wine bottle but tending to lose its high kick in the 1740s. Pre-1690 stoppers are hollow-blown; later ones pinched from solid glass, complete with finials such as the ball filled with air bubbles from 1710 or with comma-shaped tears from the 1720s. Stopper ends were ground flat to obliterate tool marks from the mid-18th century. Stopper and decanter mouth ground to ensure an airtight fit date a decanter to the 1740s or later. Tapering stoppers, no longer entirely cylindrical, date from the 1750s.

Mallet decanters: may be dated 1700–30, the six-sided or eight-sided body sometimes sloping slightly in from the nearly horizontal shoulder to the base. The neck is as long as the body or longer, encircled by an applied ring about an inch below the slightly expanded mouth, a feature with a range of shapes, rounded or knife-edged and single, double or treble.

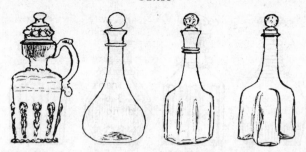

83. Decanters—early. With handle, solid-finialed blown stopper in expanded mouth, trailing ornament, about 1675. Shaft-and-globe with string ring, about 1735. Mallet shape, octagonal, ball finial with air beads and stopper not ground to fit the everted mouth, double neck ring, 1730s. Mallet in lobed or cruciform style.

84. Decanters of the 1770s–80s. Narrow-shouldered with engraved flower ornament and vertical disc stopper, 1770s. Broad-shouldered with facet cutting and cut spire stopper, 1770s. Taper with fluted neck and base and vertical lozenge stopper with bevelled edge, 1780s. Barrel, cut to suggest staves and hoops, with pear-shape stopper with scalloped edge, 1780s.

85. Decanters—early 19th century. Prussian, with prismatic cutting on neck and mushroom stopper, 1820s. Cylindrical, with two cut neck rings and mushroom stopper. With three triangular neck rings, slanting blazes on lower body, and target stopper. With feathered neck rings and convex fluted (Roman pillar) body and cut globe stopper.

In an early specimen the kick is a high cone, but is slight in those of the 1730s.

Quatrefoil decanters: date 1720s–60s, like the mallet but with the body vertically tooled into four lobes for quick cooling of its contents.

Shouldered decanters: popular 1740s–60s, and continuing to the 1800s. The shoulder may be narrow or broad, with the body slanting out or in towards the base accordingly and with the neck tall and slender. These are the earliest decanters to receive luxury ornament, engraving, gilding and even all-over facet-cutting. Some are NORWICH CUT, with shallow horizontal corrugations. An early stopper finial to this decanter may be ball-topped; spire finial stoppers date to the 1750s, ornamented in harmony with their decanters, and followed in the 1760s by flat vertical discs with diamond-cut edges and later with scalloping. Next comes the pear-shaped stopper finial.

158

Labelled decanters: dating from 1755–80 and 1810–20, of similar form but distinctively engraved with the name of the contents. Engraved 'chains' may complete the resemblance to a silver wine label. White or coloured enamelling may be noted for such labels instead of engraving and this has been reproduced. Regency label decanters are of the Prussian shape.

Champagne decanters: from the 1750s, another narrow-shouldered form with a cylindrical pocket extending into the bottle to hold ice.

Taper decanters: from 1765–80 and on into the 1800s; more slender and less sharply shouldered. The neck may be cut with facets or flutes and the base cut with a circuit of vertical flutings. In a post-1770 specimen the mouth may be widely flared. Stopper finials changed from scalloped discs to flat vertical lozenges and pear shapes.

Barrel or Indian club decanters: from 1775–1800 and self-explanatory, the bulging body curved in at the base to equal the shoulder diameter and cut with vertical flutes and hori-

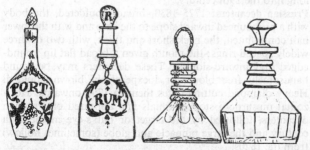

86. Decanters of distinctive types. Two label decanters and two Rodney or ships' decanters. The port decanter painted in white enamel on clear glass, with spire finial. The rum in gold with chain effect on Bristol blue glass. The ships' decanters were made in pint and quart sizes, about 1800–20.

159

87. Cordial decanter, round-footed on square plinth, with lunar cutting on stopper finial, about 1790. Two **claret jugs,** of the 1820s and the 1850s. **Square** of the 1800s.

zontal rings, to suggest staves and hoops. Here too a flaring lip was developed; a rarity is the lip with a flat surface and vertical edge. A slender barrel decanter on a square pedestal foot was introduced for cordials about 1780 and continued long into the 19th century.

Prussian decanters: 1775–1830, broad-shouldered, the body with a pronounced inward slope to the base and with the lower half comb-fluted, the neck short and thick, with two or three widely spaced rings; the mouth given a broad flat lip, round-edged and inward-sloping. These decanters may be found handsomely free blown or inexpensively blown-moulded. Heavy diamond cutting dates them to 1790 onwards. Horizontal mushroom stopper finials first appeared on Prussian decanters, followed by the target or bull's-eye in the 19th century and the large pinnacle and globe (sometimes hollow) from the 1820s.

Ships' or Rodney decanters: 1780s–1830s, designed for extra stability in heavy thick glass. The form appeared from the side as a triangle with wide base and straight sides slanting directly to the neck.

88. Four late decanters. Pillar-cut body and deep mushroom stopper, 1820s. Three of the 1850s showing typical outlines and extremely deep cutting.

Cylindrical decanters: date from the 1790s to 1830s, with vertical sides, fluted in diminishing size from the base to the lowest neck ring. Various styles of cutting are found on these, becoming especially elaborate in the 1820s and early 1830s. Mushroom stoppers were used until about 1820, then heavy pinnacles.

Neck rings are important features of Prussian and cylindrical decanters, round, square-cut, feathered, facet-cut, but after about 1815 they might be omitted and the whole neck lit with prismatic cutting.

The ROYAL DECANTER was introduced in 1828 with inward-sloping sides cut from base to neck in 12 or 14 vertical convex flutes.

Various shapes of decanter entirely covered with surface cutting appeared from the 1830s onwards and some with foot rings, especially from 1840.

Squares: in use throughout the Georgian period, early ones resembling mallet decanters but more with high shoulders and very short necks. Very many were blown-moulded from about 1745, slightly tapering towards the base as required for the

89. Candlesticks. Deep socket with rolled lip, central air-bubble knop in stem and high domed foot, about 1730. With loose sconce, double-baluster body, plain sloping foot, 1750s. With narrower socket and fixed sconce, silesian mould-shaped body and high moulded foot, about 1740. With moulded-ribbed socket, double silesian body and plain domed foot, about 1750.

one-piece mould. CARAFES for water follow decanter forms but have curved-over, out-spreading mouths.

CANDLESTICKS

The earliest known are in flint-glass of the 1680s, hollow-blown with knopped stems and high pedestal or bell feet. Solid glass candlestick stems were used from the 1690s, baluster or knopped on domed or pedestal feet, sockets and feet sometimes hand tooled with surface patterns.

The early 18th-century specimen tends to have a taller stem composed of an inverted baluster with knops above and below, such as flattened ball knops with air beads. Sockets are often strengthened with rolled-over edges and fitted with loose nozzles, saucer rimmed. Socket ornament may date from the 1710s onwards and slightly waisted outlines from the 1720s; shallow cutting from the 1740s. From the 1730s the socket lip began to be expanded, eventually becoming a large grease-pan. Feet consist of blown domes or inverted saucer shapes, often with welted rims, or are in sloping terraced outlines. The development of sharply shouldered silesian stems was reflected in spreading dome feet moulded with vertical or radial ridges.

Stems of the 1730s may have central spherical ornament, the ball, solid at first but later blown with ribbed or trellis ornament, set between knops or collars.

Shouldered or silesian stems, including inverted and multiple variants, date from 1710 onwards, often with knops as additional ornament, and tend to dominate early Georgian design.

Rib-twisted baluster stems date mainly 1730s–50s. Specimens of the second half of the 18th century are in finer quality glass. Air-twist stems were introduced in the late 1730s and in single-knopped stems from 1750; opaque white twists, 1750s–80s.

Facet-cut stems, and sockets and feet, date from the 1730s and with facet-cut knops or a central cusp from the 1750s. The socket, straight or sometimes waisted, has a loose nozzle

90. Candlesticks. Air twist stem of 1740s. Enamel twist stem as continued to 1780s. Facet-cut in simple diamonds with loose sconce and moulded foot, 1750s. With socket cut in long diamonds, cusped facet-cut stem and domed foot with sliced edge to the scalloped rim, 1760s.

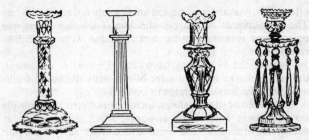

91. Candlesticks. With shouldered socket and foot cut in scale pattern, the sconce and foot in cyma outline, and tall diamond-cut pillar stem, 1780s. Simple pillar design on domed and terraced foot. Vase candlestick with elaborate sconce, fluted body and faceted square foot, 1790s. Girandole candlestick hung with lustres on a revolving glass flange with a gilded metal mount, and the circular foot radially cut beneath, 1820s.

matching the foot ornament; by 1750 it might be ornamented with scale cutting. The heavy foot is a square-shouldered dome with wide flange, often deeply ridged, and scalloped rim; more rarely it is blown-moulded with a high dome and given a welted rim.

Enamel glass candlesticks suggesting white porcelain date from the early 1760s onwards, with baluster stems, spreading dome feet painted with flowers, and painted enamel nozzles.

The main trend noted in work of the 1760s is in the neo-classic outlines, the faceted stem tapering from foot to socket being ousted by the classical column merging into a socket, saucer-shaped at first and later vase-shaped. The domed cut foot, sometimes with terraced or stepped rim, was ousted by the stepped square foot.

The late 18th century produced many cheaper moulded candlesticks, sockets, bodies and feet made as separate solid units with hand tools by pinchers (p. 137). The usual pattern has a hexagonal socket and round stem; others are hexagonal throughout. Some early specimens have barrel bodies; by the late 1780s the 'stave' ribs might be notched. Loose pinched nozzles may show notched edges to saucer rims; feet repeat the styles used on rummers.

Vase candlesticks: date from the 1780s onwards, in solid urn shapes and variously ornamented. Superbly prismatic-cut urn shapes with inverted saucer bases date from the 1820s; some have flat hexagonal feet, and round pressed feet also date from this period. Petal nozzles date from the 1820s.

Tapersticks: 4 to 6 inches high, these follow the changing shapes of the larger candlesticks, but their deep, narrow sockets lack loose nozzles. CHAMBER CANDLESTICKS are very rare, and here again fakes may be encountered.

IRISH GLASS

The Round Glass House, Dublin, was a flourishing concern between the 1690s and 1755, products covering the full range of table glass 'cut and flowered', according to a mid-century advertisement and even including 'jars and beakers of mock china'. Then the Excise Act of 1745 had its effect, forbidding export of glass from Ireland. By 1770, however, Richard Williams and Co., Dublin, were supplying all Ireland with flint-glass, and in 1780 the removal of export restrictions helped the industry. Several glass houses were established, in Belfast, Dublin, Cork, Waterford, selling more cheaply than the English because they were not subject to tax, but to some extent subsidised. The glass of the 1780s and 1790s usually has a dusky tint, but that of the 1800s is clearer—some slightly blue—and excellent for deep cutting. Blue glass compares with English Bristol blue. Blown-moulded glass may be noted also.

In 1825 the Irish flint-glass trade came under the same tax demands—10½d. per lb—as the English, who had been taxed

92. Styles of glass associated with Ireland. TOP: fruit bowls, two in
kettle drum shape and one canoe. CENTRE: moulded butter cooler;
cut scent flask; goblet; moulded square bottle; two-lipped wine
glass cooler. BOTTOM: two decanters showing the vesica pattern,
one cut and the second roughly engraved; moulded water jug
roughly engraved with the typical Cork conventional flower; claret
jug with prismatic cutting and printies.

from 1745, and the decline in trade was hastened when England began making cheap pressed glass in the early 1830s. In 1835 the Excise Commission reported that great quantities of English glass entered Ireland and all the richly-cut decanters there and heavy table ware were English made.

It must be stressed that most Irish glass followed the same designs popular in England, and neither the surface bloom nor the blue tint associated with some Irish glass can be claimed as solely Irish characteristics. In Irish glass as in English the blue tint, due to use of Derbyshire lead, had been eliminated by about 1816, but may be noted in fakes.

Marks. Unlike English glass Irish may be found with makers' marks. These include: Armstrong Ormond Quay; B. Edwards Belfast; C.M.Co (Charles Mulvany and Co., Dublin); Cork Glass Co.; Francis Collins, Dublin; Mary Carter and Son, Dublin; Penrose, Waterford; Waterloo, Co. Cork. Armstrong, Carter, Collins and Mulvany were wholesale glass sellers.

Important makers include: Belfast, Benjamin Edwards, at work 1781–1829. Cork Glass House, which became the Cork Glass House Company in 1812, a name sometimes noted on prussian and mallet decanters, which thus date 1812–18. Cork, Terrace Glass House, 1819–41. Cork, Waterloo Glass House Co., 1815–35. The vesica cut or engraved ornament is associated with the Cork glass-houses. Dublin, Chebsey & Co., Venice Glass-house, 1784–99, made fine table glass and in 1789 the magnificent lustres for Dublin Castle; the New Venice Glass-house, 1799–1802. Newry, Flint Glass Manu-

93. Typical marks found on the bases of Irish decanters.

factory, a small establishment, 1780s–1801, and another 1824–47. Waterford Glass Works (George and William Penrose) established 1784 with a works manager from the Coalbournhill glass-house near Stourbridge; under successive owners it continued to 1851, producing cut glass of a quality to compete with English work. Waterford also imported and sold English glass.

NAILSEA GLASS

This term covers a style of late Georgian and Victorian glassware produced not only at Nailsea near Bristol, but at Sunderland, Newcastle, Stourbridge, Warrington, Wrockwardine Wood, Shropshire, Alloa, Scotland, and elsewhere. The Nailsea glass-house itself was founded 1788 and closed 1873. The work is typified by the range of colours, opaque and translucent—milk-white, yellow, rose-pink, green, blue of many hues—spectacularly patterned with streaks, splotches, zig-zags in contrasting colours or more complex threads and stripes. The collector looks for all manner of gay nonsense such as walking sticks, giant tobacco pipes, coaching and hunting horns, witch balls, rolling pins, scent bottles and various styles of flask including the bellows shape and twin or gimmel form. Inevitably fakes have been plentiful for the last fifty years.

Tax impositions affected early development, until the 1845 abolition of the tax on flint-glass, and approximate periods of manufacture can be classified as follows:

1790–1820: low-taxed brownish-green bottle glass ornamented with surface flecking, mottling and encircling trails of white enamel. The flecks feel rough to the fingers and on genuine work are usually finely crazed with tiny irregular lines. Red and yellow flecks are prized rarities.

1800–20: light-green bottle glass with crackling and notched trailing ornament in white enamel.

1815–45: pale green bottle glass coloured in semi-opaque

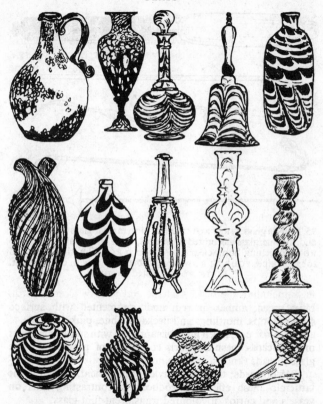

94. Nailsea glass. TOP: jug and vase of the early splashed style; decanter, bell and bottle striped. CENTRE: gimmel flask in latticinio style, post-1800; striped flask; bellows-shaped bottle with trailing; two candlesticks hollow all through. BOTTOM: striped ball; dated and initialled scent bottle with crimping, 1810s; jug; boot.

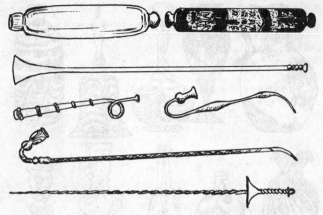

95. Nailsea glass. FIRST ROW: rolling pins, in clear glass with stopper; and in blue glass decorated with dots, both ends sealed. SECOND ROW: coaching horn, clear glass. THIRD ROW: hunting horn and tobacco pipe. FOURTH ROW: long tobacco pipe with colour twist. FIFTH ROW: twisted sword.

blue, green, amber or red, and ornamented with surface stripes, loops, mottlings and flecks in white, pink and blue.

1800s–45: pale green glass ornamented with spiralling effects of criss-cross mesh network composed of pink and white glass threads (known as latticinio).

1845 onwards: the earlier styles of ornament, including the latticinio mesh effects, introduced in contrasting tints on vessels and curios of coloured translucent flint-glass.

Mugs, jugs, tumblers, jars and flasks are widely collected, including the gimmel flask which consists of two bottles blown separately and fused together and often given a crimped or petal foot. This is often found with pink and white spiral ornament or loops of white latticinio. Flasks were sold containing toilet waters and perfumes and another favourite design copies the dressing table bellows used for powdering the hair. Giant bellows date to the mid-19th century.

Bells: made at several glass-houses, 9 to 18 inches high, and still in production. Colour combinations on genuine specimens include: blue bell, pale yellow handle with opalescent finial; opaque white bell with pink thread ornament, and opaque white hand as handle; translucent red bell ornamented with white stripes, with opalescent blue handle; red bell with colour-twist spiral handle; green bell with opaque white twist handle; opaque white throughout. All have clear flint-glass clappers.

Candlesticks: hollow from base to socket, these suggest early Georgian form, with ribbed socket, knopped stem and trumpet foot, but are in the full Nailsea colour range.

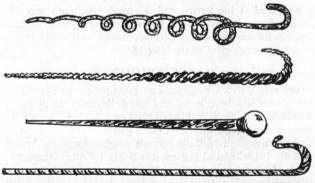

96. Nailsea glass. FROM TOP TO BOTTOM: walking stick, the snake effect emphasised by the internal colour twist; walking stick with typical tapering twist; with round head and marble colouring; with internal colour twist, crook handle and no taper.

Glass rolling pins: these may be found in the early dusky bottle glass, tapering slightly to each end. As containers first for salt, then for tea, then for comfit sweets, they progressed through the Nailsea styles of ornament until the vessel with ground-in ball-headed stopper was replaced by the solid-knobbed wall ornament. Many came from Sunderland in opaque white, the early enamel ornament lasting better than later oil colours, and the Birmingham-Stourbridge area made innumerable specimens in plain colours. Solid, heavy flint-glass rollers post-date 1845.

Witch balls: found in thick, dark bottle glass flecked and spotted and in green and blue with the Nailsea range of ornament including, eventually, transfer-printed pictures applied to the inner surface and backed with colour-marbled opaque-white. Many, like late rollers, have no openings.

Other items include **walking sticks, shepherds' crooks** and hollow **canes** filled with tiny comfit sweets. Early specimens are tapered at the ferrule end. **Poinards** are found and 40–48-in. dress **swords, riding crops** and **horns,** early small-bowled **tobacco pipes** and later specimens with larger bowls and in the finer glass of the later 1840s.

PAPERWEIGHTS

Letter-weights to Georgians and press-papers to early Victorians are widely collected and faked. Basically the design is a rounded mound or cushion of glass on a flat base containing ornament enclosed within the solid glass.

Crystal cameos or crystallo ceramie weights: made by Apsley Pellatt, 1819–35, and copied less finely by other glassmen, 1845–65, as medallion inlays. The feature of this design is a bas-relief profile portrait, known as a sulphide, usually copied from a medal or coin and frequently a head-and-shoulders of royalty such as George IV modelled as a Roman Caesar. This was cast in a china clay material and enclosed in particularly

172

clear, brilliant flint-glass. Coloured sulphides such as crests are very rare. The weight was finished by cutting the back or base with cross lines, facets, etc. The shape may be a flat plaque three to six inches across or a vertical plaque on a flat base.

Dumps: these were in production at Bristol and Nailsea by 1828, and are found in larger sizes as door porters. The dump was made in a bright watery bottle green glass at Bristol and a softer green at Nailsea, and soon after at Birmingham and elsewhere in coarser tones. Soft transparent green flint-glass was introduced in 1845. These high-crowned, egg-shaped weights appear to contain fountaining drops of water or sprays of flowers and leaves created by piercing the hot glass to form air bubbles.

A cheap dump will show a rough pontil mark, ground flat in better quality work. In one type a central core of glass was dipped in a clay mixture and appears in the finished weight as a flower pot for 'flowers' formed with a piercing tool dipped in the same composition. After 1845 coloured flowers were made and entrapped in clear glass. Garish modern reproductions lack the attractive colouring and lack, too, the silvery air bubbles or 'dew' of the Victorian specimen. Cheaper weights have the vividly coloured motifs in flat silhouette patterned with spangles.

Coloured glass paperweights: these date from 1845 onwards, when abolition of the glass tax made them practicable. First maker probably was the firm W.H.P. and J. Richardson of Wordsley, who produced *overlay* or *cased glass* weights, covering the flint-glass with layers of coloured glass so that oblique cutting edged the cut patterns with stripes of the different colours.

Millefiori work: the glass of a thousand flowers was introduced to England from France. These weights tend to be more costly and more frequently modern than the other styles, but

97. Paperweights. TOP: Apsley Pellatt weight, the face set off by deep horizontal cutting and with star cutting under the base; side view and top view of bubble-filled 'dump'; with air-formed 'flower', petals 'dew-tipped'. CENTRE: with flowers on a solid green base; side view and top view of a millefiori weight; with flowers and a moth motif. BOTTOM: top view and side view of a cased millefiori weight, the flowers seen through windows cut in the coloured surface of the glass; tazza with millefiori base; inkpot with millefiori base and stopper.

at their best are exquisite, with brilliantly coloured tiny circles, spirals, and florets cut as thin slices from rods of multi-coloured glass and made into flat carpets of massed flowers rendered vivid and magnified by the domes of clear glass.

France set the fashion in the 1840s at Baccarat, St Louis and Clichy with weights often containing the firms' or makers'

initials, but vast numbers were made in Birmingham by
George Bacchus and Sons and other glass centres such as
London and Stourbridge, so perfect that they frequently sell
as French.

English Venetian balls, the first type, now rare, date 1845–47,
containing haphazard conglomerations of coloured filigree
enamel. Early millefiori dates 1846–50, the florets arranged
within the dome of the glass itself, this being followed by the
finest quality work with the florets restricted to the flat base
and only seeming to fill the glass. Less delicate late work
dates 1870–85. The weights are found as bun shapes, cones,
ovoids, hemispheres, their bases polished clear of pontil marks
and often ground hollow to show the pattern in miniature,
or cut with stars. Overlay or cased glass may be found on a
millefiori weight, the colours ground away to offer 'windows'
for viewing the pattern inside.

CHAPTER NINE

Silver

Collectors of English silver have a wide range of pieces to delight and bewilder them. But they find the same moods expressed in design and decoration of very different collectable items. In this brief survey it is only possible to indicate something of the major trends and always, it must be understood, the collector will find both an overlapping of styles and a diversity of individual notions.

The architectural mood of Charles II's reign only gradually gave place to the rounded curves that sharpened into the clear-cut brilliancies of Queen Anne and early Georgian work, perfectly expressed in faceted stem and octagonal base, but soon overshadowed by the asymmetrical rococo extravagancies of scroll and shell, mask and monster and the chinoiserie motifs associated with the mid-18th century.

The neo-classic mood dominated the third quarter of the century with its uninterrupted curves, Greco-Roman inspired, and the collector notes among smaller detail a delight in clear-cut edges in undulating patterns to remind one of the rivalry of Sheffield plate which required edge mouldings. At this period factory processes tended to dominate and render more uniform the less expensive wares: hand raising, was replaced by flat rolled plate and spinning, and saw cutting by simpler press piercing, but increasing elaboration of detail characterised the costly creations of the master silversmiths. In all work the outline and ornamental detail gradually changed to stouter, more practical forms at the century's end when vessels tended to be more capacious and perhaps somewhat squat. To be followed in late Georgian and William IV days by the 'revived rococo', heavily flamboyant and lacking the grace of a century earlier.

Candlesticks. These moods are expressed clearly in English candlesticks. Column styles dominate those of the last quarter of the 17th century. The fixed socket surmounts the abacus above the fluted column with a second plain abacus below between the column and the spreading foot. Late 17th-century silverwork reflects the current love of S-scrolls and many variants of the baluster outline well suited to candlestick design. The baluster stick may be found in its several phases,

98. Candlesticks. TOP: pillar style of 1680s; baluster of 1700s; octagonal, about 1715; four-sided with clipped corners, 1730s. BOTTOM: with scalloped rim and base, 1750s–60s; neo-classic style, 1760s; urn socket and tapering fluted body, 1780s; gadrooned style of 1810s.

gadroon-ornamented, plain, faceted. In those of the 1730s and 1740s the baluster shoulder is emphasised and there may be a spreading nozzle. The most elaborate of this period are loaded with rococo ornament, but plain balusters are noted too and around the mid-century the scroll-based figure supporting a wide-nozzled socket.

Work of the 1760s includes the modified baluster, gadroon-shouldered, perhaps, on a square gadrooned base or fluted on a domed base edged with scallops. But by then the classic revival was prompting uncluttered outline expressed in tall corinthian column candlesticks sometimes fluted and with low relief ornament such as floral swags, masks and rams' heads. The four-sided tapering stem with urn candlesocket and square pedestal foot is associated with the 1770s and the tapering stem on a fluted base, both circular on plan, is associated with the 1780s. The styles continued well into the 19th century with some deterioration of design and with the reintroduction of heavy-handed rococo ornament.

Chamber candlesticks and wax jacks. Chamber candlesticks, too, may be found from the late 17th century, with less variation of the basic design. This consists of a shallow saucer with the candlesocket rising from a central convexity and a curving

99. Chamber candlesticks. Specimen of 1750s with snuffers under socket and extinguisher on handle; design of the 1780s and 1790s showing space for the snuffers; taper holder of the 1800s, the flexible wax taper wound on the reel and its end gripped vertically.

lateral handle supporting a conical extinguisher. The loose
spreading nozzle dates from the 1730s onwards, as do hoof
feet. By the 1760s the socket was vase shaped, with reeded
moulding towards the century's end, when the tray might be
rectangular on ball feet. Some examples of the early 19th
century lack nozzles to the wide socket rims.

For a smaller flame, convenient to carry and safe to forget,
the alternative to a chamber candlestick was the wax jack or
taper winder, and these too are collected. The flame is provided by a coil of flexible wax taper in an open frame, its end
held vertical in a spring clip. Early tapers are thicker than
those on the more common, more compact and less ornate
wax jacks of the late 18th century, when already a popular
alternative was the plain bougie box encasing the taper with a
central nozzle in the cover.

Teapots. A silver teapot is a collector's luxury. The earliest
popular designs date to Anne's reign, small and somewhat
squat with a domed lid, the body in melon outline, sometimes
delightfully strengthened with ribbing, or pear shaped, often
eight-sided. The swan-neck spout was introduced about 1705
and recurving scrolls often take the place of D-handles
from about 1710. Contemporaneous tea kettles with tripod
stands for spirit lamps show many of the same features.

Early Georgian teapots tended to become wider in proportion to height and include the globular or bullet design popular
throughout the century, variously ornamented with chasing,
flat or in high relief. The stemmed bullet pot is regarded as a
Scottish variant. The inverted pear shape with a wide foot
rim dates from the mid-century, often with a bird-headed
spout, but this was soon modified to the neo-classic urn shape
with smoothly curving spout and handle. Such designs, shaped
by hammering from the flat plate, were costly to make and in
the 1760s less expensive styles were evolved that could be
shaped from rolled sheet silver, vertical sided and either round

179

100. Teapots. TOP: octagonal with lidded spout, intended for a heater stand, 1700s; bullet shape, the lid contained in the rounded line, about 1710–20; shape associated with Scottish silversmiths and with insulated silver handle commoner by the end of the century, 1750s. CENTRE: neo-classic footed style with insulated handle, 1770s–1780s; popular style inexpensively assembled from factory-made units, on a tray to protect table top, 1770s–80s; flat-lidded, flat-hinged squat design on ball feet instead of tray, 1790s. BOTTOM: typical outline of the 1800s with flaring rim to lid opening; frequent oblong shape easily made from rolled sheet silver, with square-shouldered handle, weak spout and ball feet; one of innumerable fancy shapes of the 1830s, the melon outline revived and loaded with applied leaves and mouldings.

oval or polygonal on plan. In the last years of the century they were often enriched with fluting or reeding.

In an early specimen of the neo-classic style one looks for an accompanying silver stand on small feet, but soon the tea-pot acquired ball feet, or the flaring rim foot of George IV work. Many pots of the century's end are somewhat rounded at the junctions of side and base, capacious rather than elegant, but less cluttered with ornament than the revived rococo of the 1820s–30s.

Tea kettles. Tea kettles include many richly ornamented in high relief in the exuberant manner of the 1730s and 1740s, but they were going out of fashion by the 1760s when neo-classic enthusiasts found peculiar delight in urns. These may be found with and without spirit lamps: alternative heating methods include a cylindrical box iron heated red hot and placed in a socket inside the urn, and a perforated charcoal

101. Tea kettles. Kettle on stand, twelve-sided, with lidded spout, the kettle with wood handles, the stand, with its own lifting handles, with wood feet, about 1715. Globular kettle on stand of the 1740s–50s. Tea urn in the neo-classic manner with festoon ornament and footed plinth.

burner sending hot air through a copper tube inside the urn with a loose finial on the lid.

Coffee pots. For coffee straight-sided lantern shapes with right or left handles—sold in pairs—were soon replaced by more graceful outlines, still often straight-sided but with domed lid, swan-neck spout and moulded foot-rim. Pear and inverted pear shapes on wide foot-rims date from early Georgian days, followed by urn shapes in the 1760s, with urn lid finials and mounted on square or circular feet. The early chocolate pot in similar outlines is smaller and distinguished by the hole in the cover for the swizzle rod for stirring the drink before pouring. Later specimens resemble ewers or hot water jugs.

Tea canisters and tea caddies. For storing the tea leaves equal elegance was required when the hostess herself put them into the pot. By the 1730s it was fashionable to have three matching canisters in a decorative box; in the second half of

102. Coffee pots. Early style with domed lid, lidded spout, cut-card work to reinforce the joints, and a heavy wooden handle, with thumb rest, set at right angles to the spout, 1700s. Double-dome lid and baluster body with heavy, open spout and handle, 1750s–60s. Lighter style with dainty bead mouldings, simple, graceful outline from the urn finial to the high foot, 1780s.

the century two matching canisters and a wide-mouthed sugar box were most usual in the tea chest. Queen Anne and early Georgian canisters are box shaped. Early specimens have smalled domed lids used for measuring the tea but by about 1710 the whole top of the canister including the lid would slide off for refilling. By about 1720 an alternative was the hinged—and locked—lid in a stepped design covering the whole top of the canister. Design varied in detail but in the

103. Tea canisters. TOP: Queen Anne style shown partly open for refilling: only the dome would be opened for measuring tea into the pot. Locked canister with hinged lid and lead lining, 1720s. Spiralling vase shape of the 1760s. Bombé shaping in style of current tea chests, 1750s. BOTTOM: Chinese tea gatherers among massive scrolls in high relief chinoiserie canister of the 1760s. Vase shape of the 1770s. Simple sheet silver design of the 1780s with bright-cut engraving (*see also* Fig. 128).

104. Tea caddies and accessories. TOP: locking tea caddy of the
1780s with hinged lid and lower body fluting. Austere style of the
1790s. Massive double-lidded tea chest of the Regency. BOTTOM:
caddy ladles. Tea leaf with twisted stalk handle; shell; jockey cap;
spoon shape with clean-cut edges in contrast to Sheffield plate
work; shovel.

1740s roundly curving forms were introduced, in harmony
with bombé tea chest design, wide shouldered, waisted, with
wide foot-rim or out-curved feet. Much of the period's rococo
ornament on tea ware is more or less oriental.

Larger canisters were in demand by the 1760s when classic
vases and urns were acceptable. Tall arching handles are
associated with the period 1775–95, but by 1785 the design
was becoming sturdier. Many single canisters of this period—
caddies—may be noted harmonising with silver teapots, both
in the straight-sided styles, elliptical or polygonal on plan.
Others are square or rectangular.

Caddy ladles. Caddy ladles are widely collected, the short-
handled scoop dating mainly from the 1770s onwards. Some
of the earliest are shell-shaped but other designs range from
the jockey cap (sometimes in filigree) to the cupped hand, and
from the fruiting vine of the 1790s–1820s to the simple tea leaf.

184

Fiddle-shaped handles date from the first years of the 19th century. It may be noted that these ladles were never among the small items of silver exempted from hall marking.

Milk jugs. Small milk jugs contributed charmingly to the tea equipage from the first years of the 18th century; cream ewers were introduced in the later years of the century. The earliest are 'hot milk pots' harmonising with teapots and kettles of their day, more or less pear-shaped, often octagonal on plan, with domed lid and short, covered spout. Much the same outline was developed for the very small cold milk jug from

105. Milk jugs. TOP: lidded, with lidded spout and wood handle, fot hot milk. The earliest style for cold milk, often only $2\frac{1}{2}$–$3\frac{1}{2}$ inches tall, with applied beak spout, 1720s. Wide-rimmed style suggested by rosewater ewer, with spreading moulded foot, 1720s–30s. Three-footed for greater steadiness, though some of this date have one foot under the spout, and with daintier handle, mid-1730s. BOTTOM: three-footed cream boat, 1730s. Egg shape with three scroll feet. Boat with feet and free-standing handle, 1750s. With lip and rim of ewer type and flower embossing, 1760s.

the 1720s, pear or baluster shaped on a spreading foot rim
with an attached beak spout. As the vessel became broader,
on a moulded foot, the spout became an integral part of the
rim, rising upwards and forwards and balanced by a scrolling
handle, a feature that is noted in more elaborate forms towards the mid-century.

Three-footed jugs too may date from as early as the 1720s,
the usual arrangement at first being one foot under the lip,
noted also on some hot milk jugs where a steady stance was
equally important for the tiny vessel. Soon it became more
usual to have one foot under the handle. Shallow boats for
cream show similar details of wavy rim, forward-thrust spout,
scroll handle and shapely feet. They were usually sold in pairs
and their successive phases of ornament suggest fascinating
possibilities to the collector—some were cast in relief patterns
from the 1720s or occasionally shaped as nautilus shells; some
were hand raised and engraved or lightly chased, or worked
with low embossing from the 1740s, or ornamented with
applied motifs.

Some helmet-shaped jugs are associated with the second
quarter of the century but more date to the classic revival.
On the pear-shaped jugs of the 1740s the main change to note
is the growing abundance of embossed and chased ornament,
with rare glass-lined pierced work in the third quarter of the
century.

Neo-classic notions of design are recorded in many a graceful high-handled little jug of the 1760s and onwards but the
period is also associated with vessels in a more workaday
design, the body an inverted pear-shape, broad below the
neck and tapering to a hollow pedestal stem, often shaped by
spinning. Vase and urn jugs are found on broad foot-rims but
to represent the 1780s and 1790s flat-based substantial little
pitchers may be found, some elliptical on plan, some barrel-
shaped, as well as bail-handled vessels for clotted cream—

either pierced, glass-lined baskets or pails shaped and tooled to suggest staved buckets. Regency jugs may be vase-shaped, often reeded or with gadrooned rim and foot and sometimes raised on small feet like the companion teapot. The high handle is square-shouldered and there may be a beak spout. Even in these vessels ornament may be heavy and elaborate and 'revived rococo' decoration of the 1830s may be noted on footed pear-shapes reminiscent of the previous century.

Sugar boxes, bowls, baskets. Vessels for sugar changed down the centuries from hasp-secured boxes to covered bowls and from these to open baskets. A rare treasure to-day is a shell-shaped sugar box of the later 17th century, when sugar was

106. Milk jugs. TOP: pierced, with blue glass lining, on pedestal foot, 1770s. A typical minor style of the 1780s. Neo-classic plain sweeping lines on wide foot. Cream pail, 1790s. BOTTOM: neat helmet shape on spreading foot, end of 18th century. With oval body and gadrooned ornament, 1800s. Oval, sturdy little pitcher, 1800s. Dipping rim, square handle, gadrooned moulding, 1800s.

107. Sugar vessels and tongs. TOP: hasped box of 17th century;
lidded bowl of 1715; elaborately embossed style of mid-18th century; neo-classic style of 1780s. CENTRE: open canoe-shaped
basket, 1790s; hand-pierced openwork with blue glass lining, 1780s;
less elaborately press-pierced, 1780s; flat-based heavy style of 1800s.
BOTTOM: early tongs with arch spring and arms in round section
and shell grips; scissors type, with a spring mechanism in the central
box dating from 1749; stork design, third quarter of 18th century;
flat section spring and arms, perforated, with shell grips, later
18th century; bright-cut engraved, instead of pierced, and with
spoon grips, end of 18th century; mote skimmer with perforated
spoon bowl and barb finial.

served with wine. For the earliest tea drinkers silversmiths devised the sugar bowl, copying an oriental vessel, the domed saucer-shaped cover with a central moulded ring resting on an equally plain hemispherical bowl with ring foot. Sometimes the bowl is angular on plan and the saucer lid may have three small feet instead of the ring moulding. Such bowls continued, becoming more capacious and acquiring surface ornament, but the collector looks for ogee outlines around the mid-18th century, often high footed and loaded with asymmetrical ornament or spirally fluted, often in a three-footed design. Vase shapes may be found from 1760 onwards, with high arching handles.

Hand-pierced sugar vessels lined with Bristol blue glass may date from the 1750s onwards with matching ornament on cover, body and foot or in a lidless basket design with short-stemmed foot and swing handle. Some are footless buckets. Later piercing lacks the intricacy of early work. Canoe-shaped baskets date from the 1780s, often matching teapot and milk jug instead of merely harmonising as heretofore. In the early 19th century many follow the somewhat squat flat-bottomed capacious outlines of the milk pitcher and melon shapes may be noted with conspicuously lavish decoration from the 1830s.

It must be realised, of course, that other sugar vessels were made from the 1730s onwards to accompany tea canisters in the tea chest, larger than the canisters and opening to the full extent of the top, until the 1770s when glass bowls often replaced them.

Sugar tongs. Tongs date from the 1690s, the earliest being dainty little tools with shell grips on thin round-section arms linked by a springy bow. The scissor style was developed in the late 1730s and from 1749 this might incorporate a spring so that the shell grips remained closed until deliberately released, a usual feature by 1755. The stork is a variant of the scissor design. Simpler tongs with flat arms and a flat U-shaped

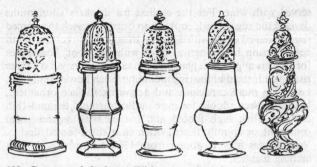

108. Casters and dredgers. With cover pierced and engraved and bayonet fastener, 1700s. Octagonal pear-shaped body, with different patterns in the sections of perforation, 1710s. Baluster body, with more formal patterns of perforation, 1720s. Double-curved body and drilled perforations, 1760s. Swirling rococo embossing on high-footed example of 1760s.

spring arch date from about 1760. At first the arms were cast, often in elaborate openwork patterns, but press piercing followed in the 1780s and unpierced, bright-cut or chased arms in the 1790s with spoon-shaped grips. From 1815 some sugar tongs were made to match old English or fiddle tea spoon patterns.

Mote skimmers. Yet another small detail of the 18th-century tea equipage is the mote skimmer. This is a long tea spoon, its finial a tiny barb and its bowl decoratively pierced. Tea dust floating on the poured cup of tea was removed with the bowl and the barb cleared the tea-leaves from the strainer inside the teapot.

Casters. For sugar, and for pepper too, casters offer the collector rich prizes. By the later 17th century they were available in sets of three for sugar and jamaica and cayenne peppers. These are vertical cylinders, plain or strengthened by in-and-out shaping, their highly domed covers fret-cut with diamonds, fleurs-de-lys and the like. Body and cover are usually secured by bayonet fasteners, lugs projecting below the rim of the cover fitting notches cut in the body moulding so that a turn of the cover makes it secure. Sometimes one finds a pull-off cover with tapering extension inside the body.

By the end of the century the cover was a little smaller in diameter than the body, and by 1705 might be enriched with a circle of applied moulding. The body is found in pear-shape, the upper half in concave outline and the lower half nearly hemispherical, and also, by the beginning of the 18th century, in the complementary baluster shape, wide shouldered and narrowing above a wide foot. Some elaboration of ornament may be noted, too, while the formal patterns of the cover piercing are particularly rich. Here as in other silver ware octagonal outlines are associated with George I's reign. The pear-shaped body with an extra curve in the swelling lower half dates from about 1750: frequently the cover is pierced less elaborately in diagonal patterns and the widely popular scrolling effect is noted in elaborate embossing on the body. Cylindrical casters with domed covers secured by bayonet fasteners, and with fret cutting in neo-classic designs, may date to George III's reign. Some are noted with pierced bodies revealing blue glass linings, intricate tracery being replaced towards the end of the century by simple pales enriched with applied ornament.

Dredgers and Muffineers. For spices, and especially for the cinnamon favoured in George III and Regency days, simpler casters may be found, 3 or 4 inches tall. Here too the earliest design is cylindrical, pierced with simple fret cutting and with an S-shaped handle. Those of George I's reign are usually octagonal and some octagonal baluster designs are particularly attractive with small bun-shaped covers, no longer fret-cut but pierced in patterns. In the 1760s the spice dredger

109. Dredgers and muffineers. Octagonal with low dome 1710s. Octagonal, still with a handle, the holes plainly drilled but making a pattern, 1720s. Double-curved body, 1760s. Taller style of muffiner, the drilled holes arranged in plain rows, 1810s. Pepper caster of 1810s.

acquired the name of muffineer, a vase-shaped or high-shouldered baluster vessel with a tall dome cover drilled with circular holes. The stemmed muffineer that evolved from this suggests an egg-cup below a tall incurved neck with a tall domed cover, soon followed by a short-necked version with a low dome. Cylindrical muffineers returned in the 1790s. Pierced, blue-lined muffineers, cylindrical or vase-shaped, date mainly to the last quarter of the 18th century. Collectors have to be on their guard, as many designs were reintroduced in the medley of muffineers dating to Victorian days.

Salt-cellars. Throughout the collector's period silver pepper casters, salts and mustard pots developed independently. Early standing salts are museum treasures, but simple trencher salts are attractive. In the late 17th century a circular piece of flat plate would be hammered into a central depression resting on the down-turned rim. This style is found elaborated into a convex gadrooned body supporting the depression and rimmed and based with moulding. Eight-sided and twelve-sided designs followed in the early 18th century, either convex or concave in silhouette and becoming rectangular with clipped corners in the 1720s, but by then more ornate designs were being developed, the bowl on a circle of palm leaves radiating from a high spreading and elaborately moulded foot. This design is found too in early 19th-century work, but with the bowl cast or spun instead of hand raised.

An alternative by 1725 was the three-legged bowl, plain at first, but soon richly ornamented, sometimes with heavy festoons between the legs, now often four. Many are noted with lion-mask legs on paw feet and these too are found in 19th-century work, some with shell ornament between mask and leg, some with three shell feet.

Hand-pierced salt-cellars lined with blue glass date from the early 1760s. Wavy rims date from about 1770. Neo-classic styles tend to show less interesting fly-press piercing. The canoe-shaped salt dates from the 1770s, too, ornamented with bright-cutting and mounted on a thin stem; often it has a bail

110. Trencher salts. TOP: gadrooned circular 1700s,; octagonal with oval depression, 1720s–30s; footed, 1730s–40s; pierced and glass-lined, 1770s. BOTTOM: pierced with simple pales under applied ornament, 1770s; canoe shape, 1770s; dipping rim and outcurving feet, 1790s; with heavy ornament, 1810s.

111. Mustard pots. TOP: tankard, early 18th century; pierced and footed, 1780s; plainer alternative, 1780s. BOTTOM: twelve-sided, with domed lid, 1790s; dipping rim and domed lid, 1790s; more elaborate footed design of the 1800s.

handle or, from the 1780s, handles rising above the pointed ends, arching or square-shouldered. Other stemmed designs are associated with the last decades of the century and also two-piece specimens in which the oval bowl and its spoon rest on a rectangular dish, elaborated in the 19th century. Plainer designs include the oblong with a dipping rim, and either a low collet foot or four small feet.

Mustard pots. Mustard sauce was popular in England for centuries and silver mustard pots are noted in late 17th-century records, but they concern the collector only from the second half of the 18th century. Among the earliest of these is the handled mustard tankard 3 inches high with a flat or domed hinged lid opened by a thumbpiece. This may have a spoon aperture, but throughout the collector's period many pots lacked this debatable advantage. Pierced pots with blue linings soon followed and these may be elaborate in work of the 1770s.

Neo-classic vases for mustard date from the 1770s onwards, with tall reeded handles, tall lid and tall pedestal foot on a square plinth. Legs appear on late 18th-century pots, matching salt-cellar design, and pots with solid cylindrical bodies, flat lidded; oval pots followed the general vogue for oval or elliptical outlines, often dipping slightly towards the centre of each side, the lid repeating the curve and sometimes centrally domed. Convex sides and barrel styles date from about 1800. Other mustard pots are rectangular, but the cylindrical outline continued also; some heavier, more elaborate pots date to the Regency and the 1820s.

Argyles. The sauce-boats and tureens that brought other keen flavours to the dining table include a curious vessel about seven inches high suggesting an ill-proportioned teapot, the design keeping to current teapot outlines from decade to decade. This is the argyle, evolved in the 1760s to keep the gravy warm. The spout is set low so that the best of the gravy is poured, and the vessel conceals a heating unit. This may be a central box iron, patented in 1774 (Fig. 112, left). The alternative is hot water filling either a central chamber or a lower compartment or the space between the outer casing and an inner lining containing the gravy—an early method that lasted into the 19th century (Fig. 112, right). As with teapots, one notes the early lack of foot-ring and consequent introduction first of a loose stand on four ball or moulded feet to protect the table and then of a flaring footrim. The argyle with a lower compartment filled with hot water lacks the slender stem of the box iron design, the body only slightly tapering above the flaring foot and the spout emerging from the base of the upper gravy compartment. The central hot water heater may be found in straight-spouted oval and hexagonal argyles towards the end of the 18th century.

112. Dinner table accessories. TOP: argyles. Fitted with central box iron for heating, inserted through upper lid opening and with a lower lid opening for pouring in the gravy, 1780s. Double-walled to hold a lining of hot water round the central gravy compartment, 1780s. BOTTOM: sauceboats. Shell shape, 1750s; with free standing handle, 1780s; double-lipped with two handles, repeating an early form, 1790s.

Sauce-boats. Silver saucers for relishes and pickles were supplemented in early Georgian England by sauce-boats for the newly fashionable pouring sauces. The canoe design has a lip at each end and a handle each side. The sides soon became higher than the lips and the latter strengthened with cast ornament. Many of the double-lipped sauce-boats with florid relief decoration, either applied or embossed, date to the early 19th century.

Single-lipped sauce-jugs dating earlier than the 1730s are comparatively rare. The wide, upcurving spout is balanced by a high double-scroll handle and the vessel rests on a wide oval foot. The 1730s saw the introduction of cheaper four-footed designs and some three footed, the feet joining the body with wide lion masks supplemented sometimes by further applied ornament cast in swags. In the 1740s the handle might be a cast fish or snake curving forward over the vessel. Shell shapes for these vessels date from the 1740s to the 1760s, often with scallop foot rings; some, bearing heavy cast ornament, date to the early 19th century. Covered tureens for hot sauces date from the 1760s, often on silver stands. The earliest are canoe-shaped with tall arching handles at the ends. Those of the 1800s may show an oblong body design with D handles and a square or round foot or four cast feet, or a half-reeded body with lion's mask and ring handles.

Dish crosses. A dining table detail noticed by some collectors is the dish cross, dating from the 1750s to the 1800s, to keep food hot at table. The pivoting arms radiating from the central spirit lamp are fitted with adjustable brackets above

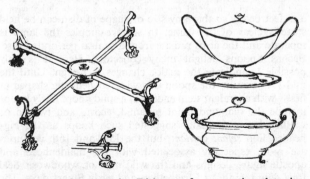

113. Dinner table accessories. Dish cross for supporting plates in a wide range of size and shape over a spirit lamp. Below is detail of one of the sliding feet. Two lidded tureens, 1780s and 1800s.

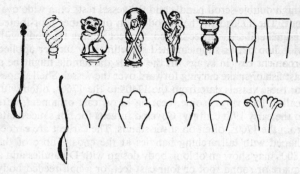

114. Spoons. TOP: silhouette of early knopped style of spoon and a selection of knops and ends, all pre-1660s—writhen, lion *sejant*, apostle (St Andrew), woodwose, seal, slipped end, mid-17th-century Puritan. BOTTOM: silhouette of spoon shape, 1660s to late 18th century and specimens of the forward-curving ends—two trifids, wavy, Hanoverian, Onslow.

and feet below so that any size or shape of dish can be held steadily clear of the flame. In some examples the lamp is separate and the arms radiate from a central perforated disc.
Spoons. Spoons delight many collectors. Here it is only possible to indicate the major changes in design. Until the mid-17th century the spoon was wide bowled—fig shaped at first—with a straight stem ending in a solid knop. Early knops include the diamond point pyramid, acorn, and twisted or writhen knop. Heraldry suggested such knops as the big-headed lion *sejant gardant*, but the 15th and 16th centuries are more especially associated with the maidenhead and apostle figure designs and the wild man or woodwose. Seal tops date mainly to Elizabethan and early Stuart days. The first break from the knop style is the slipped-in-the-stalk stem —merely widening slightly and thickening towards the end.

This developed into the stump-end hexagonal stem tapering sharply at the end and the puritan stem of about 1660, widening at the end and cut straight across. By then the bowl was egg-shaped, nearly elliptical.

The change in the 1660s affected the whole design of the spoon, the stem assuming a curve from the flattened lobed trifid end to the stem-bowl junction, now strengthened with a

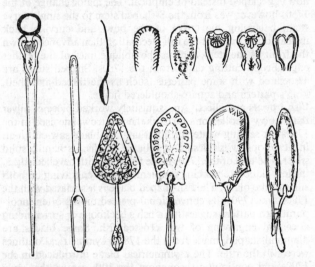

115. Spoons, etc. TOP: silhouette of spoon shape from 1750s onwards and typical spoon ends—feathered, bright-cut, thread-and-shell, king's pattern, fiddle-and-thread. BOTTOM: skewer with thread-and-shell ornament, late 18th century. Marrow scoop with smaller scoop for handle, late 18th century. Four fish slices: trowel, perforated, about 1770; fish shape, 1790s; blade no longer symmetrical, 1800s; with spring-controlled secondary blade, from about 1800.

V-shaped tongue which soon extended down the back of the bowl, known as a rat tail and becoming an ornamental feature. The notched end was followed by the wavy end in the 1690s. In the early 1700s the upcurved end, a plain semicircle, was given a tapering central ridge.

The scrolled Onslow pattern dates from about 1750, with a waisted stem widening slightly at the junction with a bowl now egg-shaped instead of elliptical. The major change of the 1750s however was from the S-shaped stem to the single curve stem, balancing the curve of the bowl and curving back instead of forwards at the tip. Decoration then advanced down the front of the stem, such as the oblique lines of the feather edge. Bright-cutting dates from the 1780s. Shaped stems are associated with some patterns, such as the thread-and-shell, king's pattern and square-shouldered fiddle.

Fish trowels and slices. An exquisitely worked piece of silver that is now a collector's rarity is the fish trowel devised in the 1750s for serving whitebait, its triangular blade saw-cut in an intricate openwork design of foliated scrolls, its handle solid silver. The tool of the 1770s is the fish slice with bevelled edges, the less elaborate piercing supplemented by engraving on both sides of the blade. The fish-shaped blade is associated with the 1780s and 1790s, its conventional pierced motifs often incorporating a pattern suggesting a fish's backbone or surrounding a central engraving of two crossed fish. Some blades are diamond-shaped, made from the 1780s: symmetrical outlines were still the rule. The asymmetrical blade introduced in the 1790s and continuing throughout the 19th century has only one bevelled edge in a simple curved outline in contrast to the incurved undulating outline of the opposite, blunt edge. The handle is of silver, ivory or wood, the ivory plain surfaced at first and often stained green, but later turned or carved in its natural colour.

One may find the asymmetrical fish slice for the left hand

too until the arrival of the companion fork in the 1820s. A more elaborate alternative is the fish slice with a second, smaller blade controlled by a lever or a spring so that it can be lowered over the main blade to hold the fish steady while serving it. Table knives for fish appear to have been introduced in about 1820 and forks considerably later.

Skewers. Skewers in silver, like fish trowels, date from the introduction of carving at table by host or hostess. Early silver skewers follow designs in wood with 5-inch handles, but by 1750 a new type was in use, resembling a bodkin, cut from flat plate and topped by an eye, elongated at first, oval with shell or other ornament by 1760 and round by 1765. Spoon patterns for skewer ends are noted from 1770 and some are shaped as arrows.

Marrow scoops. The marrow scoop is an elongated spoon for extracting bone marrow at the dining table, in use from the late 17th century. One end is a long narrow spoon, straight-sided and rounded at the end, at the other end is a still narrower scoop. By the early 19th century the scoop was longer and deeper and the smaller scoop narrowed a little towards the central stem. Later specimens have only the one end as a scoop, with a spoon handle at the other. Scoop ends are also noted as handles on otherwise normal spoons.

Monteiths, funnels and ladles. Many lovely pieces of silver are associated with the service of wines. A vessel worth mentioning, if only to clear up a frequent misapprehension, is the monteith. This is often regarded as a punch-bowl, but the characteristic undulating rim, most frequently removable, was intended to support drinking glasses by their feet so that the bowls might cool in the vessel's iced water. Wine strainers or funnels, gilded within, became popular in the 1760s for filling clear glass decanters.

Ladles may be traced in their chronological sequence. Punch-bowls of the 1690s were usually matched by ladles with

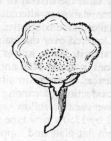

116. Drinking accessories. LEFT: monteith, about 1700. RIGHT: wine funnel, about 1770.

cylindrical bowls and long, flat, spoon-topped stems. Queen Anne examples, still cylindrical, have hollow cylindrical handles and from the 1720s the handle might be engraved and chased. In the 1720s the bowl might be hemispherical with outcurved rim. Many ladles made before 1750 have turned hard-wood handles, the bowls oval from about 1725, egg-shaped later in the 1720s, oval with lips at both ends from the early 1730s, and in escallop shell outline from about 1740. Some are embossed.

In the 1760s hot toddy became popular, and as wood handles proved unsuitable ladles are found with silver rod between ladle and handle, pre-dating the introduction of whalebone handles, usually on hemispherical ladles with incurving sides and everted rims. Shapes from earlier periods were continued for some expensive specimens and further confusion may be caused by the insertion of coins in ladles, with dates from earlier reigns.

Wine labels. Wine labels for bottles may be dated as early as the 1720s. Plain shapes were used for hanging on bottles, rectangular, crescent—dating from the 1730s—and escutcheon

—from the late 1740s. Ornament such as feather edging dates from the 1740s, piercings and crestings from about 1770, and embossing from about 1790. Oval labels are associated with the late 1770s and pointed ovals with the 1780s, but plain rectangular labels with clipped corners continued most popular and one finds increasing numbers of labels with saw-cut lettering. Plain neck rings, engraved with the name of the wine in two places, also date from the 1780s, augmented by rings with hinged labels from the mid-1790s. Cork bottle stoppers

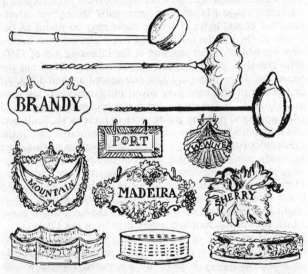

117. Drinking accessories. TOP: three ladles of about the 1720s–30s, 1760s and 1780s. CENTRE: wine labels. The brandy and port labels date from the 1760s or 1770s to about 1800; mountain to the late 18th century; w. wine, early 19th century; madeira and sherry, 1820s. BOTTOM: three wine coasters, 1780s, 1780s, 1810s.

mounted with labelled silver caps, some with elaborate relief ornament, may date 1825–60.

More elaborate labels are associated with glass decanters, becoming larger and more ornate from the 1770s. Hand raised examples rarely date later than 1810 but die-struck labels of the previous twenty years are beautifully made. Some heavy, cast labels are also found. Regency labels frequently bear soldered borders cast in ornamental relief. Heavy cast labels with extremely wide borders are associated with the 1820s. Vine leaves with perforated lettering date from 1824, following the single saw-cut letter on a rectangular label. Even silver-mounted boars' tusks and tiger claws may be found as de-canter labels, but the fashion died when labelled wine bottles were introduced under sanction of the Licensing Act of 1860.

Wine coasters. Wine coasters, to protect the table from the rub of bottle or decanter, were introduced around 1760. At first both rim and base were silver, but boxwood bases were usual from 1775, the early everted rim becoming straight and taller and hand piercing giving place to press work. Scalloped and undulating rims date from the 1780s onwards and in the 1790s embossing, piercing and fine, bright-cut engraving were variously combined. Bottle stands of this period may be dis-tinguished from decanter stands, being narrower and taller. Florid ornament dates from about 1815 onwards and footed bottle stands from the 1830s. From the 1790s decanter stands might have everted rims and from 1810 the sides might curve a little outwards. Double coasters date from the 1790s.

Posy holders. Some of the most delightful small silver fur-nished the finishing touch of elegance to the costume of lady or gentleman. Posy holders are associated especially with social occasions of early and mid-Victorian days. A silver specimen is a welcome rarity setting the style for the countless thousands cheaply but delicately manufactured in gilt metal. The simplest design is a tapering funnel, often curved into a cornucopia, the most usual alternative being a cup mounted on a stem or crook handle, often of mother of pearl. There may be a pin across the mouth which can be thrust through the posy to hold it and which fits perforations in the rim—screw-threaded in late specimens.

Alternatively the mouth may be petal-shaped with a sliding ring to compress it round the flower stalks, or the stalks may be pressed among downward-projecting prongs. A finger ring on a delicate chain is usual, freeing the hand for dancing, but in several designs the stem handle or the side of the cornucopia conceals legs which spring outwards when released so that the flowers can be set down without disarray. The collector looks for holders in cast silver finely chased and double gilded or in gold or silver filigree, the cup formed of petals filled with delicate openwork flower and leaf designs and the stem of coiled milled wire. Some silver specimens are mounted with agate or with tiny silhouettes or carved cameos; others have minute reducing mirrors.

118. Posy holders and card cases. Three posy holders: funnel with finger ring and pin; with stem handle held by cap on chain which when released springs out as three feet; cup-and-stem design with pin on chain. Card case in filigree with pull-off lid. Card case with hinged lid, the ornament of asymmetrical scrolls and building worked in high relief.

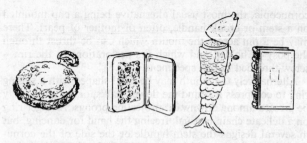

119. Vinaigrettes. Watch shape with spring lid, Regency. Plain box shape showing early, decorative grid. Flexible fish with hinged head. Book, speciality of Gervase Wheeler, 1830s.

Card cases. Card cases, exquisite in silver filigree, are elegancies in demand throughout the 19th century. The collector of silver card cases looks for a more or less rectangular box, 4 inches by 3 inches by $\frac{1}{2}$-inch thick, either with a sliding lid or opening on a small hinge on one of the narrow edges and secured by a spring catch. A slightly thicker design for men opens lengthways like a book with a number of gilt-rimmed compartments, and there are more elaborate variants. Victorian cases tended to be lighter than earlier work and lightest of all are the press-embossed cases of the 1890s. Ornament varies from high relief effects to flat engine turning. Many collectors look for views of famous buildings which were a speciality of Nathaniel Mills of Birmingham and others, appearing on card cases from about 1840 and also on snuff boxes and vinaigrettes. Engraved views were succeeded by low relief pressing and chasing, and these by high relief motifs such as Westminster Abbey, St Paul's Cathedral and Windsor Castle. Hallmarks may be found on the case exterior in specimens pre-dating the early 1840s and thereafter on the projecting rim. Filigree was exempt from hallmarking.

Vinaigrettes. The vinaigrette is the silver box at its smallest and most exquisite, opening to reveal an inner lid perforated and thickly gilded, enclosing a wisp of sponge soaked in aromatic vinegar. It was the successor of the now rare pomanders and pouncet boxes and served a similar purpose of mitigating the unwholesome odours of less hygiene-conscious centuries. Rare early specimens dating from the late 18th century are round or oval, their lids flat-chased or bright-cut, but common examples are either rectangular or in some imitative design, suggesting a miniature book, watch, reticule or other 'toy'. Some are lockets; some small enough to set in finger rings; some shaped as flexible fish; and the spun shapes of egg and acorn, opened by unscrewing, are found in vinaigrettes as well as in nutmeg graters. Late Georgian specimens are characterised by pierced grids rendered superbly ornamental with filigree, pictorial engraving or bright cutting, but vinaigrettes of the 1830s and onwards tend to have simpler grids with round, drilled holes in contrast to their more emphatic lid ornament, where the main change is to more rectangular outlines with massive looking enrichment. Even by the mid-19th century the fashion was waning.

Nutmeg graters. Pocket nutmeg graters have a longer history. They were in use in the late 17th century, but those found to-day date mainly between the 1770s and the 1830s, when hot toddy was popular. Some made before 1790 were exceptionally small to escape assay requirements and the general design of a rough-punched rasp protected by a case that would also contain the nutmeg was developed into various attractive 'toys'. Some of the earliest are cylinders $2\frac{1}{2}$–3 inches long, containing tubular graters. Box shapes may be found, dating from early Georgian days, heart-shaped, oval, rectangular and so on, the lid and base both hinged to open, giving access to grater and nutmeg. Egg shapes are found, too, larger after 1790, opened by unscrewing, and acorns, walnuts and nutmegs.

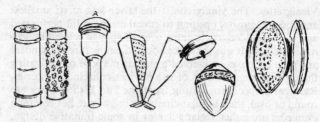

120. Pocket nutmeg graters. Early cylindrical type with rough-cut cylindrical grater, 1700s. Mace design with corkscrew in stem. Vase shape showing how it is hinged at the foot. Acorn with bright-cut ornament. Shuttle shape. All later 18th century.

As the dried outer covering of the nutmeg was sold as the spice called mace some graters may be found shaped as official maces. The stem contains a corkscrew and sometimes also a tubular grater. The urn shape opening vertically on a hinge in the foot dates from about 1780 onwards. The grater itself may aid in dating a specimen—usually silver until 1739, with unevenly placed holes; then of hammered sheet steel, silver framed, until the 1770s; then of tinned rolled steel and, from the early 1790s, of blued steel with symmetrical perforations in concentric circles in the best work.

HALLMARKS

Hallmarks, viewed with caution, can greatly help the silver collector. Since the Middle Ages goldsmiths and silversmiths have been required to submit their wares for assay. The row of marks on a piece of silver testify to the sterling or high-standard quality of its metal and show the town where this quality was tested or assayed, together with the date, the maker and, between 1784 and 1890, the payment of excise duty. It is important to note the shape of the punch mark surrounding

1696	1716 A	1736 a	1756	1776 a	1796 A	1816 a
1697	1717 B	1737 b	1757	1777 b	1797 B	1817 b
1698	1718 C	1738 C	1758	1778 c	1798 C	1818 c
1699	1719 D	1739 d	1759 D	1779 d	1799 D	1819 d
1700	1720 E	1740 e	1760	1780 e	1800 E	1820 e
1701	1721 F	1741 f	1761	1781 f	1801 F	1821 f
1702	1722 G	1742 g	1762	1782 g	1802 G	1822 g
1703	1723 H	1743 h	1763	1783 h	1803 H	1823 h
1704	1724 I	1744 i	1764	1784 i	1804 I	1824 i
1705	1725 K	1745 k	1765	1785 k	1805 K	1825 k
1706	1726 L	1746 l	1766	1786 l	1806 L	1826 l
1707	1727 M	1747 m	1767	1787 m	1807 M	1827 m
1708	1728 N	1748 n	1768	1788 n	1808 N	1828 n
1709	1729 O	1749 o	1769	1789 o	1809 O	1829 o
1710	1730 P	1750 p	1770	1790 p	1810 P	1830 p
1711	1731 Q	1751 q	1771	1791 q	1811 Q	1831 q
1712	1732 R	1752 r	1772	1792 r	1812 R	1832 r
1713	1733 S	1753 s	1773	1793 s	1813 S	1833 s
1714	1734 T	1754 t	1774	1794 t	1814 T	1834 t
1715	1735 V	1755 u	1775	1795 u	1815 U	1835 u

121. London date letters.

209

122. London hallmarks.

FIRST ROW: typical marks for a piece assayed in 1561. Leopards head and lion are in the style used 1548–1678.

SECOND ROW: 1681, in the style used from 1679 to the beginning of high standard silver, March 1697, and again 1721–9.

THIRD ROW: high standard marks, Britannia and lion's head erased, as 1697–1720. This letter began May 1697.

FOURTH ROW: 1737, in style of 1729–39. Shield for the date letter also changed 1739.

FIFTH ROW: 1741, in style of 1739–55. The maker's mark is of Paul de Lamerie.

SIXTH ROW: 1799, with leopard's head and lion in style of 1756–1820; date letter shield had clipped corners from 1776; duty mark of monarch's head added 1784 and changed to this style 1785, changing again for each new monarch.

SEVENTH ROW: 1862 with leopard's head and lion approximately in the style of 1821–1895. Victoria's head duty marks 1837–1890.

each motif as this was changed frequently and deliberately. The following are among the marks that may be noted on silver assayed in the British Isles.

Heraldic lion walking to the left. The mark of sterling quality silver. Until 1820 the head was turned full-face in the heraldic position known as *passant gardant*. Since 1821 it has looked straight ahead.

Heraldic lion's head; the so-called leopard's head. Mainly used as the mark of London-assayed silver, but sometimes found on provincial silver, being used, for example, by Chester 1720–79, Newcastle 1720–1884 (crowned until 1846–47), Exeter 1720–78, York 1776–1848. The head bore a crown until 1821. Both lion and leopard's head appear also on Canadian silver of the 18th century and on the Jamaican silver of J. Ewan & Co.

Town marks. The town marks of other assay centres are sometimes noted. Many such marks were taken from the town's coat of arms. These vary greatly because many silversmiths applied their own versions of their town marks. Assay offices in England are now limited to London (leopard's head),

123. Edinburgh and Dublin hallmarks. TOP: Edinburgh hallmarks for 1769 (thistle introduced in 1759). BOTTOM: Dublin hallmarks for 1739. Harp crowned from 1637. Hibernia duty mark from 1730 and used with monarch's head duty mark from 1807 when Hibernia might be considered rather as a hall mark.

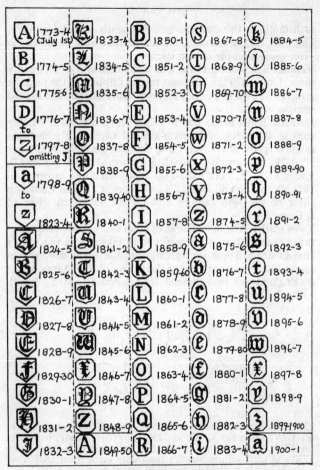

124. Birmingham date letters.

212

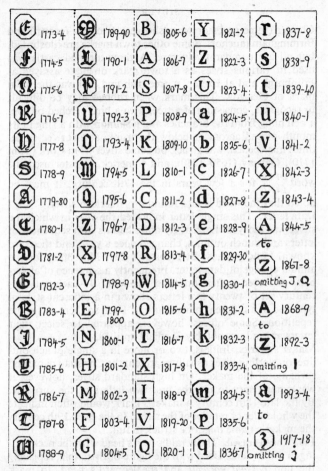

125. Sheffield date letters.

Chester (three garbs or wheatsheaves), Sheffield (crown) and
Birmingham (anchor). Some other town marks are illustrated,
but all are comparatively rare. A three-turreted castle was
used in various styles as a town mark on plate assayed at
Edinburgh and at Exeter. A tree, fish and bell was the town
mark of Glasgow. This mark when rubbed may be difficult
to recognise, consisting of a tree, with a bird perched on top,
a bell hung from the branches and a salmon with a ring in its
mouth placed across or below the trunk. STERLING, sometimes mis-spelled, was struck on some silver from Cork (from
1710), Galway (1650–1730), and Limerick. Chester used the
word $\frac{\text{STER}}{\text{LING}}$ for a few years in the 17th century. It must be
noted that the word is also found on American silver.

Date letter. This single letter indicated the year in which the
silver was assayed. Each assay office had its own sequences of
letters and punch outlines, changed once a year, and these are
known. London chose St Dunstan's day, May 30th, for the
annual change of date letter. Frequently a sequence of alpha-
bets was used—often omitting the letter J—each quarter-
century set of twenty-five letters shown in a different style of
type and in a different punch outline. Even so there was some
repetition. Some offices, however, appeared to select their
letters at random, notably Sheffield until 1824.

Maker's marks. Initials, two or more in a single punch outline, on sterling silver usually represent the Christian name and
surname of the maker. On high standard silver, however, it
was compulsory to use the first two letters of the surname.
By the late 18th century a maker's mark would often indicate
the wholesaler or retailer of the silver. In the early 19th century
the maker's name might be struck in full.

Lion's head erased. The heraldic lion's head with the neck ending in a wavy line. Used with the figure of Britannia, replacing
the lion *passant gardant* and the leopard's head, to mark

CHESTER   BIRMINGHAM   SHEFFIELD

NORWICH   NEWCASTLE

YORK   LEEDS

EXETER   HULL

GATESHEAD   KING'S LYNN   LINCOLN   TAUNTON

126. Provincial hallmarks.

(Note: in all cases the outlines of the punch marks varied.) CHESTER (left) mark used 1700–20, (right) mark used 1687–97 and 1779 to present day. (In the period 1720–79 the marks were the leopard's head and lion *passant gardant*.) BIRMINGHAM from 1773. SHEFFIELD from 1773. NORWICH (left) 1565–1697, (right) 1624–97—this mark of rose and crown used in addition, but replaced by rose and crown on separate punches 1645–87. NEWCASTLE (left) pre-1673, (right) 1673–1884. YORK (left) 1483–1510 (half fleur-de-lys, half lion), (centre) 1632–98 (half fleur-de-lis, half rose crowned), (right) 1701–17 and 1776–1857. LEEDS 1650–1702. EXETER (left) pre-1701 (often with pellets round it), (right) 1701–82. KINGS LYNN 1620s–40s. LINCOLN 1560–1706. TAUNTON 1640–90.

127. Scottish hallmarks.

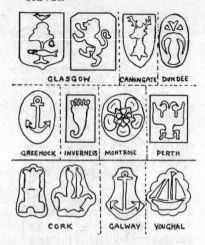

GLASGOW from 1681 (bird, tree, bell and fish). In addition to a lion rampant from 1819. CANONGATE 1680–1836, together with anchor and cable from c. 1790. DUNDEE 1628–1809 (lily pot). GREENOCK 1758–1830. (Alternatives include ship or green oak.) INVERNESS 1715–1815 (cornucopia) together with letters INS. Letters alone—1880. MONTROSE 1670–1811. PERTH 1710–1856. (Previously lamb and flag from 1675.) CORK pre-1715. (Very varied because each man his own mark. Sometimes the town mark of ship between two castles on one punch. After 1715 the word STERLING.) GALWAY also used word STERLING. GALWAY and YOUGHAL very rare.

silver of the high standard compulsory for plate when coin became short, 1697–1720, and permissible ever since; it was in considerable use in the 19th century. This silver contained less alloy than sterling silver.

Britannia. A seated figure used, with the lion's head erased, on high standard silver, which is sometimes called Britannia standard silver. A figure of Britannia also appeared on silver made for export and thus exempt from duty, from 1784 to 1890, but this was accompanied by the lion *passant* instead of the lion's head erased.

216

Hibernia. A somewhat similar figure, but leaning on a harp, may be noted on Irish silver. This was a duty mark used on Irish silver from as early as 1730 until the Union of 1801. Thereafter the English duty mark of a monarch's head was soon used and Hibernia became the town mark of Dublin.

Monarch's head. This indicated duty paid and was used from December, 1784 to 1890. Here again shape of head and punch outline may help in dating, although on provincial work there was usually a time lag in introducing the new sovereign's head. Two impressions of this mark might appear on a single piece of silver assayed in 1797–98, indicating payment of the duty doubled that year.

Thistle. The sterling standard mark introduced in 1750 on Scottish-assayed silver, but not used on Glasgow silver until 1912.

Lion rampant. Standard mark compulsory on Glasgow silver from 1819. Lions rampant crowned are frequently noted on Dutch silver.

Harp crowned. Irish standard of fineness mark.

Elephant and **H & Co** and **A.** Calcutta silver by Hamilton & Co., who emigrated to Calcutta from Inverness in about 1780.

Unfortunately some silver was exempt from hallmarking. Many small articles weighing less than 10 pennyweights were exempt from 1739 and further exemptions followed in 1790, including any article of less than 5 pennyweights, except a few specified such as caddy ladles and bottle tickets.

Fakes. It is unnecessary to do more than quote from page 101 of the *Report of the Departmental Committee on Hallmarking* (H.M.S.O.), 1959: 'Since it was set up in 1939 until 31st December, 1957, the Antique Plate Committee has examined 14,017 pieces of plate; of this number 6,337 pieces have been passed as genuine and 7,680 have been rejected. In addition 2,335 pieces have been examined at auction sale rooms, of which 580 were passed as genuine and 1,755 were withdrawn from sale.'

CHAPTER TEN

Sheffield Plate and British Plate

The finest characteristics of the silversmith's craft, grace and beauty of line and delicacy of workmanship, are to be found in Sheffield plate. Indeed, to many a collector there is a subtle charm about Sheffield plate's peculiar lustre that is lacking in the cold loveliness of solid silver. Yet, for more than a century in England, Sheffield plate was produced at less than one-fifth the cost of solid silver.

The manufacture of Sheffield plate, one of the few crafts entirely English in origin, dates from 1743 when the process was discovered by a Sheffield man, Thomas Bolsover, who fused a thin sheet of silver to a brick-shaped ingot of copper and passed them through heavy hand rollers, gradually reducing thickness while relative proportions remained unchanged. Bolsover, who made small boxes with pull-off lids embossed in low relief, named his process Copper Rolled Plate; the earliest use of the term Sheffield plate so far noted dates to an advertisement of 1771.

Bolsover's first competitor was Joseph Hancock, who evolved a way of increasing the plate's resemblance to solid silver with the lapped edge, and established a factory in 1758. He soon entered the field formerly held by the silversmiths and for the first time domestic ware was made in Sheffield plate such as teapots, coffeepots and hot water jugs, all tin-lined, and also candlesticks.

Plating soon became an important trade in Sheffield and Birmingham and by 1790 elaborately illustrated pattern books were issued, the earliest being a folio of 84 engraved plates issued by John Green, Sheffield, showing more than 500 different articles. The Sheffield platers copied all the 18th-century and early 19th-century styles in silver.

It is important to realise that the terms used for designs must be taken as trade definitions rather than as in any way related to the dates of the monarchs named. Thus the earliest domestic ware in this material, developed from 1762, consisted of teapots, jugs, waiters and so on, in the style of silver plate made in the reign of George I (1714–27), but now usually termed 'Queen Anne' (1702–14). These styles continued in Sheffield plate until 1790, but silver plate in the George II (1727–60) style was also copied from the early 1770s, displaying raised or indented spiral fluting.

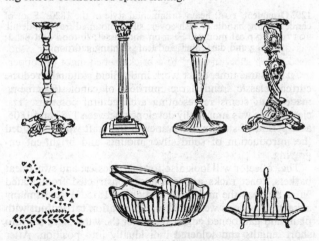

128. Sheffield plate. TOP: candlesticks. Made in the 1750s in George I style, known as 'Queen Anne'; Early neo-classic style, 1760s; Egyptian style, 1790s; heavily ornamented style, 1830s. BOTTOM: later 18th century. Two details of bright-cut ornament; two specimens of wire work, cake basket and 'Gothic' toast rack, 1790s.

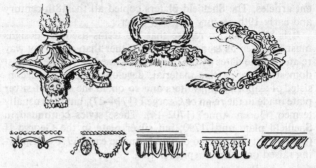

129. Ornament. TOP: heavy ornamental style of the 1820s. Foot of candelabrum; handle of dish-cover; silver-mounted tray rim detail. BOTTOM: typical mounts. Festoon and tassel; festoon and bead; egg and dart; shell and leaf; slanting gadroon.

At the same time, other work in Sheffield plate reflected the current classic trend, large numbers of candlesticks being made with stems representing architectural columns. The classic style was more fully developed between 1785 and 1805, at a period of structural advance in the craft which included the introduction of solid silver mounts and bright-cut engraving.

The collector will look also for cake, dessert and sweetmeat baskets, toast racks and epergnes constructed from plated wires between the mid-1780s and about 1815. Wires of many attractive sections were used and decoration carried out with plain and gadrooned edgings. At first the wires were cut into short lengths and soldered individually into position. After about 1800 wire work was made by bending lengths of wire into continuous curves forming patterns.

The Empire style became fashionable in Sheffield plate early in the 19th century and continued throughout the

Regency years, characterised by expansive representations of winged lions, lion masks, sphinxes and leaf and wicker work, with much fluting. Shells, dolphins and oak leaves interspersed with gadroons composed fashionable edgings. After 1815 patterns were elaborated and are difficult to classify as the range was so extensive. There was much pierced work. During the 1820s much Sheffield plate was decorated with applied bouquets, fruit, flowers and fruiting vine. The largest articles ever to be attempted in Sheffield plate were made between about 1820 and the late 1830s, the finely designed bodies being worked up by spinning. Collectors should inspect their hollow-ware for evidence of spinning as this inevitably dates a piece later than 1820, when a special copper was evolved for the purpose. This was softer and more malleable than that normally used for plating and other purposes, yet capable of withstanding the fusing process.

The range of articles available for the collector of early 19th-century Sheffield plate is indicated by an advertisement by Harrison & Co., a plating firm of Sheffield, in 1839: 'Tea Services, seventeen elegant patterns consisting of Tea Pots, Coffee Pots, Sugar Basins, gilt inside; Cream jugs, gilt inside; Epergnes; Celery Stands; Tea Urns, all sizes; Corner Dishes, oblong shape; Corner Dishes, melon shape; Corner Dishes, with warmers for hot water; Kettles, plain or chased; Kettles with stand, and Lamp for Spirits; Bread Baskets; Cake Baskets; Cruet Frames, for from four to eight Glasses; Egg Frames, with gilt Cups; Pickle Frames, for two or three Glasses; Liquor Frames; Dish Covers, from 14 to 20 inches diameter; Table Candlesticks, from 8 to 12 inches high; Branches to match ditto; Waiters, shaped pattern, from 8 to 20 inches; Communion Services; Chamber Candlesticks; Cups, embossed or plain; Muffin Plates; Mustard Pots; Salts, gilt; Ditto with rich cut Glass Saucers; Snuffers, Table; Snuffers, Chamber; Knife Rests; Decanter Stands; ditto Labels; Toast

Racks; Wine Funnels.' Tankards and half-pint mugs were made by the thousand.

EDGINGS AND MOUNTINGS

These provide a close guide to period and may be grouped into eight easily recognised classes:

Sheared edge (1743–58). During this period the metal was plated on one side only and when sheared a strip of red copper was visible on the raw edge. This defect on Sheffield plate limited its uses.

Single lapped edge (1758–80s). This was introduced by Joseph Hancock of Sheffield and required a thicker coating of silver than formerly had been applied. The plated copper was cut with a blunt tool so manipulated that the layer of silver extended beyond the edge of the copper, to lap over and effectively conceal the red edge.

Double lapped copper mounts (1768–early 19th century). Paper-thin flat ribbons of copper were prepared by plating with silver on both sides and on the edges. This method was the immediate forerunner of plating on both sides of copper sheets. The ribbon was soldered to the silvered edge of the plate so that it protruded over the edge and could be lapped over the copper edge and lie flat against the underside. So skilfully was this carried out by the Georgian platers that it is difficult to detect the joins upon the plated surface.

Silver lapped mounts (1775–1815). These followed in the early 1770s when Sheffield platers made the big advance of silver plating both faces of the copper sheet. This still left a streak of copper visible on the sheared edge of the plate. A narrow ribbon of paper-thin silver, which might measure as little as $\frac{1}{16}$ inch wide, was passed through a hole in a draw-plate, thus making a fine-bore tube. The seam was then opened throughout its length to suit the gauge of the plate upon which it was to be mounted and the resultant U-shaped silver wire was fitted over the edge of the plate and soldered. The joins on both surfaces were vigorously burnished until practically invisible.

Solid silver mounts (*c.* 1780–*c.* 1830). These, cast and hand-chased in sterling silver, are found only on fine Sheffield plate. They were hard soldered into position and are sometimes difficult to distinguish from stamped mounts finished by chasing.

Drawn silver wire mounts (1785–1820). Silver wires, either of pure metal or alloyed with brass but better than sterling, were drawn in a range of shapes, their cross sections being flat, half-round, hollow U, sharp L, and other angles and curves. These were filled with lead-tin alloy and could be hand-shaped quickly to fit the piece they decorated. Before such a mount was applied to the edge of an article silver wire $\frac{1}{32}$ inch thick was soldered beneath the rim.

Silver stamped mounts (from the early 1790s). The earliest of these were in bead, thread and gadrooned patterns, but early in the 19th century the scope of design was widened to include festoon and bead, leaf and scroll, egg and dart, laurel leaf, scallop shell and scroll and other patterns. Underseams were burnished until invisible. Until about 1815 mounts were stamped from silver plate so thick that sections could be soldered into position after filling the back hollows with soft solder. Thinner silver was used for the wide, elaborate rococo designs stamped in high relief from about 1815. These were soldered to edges in which the copper had been concealed by silver lapped mounts. The division between any two mounts may be detected.

Improved silver stamped mounts (from 1824). By this method the junction between the plated surface and the mount was rendered invisible. After the edge of the ware had been shaped to follow the indentations of the mounting, the bare copper edge was concealed with drawn silver wire soldered into position. This was hammered until it extended a little beyond the ornamental silver edge. The projecting part of the soldered silver edge was then removed by filing. Burnishing completed the process.

Electrotype mounts (from mid-1840s). These mounts were made by the electro-deposit process invented by Elkington of Birmingham. They may be recognised because slightly lighter in hue than the sterling silver fused to the copper.

Until the platers began covering both sides of the copper sheet in the early 1770s it was customary for hollow-ware such as dish covers and hot water jugs to be tinned inside and for flat-ware to be tinned on the back. Trade catalogues as late as the 1820s described large trays and waiters as having either 'tinned' or 'plated' backs.

MARKS

These form an important means of identification and dating.
1. Until 1784 it was illegal to strike a name or mark on Sheffield plate. Some authorities, without any justification, claim that until 1772 Sheffield plate might be struck with imitation hallmarks. Such plate, always silvered on both sides, dates from the late 1840s or is a modern reproduction.
2. The law was amended in 1784 so that Sheffield platers could mark their ware with a personal emblem or trade mark. These had to be registered at the Sheffield Assay Office. The majority of firms chose not to register marks, preferring to issue their ware unmarked. Registration continued until 1835.
3. A crown might be struck on fine quality Sheffield plate from 1820 to 1835, thus distinguishing Sheffield ware from the lightly silvered French importations.
4. Because of this, in 1821, platers began marking some of their productions with a stamp stating the proportions of silver and copper such as BEST SHEFFIELD HEAVY SILVER

130. Makers' marks on Sheffield plate.

FIRST COLUMN, READING DOWNWARDS: *fleur-de-lys* of I. & I. Waterhouse and Co, Sheffield; Thomas Small, Birmingham; two of Aaron Hatfield, Birmingham, all early 19th century. *Sun* of Matthew Boulton, Birmingham, the mark registered 1784 but more often found on articles made after 1805.

SECOND COLUMN: *cross and orb* used by Blagden, Hodgson & Co., Sheffield, but never registered, and absorbed by Hawksworth, Eyre & Co. in 1833; by Samuel Roberts & Co., registered 1786; George Bott Dunn, Birmingham close platers; Walker, Knowles & Co., who were using it 1845. *Phoenix* used by Waterhouse & Co., Sheffield, registered 1836 and often found on tea urns, wine coolers etc.

THIRD COLUMN: *crossed keys* used by J. Parsons & Co., registered in 1784. This version registered by John Green, 1799, who had been one of Parsons' partners; by Henry Wilkinson & Co., registered 1836. *Hand* used by Nathaniel Smith, registered 1784, re-registered 1810 by George Smith, Tate, William Nicholson and Hoult. This firm was taken over by John Watson & Son between 1828 and 1837 and they in turn sold to Padley Parkin in 1849 who continued the hand mark. *Crossed arrows* used by T. & J. Creswick, Sheffield, registered 1811. This mark may be difficult to find. *Bell* used by Roberts, Cadman & Co., Sheffield, registered 1785 but more often used after 1810.

PLATING 80 dwts to 8 lbs. or SHEFFIELD LIGHT SILVER PLATING 50 dwts to 8 lbs.

5. Imitations of hall marks on silver date from 1836 onwards: a row of five marks was usual including a simulated monarch's head duty mark.

6. It is an offence to describe as Sheffield plate any ware in which silver has not been fused to copper. A subterfuge adapted with electro-plated goods to keep within the law was to mark such ware SHEFFIELD PLATED.

BRITISH PLATE

This is a seldom named but very common variant of Sheffield plate for which it is often mistaken. It was patented in 1836 by Anthony Merry and its development virtually ended the manufacture of Sheffield plate. It enjoyed a quarter of a century of success before itself being eclipsed by still less costly electroplate. British plate's triumph lay in replacing the copper with a silver-coloured alloy, known as german silver but containing no silver at all. To this was fused a film of silver. British plate possessed the attributes of Sheffield plate including silver mounts, but was harder, more durable, virtually the colour of sterling silver and did not show pink when worn. Another advantage was that units could be assembled with hard solder, a much less costly process than hand-working the seams. Yet another cost reducing factor was the amount of silver required for plating. On copper the silver tended to tinge unless a coating of substantial thickness was applied. Two types of silver mounts decorated British plate: improved silver mounts and electrotype mounts as used on Sheffield plate (8 and 9 in the list of mounts above). British plate was usually struck with punch marks, one of them containing the maker's initials, closely resembling silver hall-marks in size, design and placement. The goods made covered the same range as Sheffield plate.

131. British plate. A pseudo hallmark such as was customarily struck on British plate. The maker's mark shows it to have been made by or for G. R. Collis and Co., 30 Regent Street, London.

Roberts's plate. This competitor with Sheffield plate was short-lived—patented in 1830 and out of production in 1837. The basis of copper was doubly masked, being fused first with german silver and then with sterling silver over this. The silver could be applied in a thinner film than was possible on Sheffield plate, for when it partially wore off the defect was scarcely perceptible.

Plating on Britannia metal. Introduced in the early 1820s. A sheet of pure silver was laid on a flat surface and well heated. Molten Britannia metal was poured over this. The two metals fused and when cold could be rolled into sheets. This process was soon abandoned because of difficulties in assembly, but examples are sometimes found.

CHAPTER ELEVEN

Pewter and Tin

When domestic pewter left the pewterer's shop it was burnished to a high silvery lustre, which use soon oxidised to a dull grey. As late as 1668 the Pewterers' Company laid down that there was no distinction in pewter other than fine and lay. By 1692, however, three qualities were recognised, hard metal, trifle metal and lay metal. Hard pewter was 50 per cent. more costly than trifle pewter, which in its turn was 20 per cent. more costly than lay metal.

HARD METAL

Hard metal or plate pewter, an alloy of tin and 4 per cent. of bismuth was marked with an X. Designated by the Company as 'extraordinary ware', it emits a bell-like ring when struck. The Company also fixed high retail selling prices and in 1697 they agreed that members of the craft might mark it with some such legend as 'Superfine Hard Metal', 'Superfine French Metal', or 'Superfine White Metal'. In the 1750s an even harder plate pewter was evolved. This pewter, described by the Company as 'better than extraordinary', has a whiter polish than former metals and when struck emits a mellow sonorous ring. It was distinguished from earlier plate metal by being marked with X surmounted by a conventional crown. From these metals were made best quality tankards, spoons and flatware shaped by hammering from the plate. Its successor was Britannia metal.

TRIFLE METAL

This was the finer quality of the two metals authorised by the Pewterers' Company until 1692. It bears a coarse resemblance

228

to hard metal and was cast and turned and used for ordinary quality domestic ware and such articles as ale-house pots, candlesticks and funnels. It consists of an alloy of 79 per cent. tin, 15 per cent. antimony and 6 per cent. lead. London-made flat-ware of trifle metal was rendered more wear-resistant by hammering or planishing like silver to give it compactness of texture. The bouge—the rise of the dish or plate between base and rim—received extra hammering, the marks remaining in a series of concentric rings, which were skimmed from the upper surface but remained visible on the underside.

LAY METAL

This consists of 75 per cent. tin and 25 per cent. lead, which it rather resembles in surface coarseness, and was used for wine measures, chamber pots, still heads and so on, but not for drinking vessels until after about 1820, when the Company ceased to exercise autocratic control over its members.

From 1692 to the 1820s the sizes and weights of pewter were standardised. Those that follow, taken from *The Complete List of Pewterers' Goods*, published in the late 1760s, will form useful guides in the detection of fakes whose sizes and weights rarely comply with the Company's requirements.

BRITANNIA METAL

This was a hard form of pewter evolved in the early 1790s from crowned X plate pewter. If struck with a wooden rod it emits a clear ringing tone. Ingredients approximated 90 per cent. tin, 8 per cent. antimony, and 2 per cent. copper, but proportions varied with different makers who marketed the metal under such names as queen's metal, Argentine plate and Ashberry's metal. An extensive variety of goods was made by factory methods, such as stamping with dies, casting in moulds, and, from 1820, spinning hollow-ware in the lathe. When polished this silvery white metal faintly tinged with blue became highly lustrous and could be mistaken for silver when in use. Its lustre required to be maintained; once the surface was allowed to oxydise its original sheen could not be recovered. The Jury of the Great Exhibition reported of tea and coffee services: 'They are an imitation of silver, but the forms might be very advantageously imitated in that metal.'

Britannia metal was used for a wide range of table ware among those who could afford neither silver nor Sheffield plate and were weary of the monotonous plainness of pewter. The collector will find tea and coffee services, tea canisters, soup tureens, gravy dishes, every variety of vegetable and side dish, cruet frames, dish covers, tankards, beakers, measures, hot water jugs, trays and waiters, mustard-pots and salt-cellars, candlesticks, fruit baskets, card trays, flower vases, wine coolers and so on. None of these was engraved in the style of Sheffield plate, but in 1842 a method of engraving was evolved by the use of rollers or dies patterned with appropriate dots and lines.

Names or trade marks were impressed on the under-surface of good quality Britannia metal. John Vickers of Sheffield, who is believed to have made the first Britannia metal domestic ware and was responsible for most of the output until about 1810, marked his ware until 1817, I VICKERS in small roman capitals. The type was then enlarged. After 1837 the address BRITANNIA PLACE SHEFFIELD was added below. John Dixon, established in Sheffield, 1806, became renowned for the excellence of his design and workmanship and impressed the trumpet and banner mark. Eight crossed arrows were used by Broadhead & Atkins from 1832. Most makers impressed their names only, such as Kirby, Smith & Co., from 1797; William Holdsworth from 1800; John Parker from 1821; J. Wolstenholme from 1828; P. Ashberry from 1832. When a pattern number is impressed the piece is in Britannia metal and not the earlier pewter.

MARKS

During the reign of Henry VII the Pewterers' Company made it compulsory for every pewterer to stamp his productions with his private touchmark. These marks had to be registered with the Company on a special plate known as a counterpane or touch plate. The earliest of these touchmarks were small initials and in general the smaller the mark the earlier the piece. The inclusion of a small circle of beads or dots suggests 16th- or 17th-century origin. When a date is incorporated in the design it refers to the year in which the mark was registered and could not be changed without a general order of the Pewterers' Court. Touchmarks are always impressed, never engraved. Typical marks on Britannia metal are detailed on page 230.

Crowned rose. On 17th December, 1697, the Pewterers' Company ordered that 'no Member of the Mistery shall strike any other mark than his Touch or Mark as struck upon the Plate at the Hall; and the Rose and Crown Stamp when intended for export; and the letter X upon extraordinary ware.' The Tudor rose, three times repeated in a chevron, appears in the Pewterers' coat of arms. Collectors will find examples of the crowned Tudor rose in a variety of forms, in some instances with the pewterer's initials at the sides. The crowned rose differs in detail with each pewterer and its frequency suggests that during the Georgian period it was struck on pewter intended for the English market.

132. Marks used by 19th-century London block tin maker I. B. Finch.

133. Pewtermarks. LEFT: Samuel Ellis, London. Received permission to strike his touch 10th Nov. 1721 (the fleece). The letters HN denote the name of the owner Henry Newman. The X crowned above signifies hard metal or extraordinary ware (the mark controlled by the Pewterers' Company). RIGHT: marks of John Duncumb or Duncomb, Birmingham. Refused admission by redemption in 1706. The mark also shows his rose and crown. His marks are taken from the armorial bearings of the Duncombes, Earls of Feversham. The rose and crown was used as a quality mark from mid-17th century. Continental pewter may have the maker's initials in the rose on the crown.

Excise marks. From 1824 each county and borough was required to verify the capacity of all measures and drinking vessels in which liquor was sold by measure. Each was tested brim-full and then stamped with an excise mark composed of a local badge or emblem; the monarch's cypher—G.R., W.R., or V.R.; and various letters and numerals indicating the year and the testing official concerned. In 1877 the excise marks were standardised throughout the country and consisted of a conventional royal crown and the monarch's cypher, with a number representing the testing office and a date letter beneath. These excise marks were struck on the pewter by a weights and measures inspector of the Board of Trade.

Imitation silver marks. Imitations of silver hall-marks were struck on much pewter during the period about 1650–1800. The small shield-shaped punch marks displayed crude versions of the leopard's head, lion *passant gardant*, date letter and maker's initials. To the casual observer these appeared to be genuine silver marks. They were struck in the same positions as those chosen by the assay office when striking hall-marks on silver. On a tankard, for instance, they were struck across the cover near to the thumb-piece and upon the body to the right of the handle immediately below the rim. On flat ware, until about 1730, they were struck on the rim or bouge; afterwards, in the centre of the under-surface.

Crowned X. The letter X or X crowned, as already explained (p. 228) distinguished best plate from trifle or lay metal.

DECORATION

Little was used on English pewter until the early 1660s, when large floral devices in broken or wavy line work were produced by what was then known as wriggled or joggled work, carried out by tapping a blunt chisel while rocking it from side to side. As similar decoration is found on brassware made half a century earlier it is reasonable to assume that some pewter

134. Excise marks. Until about 1877 each borough and county had its own stamp, usually town or county arms, sometimes with figures or letters. Since 1877 the mark has been the crown, sovereign's initials and a number representing the town and a letter for the date.

also was decorated in that way from the beginning of the 17th century.

From early in the 18th century, decoration with the graver might be used, a fragment of metal being removed at each cut. Alternatively a tracer was applied, the tool being held vertically and struck with a hammer, without removing the metal but merely displacing it and forming a furrow. Deep engraving is seldom found as this would tend to weaken the pewter. Engravers journeyed from pewterer to pewterer, executing commissioned decorations with their own tools. Silver engravers' advertisements and trade cards show that they might decorate pewter, too, calling this branch of their craft 'scratching'.

Pewter might be engraved with portraits, animals, birds, foliage, flowers, coats of arms, crests and cyphers, symbolic motifs and other ornament. An owner's initials might be punched, engraved or stamped, three letters being placed as if at the corners of a triangle. The single letter at the apex indicated the owner's surname, the lower left-hand letter the man's first name; the right-hand initial that of his wife. This custom continued until towards the end of the 18th century. There might also be the date when the pewter was bought and its inventory number.

FLAGONS

Originally these were ecclesiastical vessels of approximately two quarts capacity used for Communion purposes, one containing wine and the other water. They eventually became lay vessels, for in 1760 the *London Chronicle* reported that James Shoesmith, for stealing three pewter flagons from a Fleet Street tavern, was transported for seven years and branded on the hand.

It is doubtful if pewter flagons were used until early in the 17th century. These were tall vessels of thick metal, the body slightly conical with straight sides and no spout. A slightly spreading moulded skirt with a beaded rim served to lift the base a little above the table; similar moulding, inverted, encircled the mouth. The lid of an early flagon was raised by means of a towering thumb-piece fitting into a pair of strong hinge lugs cast on the top curve of the D-shaped handle which extended two-thirds down the body. The bun-shaped lid was designed with a profile matching that of the foot. By 1615 the flagon was tending to become lighter in weight, the thumb-piece more slender and with a backward tilt.

In the second quarter of the century the foot ring became more expansive and contained more curves than formerly. The thumb-piece became wider and flatter and might be pierced with a heart shape. The handle became S-shaped and extended to a point immediately above the foot moulding to terminate in a flattened tail which might curve upward. From about 1640 a short strut might connect the lower curve of the handle with the body. At about the same time appeared the knopless flat lid and the hammer-head thumb-piece which was common until about 1760.

The flagon body from 1660 might be encircled with reedings, often singly, but more often in pairs, dividing the body surface into a series of plain bands, alternately narrow and wide. A flat, shallow dome rose from the knopless lid, but by 1665 the beefeater lid was in fashion, its profile resembling that of a beefeater's hat. The body might be plain or have reeding encircling each end or above the cavetto moulding at the base. The lip rim was finished with plain, narrow beading. Twin-ball thumb-pieces shaped to fit the thumb and backward sloping were common, variants of their terminals including acorns, buds, links, pomegranates and shells. This type of flagon, with local variations, continued well into the 18th century. The cover lip from about 1690 might be provided with a flat-surfaced frontal projection, generally with a scr-rated edge. The lid might be double domed and the handle perhaps end in a dolphin-tail finial.

Flagons with beaked lips had appeared in England by about 1720; already for a century they had been in use on the Continent. By the late 1720s the lid was extended to cover the spout opening, this extension sometimes having a serrated edge. At about the same time appeared the re-curved scroll handle with its ornamental terminal, although the S-shaped and D-shaped handles continued in general use until the 19th century. By 1750 the profile of the skirt was re-designed to form a continuous line with the tall body, now tapering appreciably towards the lid. From the 1790s the flagon base was encircled with a narrow band of moulding matching similar decoration at the lip.

The York flagon, with its acorn-shaped body, its double domed lid and heart-and-leaf spray thumb-piece, was in use between about 1725 and 1760. The bodies of early examples were plainly smooth, the sides of the upper body being vertical. By 1750 the upper part was tapering and might be encircled with reeding, as was the outer perimeter of the near-spherical lower body. In late examples the spout projected from the body in a bolder curve than formerly. The S-handle extended to the bulge of the body to which it was directly soldered. A light moulded foot ring encircled the base.

The Oxford flagon, a Regency innovation, had an urn-shaped body and a double domed lid which left the spout uncovered. A perforated strainer was fitted behind the spout.

FLAT-WARE

Chargers and dishes. Wide-rimmed flat-ware used for the service of large joints, game and so on were sold as chargers until the 17th century. They were circular and made in four sizes: great chargers, 7 lb; chargers, 5 lb and $3\frac{1}{4}$ lb; lesser or small hollow chargers, $2\frac{3}{4}$ lb. Late in the 17th century they were recorded as dishes, still circular, their rims shaped like those of plates and in eighteen sizes: 28 inches diameter, 19 lb 12 oz.; 24 inches, 13 lb; 21 inches, 9 lb; 17 inches, 5 lb; 14 inches, 3 lb; $13\frac{1}{2}$ inches, $2\frac{3}{4}$ lb; $12\frac{1}{4}$ inches, $2\frac{1}{4}$ lb; $10\frac{3}{4}$ inches, $1\frac{3}{4}$ lb. Oval dishes did not appear until the 1770s, the shape being introduced by the potters.

Plates. Early pewter plates were of four types with standardized weights, $2\frac{1}{2}$, $2\frac{1}{4}$, 2, and $1\frac{3}{4}$ lb each. All were broad-rimmed with plain edges and shallow bouges, the bouge being the rise from base to rim. From the last quarter of the 16th century the rim might be strengthened with a narrow, low edge, usually oval in section. The bouge was deeper and less abrupt in its fall than formerly, a feature retained throughout the remainder of the pewter period. During the first half of the 17th century the edge was hemispherical in section and the rim usually encircled with two closely-spaced chased lines, the space between being slightly concave. These and most earlier plates were horizontally rimmed; some existing examples have a slight rise from the top of the bouge.

From the mid-17th century until early in the 18th century three types of raised edge encircled pewter plates. Until about 1690 the width of the rim might be half that formerly fashionable and its edge strengthened with oval beading. This type of rim rose slightly upward from a circle cut deeply into the rim-bouge junction, the upper surface shaped in the form of simple moulding. A second, less common, type had a wide horizontal rim bordered with triple reeding and a beaded edge, oval in section. A third type, now uncommon, had a rim of similar width decorated with simple moulding twice as broad as the triple reeding, and a beaded edge of circular section.

A broad rim with single reeding and a wide, shallow beaded edge was usual during the first half of the 18th century. With the decline of the pewterer's craft from the 1760s plain rims became usual. Facing competition from the Staffordshire potters, the pewterers also made octagonal plates, at first with plain rims, later with double or triple reeded borders, gadrooning, or a combination of beading and reeding. Wavy-edged plates, copying silversmiths' fashionable designs, were also made and may be found as follows: with five lobed rims, their edges being reeded, gadrooned or plain; with scroll and shell decoration in relief; eight-lobed, with plain, single or double-reeded edges.

The standard sizes and weights of London-made plates in the 18th century were: 9¾ inches, 16 lb a dozen; 9½ inches, 14 lb; 9¼ inches, 13 lb; 8¾ inches, 11 lb; 8½ inches, 9 lb 10 oz.; 7¾ inches, 7½ lb a dozen. In some parts of the country the two smaller sizes were 9 lb and 7 lb a dozen and elsewhere 10 lb and 8 lb a dozen.

MARRIAGE PLATES, usually in pairs, were customary presents in pewter from Elizabethan days until the 1790s. Early examples might be decorated with wriggled work or line engraving and the wide rims inscribed with appropriate mottoes or posies, the flat centres displaying pictorial scenes. They were bought from stock, for the initials of husband and wife are generally in a different hand from other inscriptions.

SERVICE PLATES, for pies and cheese, were equal in weight to dishes and plates of the same diameter, for these, being flat and without rims, were cast stronger than dishes or plates. In most instances such a vessel was raised on three ball feet and the surface edge encircled with ornament as on contemporaneous plates.

DESSERT PLATES, known contemporaneously as banqueting dishes, were widely used. About six inches in diameter and weighing about one pound, such a plate has a concave rim rising from a flat base and encircled with a scalloped edge. The inner surface might be plain, decorated with punched work or enriched with simple designs in low relief. From early in the 17th century a pair of thin ring handles might be attached diametrically opposite to each other. In the second half of the century a pair of flat handles with surface decorations was fashionable. By the 18th century dessert plates were made shallower and continued without handles until the early 19th century.

DOUBLERS, used for serving semi-liquid foods known as spoon-meat, are referred to continually in 17th and early 18th-century inventories. These were flat-bottomed plates with exceptionally deep depressions, rather deeper than the Georgian soup plates by which they were superseded. The wide rim sloped slightly up to the edge, which matched with contemporary plates.

SAUCERS, deep rimless vessels measuring about six inches in diameter, were used for the service of the sauces considered essential with many preserved foods. They were made in tens of thousands until the mid-18th century.

Voiders were oval trays of lay metal used in large establishments for clearing away soiled dishes, left-overs and scraps removed from the table during a meal. They were superseded by trays of tinned iron in the 1730s.

Trenchers. For centuries it was the custom for food to be served individually on pewter plates. Meats and other foods that required cutting were then transferred by the diner to a flat square or disc of pewter known as a trencher. In this way the various pieces of flatware used during a meal were saved from becoming scarred by steel knife blades. Trenchers weighed between 9 and 14 oz. The plate trencher was square or slightly rectangular with a low rim in the form of a wide inverted U. Trenchers were cleared of marks after each meal by scraping with a special tool; a large establishment would include an employee specifically known as the trencher scraper.

Garnish of pewter. A set of flat-ware consisting of twelve each of chargers, dishes and plates. These were displayed on tiers of shelves in the kitchen, their backs facing outward.

Sauce boats. These were made in pewter during the second half of the 18th century, but are now difficult for the collector to acquire. The design may include a single ringed foot, or three cast feet. They were made in three sizes: $4\frac{3}{4}$ inches weighing 14 oz.; 4 inches, 11 oz.; $3\frac{1}{2}$ inches, 8 oz., the measurement being across the boat at its widest part.

Spoons. When new they weighed between 2 lb and 1 lb. 6 oz. a dozen.

Tankards. Early in the 17th century 'tankard pots' sold retail at prices fixed by the Pewterers' Company: quart, 2s. 6d.; pint, 1s. 8d.; half-pint, 1s. 3d. The most familiar cylindrical style is to be found from the 17th century to the 19th, made from sheet metal vertically joined in an invisible seam and with a disc base inserted as instructed by the Company. When they became standardised in the 18th century—known to the pewterer as ale-house pots—tankard capacities and weights, without lids, were as follows: 1 gallon, $6\frac{1}{4}$ lb; 3 quarts, $4\frac{1}{2}$ lb; 2 quarts, $3\frac{1}{4}$ lb; 3 pints, 2 lb 2 oz.; 1 quart, $1\frac{3}{4}$ lb; 1 pint, 1 lb. 1 oz.; one penny pot, 13 oz.; $\frac{1}{2}$ pint, 11 oz. Three sizes were made with lids: 1 quart, $2\frac{1}{4}$ lb; 1 pint, 1 lb 7 oz.; $\frac{1}{2}$ pint, 1 lb 1 oz.

In the early 17th century the vessel was vertical-sided, its rim strengthened by narrow moulding and its base encircled by wider convex moulding to lift it a little above the table. Frequently the design included a hinged cover, smoothly convex at first in a curve that continued slightly over the vessel's rim. By the 1640s this lid was replaced by the single-step cover, shaped like a beefeater's hat and sometimes known as the beefeater lid. This had a flat rim $\frac{3}{8}$–$\frac{1}{2}$ inch wide encircling a low, vertical-sided, central lift.

For drinking, the lid had to be raised and held upright and for this purpose the drinker pressed upon a thumb-piece attached to the lid directly above the tankard handle. This thumb-piece was known to the pewterer as a lever, purchase

135. Pewter tankards. TOP: (left) 1640s; (centre) 1650s; (right) 1660s. BOTTOM: (left) 1670s–80s; (centre and right) 1690s showing transitional forms.

or billet. In the early pre-1660 vessel it was merely a thick vertical lever shaped to fit the thumb and soldered to the loose leaf of the hinge which fitted into a pair of strong lugs either cast with the handle or soldered to its upper curve and to the lid. In the mid-17th century the thumb-piece became somewhat wider and flatter and might end in a twin-dome or twin-ball. The handle was in the curve known as the swan-neck, invariable until early in the 18th century and still used in the 19th. At first it was cast hollow, light in weight and semicircular in section. At the upper end it was sliced across vertically, providing little thickness for soldering to the body. At the lower end the handle finished in a short tail or heel-shaped slice sometimes bearing an applied shield engraved with the owner's crest or cypher.

The tankard of the mid-17th century tended to lose the

square silhouette and became slightly tapered. The base moulding developed into a wide-spreading and deeply concave skirt, but this was replaced by narrow moulding in the 1660s. The general design of a post-Restoration 17th-century tankard showed a slightly tapering body, often of greater diameter in proportion to height than at any other period. By 1675 the foot moulding had become deeper, more elaborately shaped and more boldly convex; subsequently this was matched by the moulding that encircled the vessel's rim below the cover. In some instances additional strengthening moulding was introduced half-way down the body but this did not become a regular feature until the 18th century. The cover in the 1660s had its rim extended to a point in front and decorated with a chased encircling line. Before the end of the decade a new alternative was the double-step cover, its broader rim chased or engraved with three or more concentric rings. The front of the rim was extended, sometimes fretted, and its edge serrated.

Before the end of the century some covers were raised in three or four steps, but these are uncommon. A more frequent forerunner of 18th-century design was the cover with the single step leading to a tall, narrow central dome. The obvious development of this was the rounded double-dome cover which may be dated from the 1690s, but is mainly associated with the 18th century. The extended serrated lip, unperforated, continued until about 1715. The thumb-piece for raising the lid might end in a scroll design. Volute scrolls, beaded scrolls, corkscrews and ram's head patterns continued popular until about 1715, as well as double acorns and the fleur-de-lys, and the familiar late Stuart love-bird motif with the birds beak-to-beak.

Such a tankard was equipped with a more durable handle, more expansive at the top and sliced obliquely to ensure a stronger soldering joint; in addition there might be a strengthening lug extending almost half-way down the tankard body. The tail might end in a twin spiral, a heel-shaped slice or an applied shield. By the end of the 17th century the swan-neck handle was a massive affair and more boldly curved than formerly.

In conformity with the curving outlines characteristic of the Georgian period until 1760 was the tulip-shape tankard copied from the silversmiths. The body still tapered upwards from base to rim, but was curved in a swelling bell or more pronounced tulip outline, the rounded base being supported by a concave moulded foot ring, its diameter approximating

136. Pewter tankards. TOP: (left) 1700s, showing completion of double-dome and moulding round body; (centre) early Georgian bell, suggesting beginning of tulip; (right) mid-Georgian tulip. BOTTOM: (left) late Georgian tulip; (centre) early 19th century barrel; (right) mid-19th century style, sometimes glass bottomed.

that of the widest part of the body. To complete the curved silhouette the vessel had a double-dome lid with moulded rim. The thumb-piece was usually a volute scroll, and after about 1730 the handle might be the most ornate style of recurved scroll, in use until the 1830s, often with a short strut between the body and either one or both terminals.

For some twenty years from about 1760 the tulip tankard was modified to an ogee outline with a more boldly modelled foot rim. The lid was edged with cavetto moulding in a style that was never superseded as a standard pattern. The thumb-piece, too, became lastingly established as a more graceful feature with perforated ornament. The plain handle that marked the beginning of less careful craftsmanship dated from about 1790 onwards, its tail soldered flatly on to the body; this handle, too, might have a strut between the body and its upper terminal. By then the tulip shape was out of favour and the tapering cylindrical body was in vogue again, but with the late 18th-century details of lid, thumb-piece and handle that indicated its period.

Many more tankards found to-day date only to the 19th century, including the late Georgian barrel-shape and the heavy-lidded cylinder with a glass bottom popular among young Victorians.

When the tulip-shape was revived in about 1810 it was distinguished by a vertical rim. Such vessels were known throughout their period as wine pots and were made in seven sizes of much heavier metal, with and without covers: 1 gallon, 9 lb with cover and 8½ lb without cover; 2 quarts, 5 lb and 4 lb 10 oz.; 1 quart, 3 lb and 2 lb 11 oz.; 1 pint, 1 lb 14 oz. and 1 lb 10 oz.; ½ pint, 13 oz. and 10 oz.; quartern, 7 oz. and 6 oz.; ½ quartern, 5 oz. and 3½ oz.

Teapots. These were made in plate metal from the 1760s in shapes resembling plain silver in five standard sizes and weights, including a hardwood handle of about 1 ounce;

1 quart, 1 lb 8 oz.; 1½ pints, 1 lb 4 oz.; 1 pint, 1 lb 1 oz.; ¾ pint, 14 oz.; ½ pint, 10 oz. These were struck with the crowned X indicating high quality metal. The majority of existing teapots are in Britannia metal (*see* p. 229).

Until 1820 Britannia metal teapots tended to be small owing to limitations of manufacturing processes. Sections for building hollow-ware were chiefly produced by drop stamping, which enabled bodies to be decorated inexpensively with designs in relief. Between 1820 and 1850 large numbers of teapot bodies were shaped by spinning in the lathe. In the mid-1840s a process was evolved by which a teapot, sugar basin or other hollow-ware could be cast in a solid piece with thin walls and relief ornament.

Wine measures. The baluster wine measure with a hinged lid was designed by the Pewterers' Company in 1615 in an effort to combat the short-measure evil. It was laid down that these measures should be in lay metal and seven sizes were designated: gallon weighing 10 lb; pottle or half-gallon, 6 lb; quart, 3 lb; pint, 2 lb; half-pint, 1 lb; quarter-pint, 8 lb the dozen; half one-quarter-pint, 4 lb the dozen.

The various features were chosen so that a customer could detect by a casual glance if the measure had been manipulated against him. The gauge of the metal was required to be thick enough for the soft lay metal to defy the stresses of everyday use. The curve of the body was such that inward dents calculated to lessen the vessel's capacity were easily visible. Generally speaking, compared with pre-1680 measures, the curve became bolder in those made between 1680 and 1824. Better to reveal dents in the surface, it became customary from the mid-18th century to introduce two pairs of closely placed lines incised a little above the shoulder and below the bulge. Single lines encircling top and bottom edges of the vertical rim made it apparent when the rim had been cut down in a slant from the handle.

This vertical lip rim, occupying between ten and fifteen per cent. of the vessel's total height, could not otherwise be misshapen to lessen capacity without at once making the deceit visible. The diameter of the rim and the maximum diameter of the base, of a type known to contemporary pewterers as the broad bottom, were made equal so that any attempt made by the publican to squeeze either would distort the harmony of the vessel's shape.

The broad bottom was made without a foot ring so that it could be seen if the flat base were topped up in a slight concavity to provide short measure. The base was set in the bottom so that the vessel stood flat upon the serving bar, and it fitted snugly against the inward curve of the lower body rim in which it was soldered and then trimmed to a sharp angle. The incurve of the body neck was such that the neck diameter was smaller than the base diameter: proportions were about eight to five in the Company's standards. This prevented the insertion of a pewter disc as a false bottom.

The lid prevented a thumb from creeping over the handle and so reducing the quantity of the liquor. The lid's upper surface was ornamented with three circles cut into it with a turning tool, either as narrow incisions cut with a sharp point or as wide, shallow gutters gouged into the metal. These circles included one near the edge, another in the centre, and a third midway between. They served to indicate if the lid had been tapped down into the body of the measure. This would be virtually unnoticeable in a flat, unmarked lid but the incised circles would become distorted under such treatment. The lid, hinging from the handle and resting on the rim-surface, would indicate if the lip rim had been shortened by having a downward slope instead of closing horizontally.

Pewterers were not allowed to deviate from these standardised features. They were permitted, however, to use discretion in regard to handle and thumb-piece design, which for the most part followed those fashionably used in tankards.

The wine gallon had by custom been considered to contain 231 cubic inches of liquor and the pewterers' standards had been in accordance with this, but no legal standard existed until 1707, when an Act of Parliament was passed establishing this measurement, which continued until 1824 and applied also to spirits, cider and perry. Ale and beer had been sold by Winchester measure: 272·2 cubic inches to the gallon, slightly less than the imperial gallon of 277·463 cubic inches.

After 1824, when the imperial system of weights and measures came into operation, standardizing all measures throughout the country, pewter measures were no longer required to follow the baluster design. This was continued, however, but without a lid and with the addition of a foot ring. Each measure was now tested and struck with an excise mark.

Fakes. Old shapes have been copied in alloys resembling the old formula for plate pewter. Touchmarks may be applied after the ware has left the workshops and it may be scratched, dented or otherwise 'antiqued' by burying or treating with acids. The writer has seen new pewter 'aged' by immersion in a galvanizing pickle vat.

TIN

Domestic ware cast and turned from solid tin was made contemporaneously with pewter and in similar patterns. The 1638 charter of the Pewterers' Company gave the Company jurisdiction over 'every maker, worker, or manufacturer of Tin, Pewter and Lay Metal.' Tin men were not permitted to make pewter, but were compelled to register their marks at Pewterers' Hall and to strike their work with such marks.

Silvery-white tin table ware is continually mentioned in household inventories from the 16th century to the mid-19th century, usually entered in the same group as pewter, each metal being distinguished by name. Tin was more open textured and rougher of surface than pewter so that fragments of food might become embedded in it, causing it to need vigorous scouring. The metal would not cast satisfactorily into relief decorations.

Georgian tin ware until the 1770s may be distinguished from earlier ware, which had a silvery tinge. Improved smelting processes during the final quarter of the 18th century, however, recaptured the silvery hue and by 1800 'tin ware manufacturers' in London outnumbered pewterers, many of them marking their productions with the inscription 'English Block Tin'. An advertisement in the *Birmingham Gazette*, 1821, announced the sale of 'a large assortment of Block Tin Ware: Teapots, pitchers, bowls and ewers, tumblers, quart and pint beer pots, lamps.'

CHAPTER TWELVE

Brass

English brass was used for a wide range of domestic ware, from hand-wrought warming pans to cast candlesticks and cooking pots heavily tinned inside. It is a wonder that brass ware such as chestnut roasters and skillets can be dated at all. But collectors soon become aware of the main changes down the years in the colour and texture of the metal itself. Brass goods can be grouped into five clearly defined classes in accordance with chronological improvements in materials and manufacturing processes. Brass was not made in England on a commercial scale until about 1585. Domestic inventories distinguish between brass and latten, the latten consisting of brass ingots hammered into tough, close-textured sheets for working.

1. Until the 1690s brass was an alloy of copper and calamine and was described by the Founders' Company as 'hard, flawy and scurvy and difficult to work'. This brass teemed with tiny bubbles so that the surface of finished castings was marred by pitting. Latten made from this brass tended to split while being worked, was of poor colour, lacked brilliance and was uneven and pitted of surface. Brass workers preferred to use imported plates.

2. Improvement in the manufacture of copper and in the casting techniques for brass were made during the 1690s, the alloy being rendered softer, more pliable and lighter yellow in colour by the addition of 7 lb lead to each hundredweight of copper-calamine. Bubbles were fewer and surface blemishes shallower than formerly.

3. Copper was refined by a new method from 1725 and within

a few years English brass was more attractive in colour. The spring rolling machine dates from the same period: latten could now be made by rolling the brass into sheets of uniform thickness, although hammering continued for thick sheets until the introduction of steam-driven machines in the early 19th century. The new plates enabled brass workers to extend the range and volume of their productions to include saucepans in ten standard sizes, potage pans in fourteen sizes, soup pots, charcoal braziers, frying pans, pastry pans, basins and a hundred other things.

4. A major change in the composition of brass was introduced in 1770 by James Emerson who patented an alloy of copper and zinc, described in 1786 as 'more malleable, more beautiful, and of a colour more resembling gold than brass containing calamine.' This alloy cast into clear-cut modelling without pitting, in a manner formerly possible only by the costly use of princes metal and pinchbeck. Such articles as inkstands, girandoles, pastille burners, paperweights, busts, figures of animals and watch stands were now cast and might be double-gilded.

5. Complicated single-piece castings in a brass composed of copper and zinc date from about 1860.

CANDLESTICKS

Seldom will a collector discover an example dating earlier than about 1700. Seventeenth-century specimens were either hammered from latten or cast in solid brass and turned. Until about 1690 candlesticks were fitted with expansive drip pans, but when candles improved in quality at this time the pans were abandoned in favour of socket rims expanded into saucer-shaped nozzles. Until about this period, too, the socket was pierced with an aperture to facilitate removal of the candle end. Originally the aperture was a vertical oblong, but this

137. Candlesticks. Late 17th and early 18th centuries. Upper section cast solid and drilled, foot cast and turned, third quarter of 17th century. Made from hammered brass plate, late 17th century. Socket and stem formed of two turned castings with the base a separate solid casting, late 17th century. Two examples of socket and stem halves formed as two hollow vertical castings brazed together, with added cast foot, early 18th century.

was superseded by a small circular hole about the size of a pea drilled in the centre or upper half of the socket.

Early in the 1690s brass workers evolved a process by which socket and stem of a candlestick could be cast in two vertical halves which were brazed together, leaving the centre hollow. A substantial foot was added, deeply concave beneath. This required less metal than formerly at a time when cast brass cost 1s. 7d. a lb at the foundry. One can just detect the line of the brazing down the sides of the stem. This began a widespread vogue for domestic candlesticks in brass. Collectors look for curving baluster-shaped stems on the octagonal, hexagonal or highly domed circular feet associated with the first quarter of the 18th century. In some stems the main swelling curve was acorn-shaped, this acorn becoming longer and longer until it was really an inverted vase outline. The socket at this period had high convex moulding around the lower rim.

138. Candlesticks. 18th to early 19th centuries. Lobed, 1740s–50s; lobed stick of kitchen quality, 1740s–50s; two specimens of neo-classic design, with square and round pillar bodies, later 18th century; characterless style of early 19th century.

Candlesticks with hollow cylindrical stems shaped from hammered plate were made, a slot in the stem being fitted with an adjustable slide for ejecting the candle end from the socket.

From early in the 1720s the octagonal foot might support a slender octagonal stem cast solid and faceted. There were several variants to the lobed foot of the 1740s, at first with four lobes, then with six. Until 1760 the lobes were accentuated by grooving the surface of the foot; then from about 1770 scalloped rims were usual. These were the parlour candlesticks: throughout this period large numbers of kitchen candlesticks were made and in these the cylindrical stem's only ornament was a central bulge and the foot was a plain low dome.

The third series of brass candlesticks date from the early 1770s and include the majority of to-day's antique examples. By then casting techniques had become so much improved that a hollow stem and socket could be cast in a single piece, the foot being cast separately and brazed to the stem. Best quality candlesticks were tinged a beautiful golden colour by a heat and acid process, then burnished. The demand for the new and cheaper candlesticks became enormous after the 1770s.

The fashionable candlestick from about 1760 was square-footed, at first with a plain edge. Moulded edges were preferred by about 1770 and gadrooned edges a few years later. The most characteristic candlestick pattern from the mid-1770s was a stepped foot supporting a column, plain or fluted, and complete with a capital in the architectural manner. Many other 18th-century candlesticks had thin, vase-shaped stems.

The stem in the form of an elongated, inverted cone was typical of what could be achieved with a single casting from the 1780s until the mid-19th century. This might be round or square in section and was usually fluted. It rose from a high pyramid or domed foot encircled by an incised line, or a single concave moulding in early work. The socket was vase-shaped with an expanded rim forming a sconce. The series of swellings known as gadrooning might decorate the socket-base and the upper surface of the foot.

From the 1780s, too, one may hope to find a candlestick with a substantial vase-shaped stem, tending to be over-elaborated by additional knop swellings. By 1810 the knops were usually shapeless and spoilt the design. The wide, circular foot of this series rose in low, moulded curves into a dome of medium height.

The telescopic candlestick had a considerable vogue from about 1800 until the third quarter of the century. This consisted at first of a trumpet-shaped foot rising as a lower stem into which slid the upper stem supporting a vertical-sided socket with its rim expanded into a nozzle.

Among 19th-century brass candlesticks one must pick warily, however, for by the second quarter of the century the earlier Georgian designs were being repeated, taking their

253

139. Chamber candlesticks. With extinguisher, 18th century; with glass shade and ventilated base, two specimens of the early 19th century.

place among more easily recognised and dated pieces on oval or oblong feet.

It is easier to know the later 19th-century work. From about 1860 the whole candlestick, foot, stem and socket, could be cast in a single piece. Most of the earlier patterns were copied. The majority of so-called antique brass candlesticks are made by this method.

Chamber candlesticks. These were intended for carrying from room to room, for lighting the way upstairs and so on, and were made from plate brass. Their design consisted of a shallow saucer with a central convexity supporting a candlesocket, and slightly curved lateral handle shaped from flat brass strip. It was equipped with a conical extinguisher, seldom present on a remaining example. A flat, horizontal pear-shaped handle was fashionable from about 1680. The collector will rarely find an example made earlier than the 1730s, when the socket might have a detachable nozzle with a spreading sconce and the handle might be scroll-shaped, curving upward and outward, its terminal about two inches above the rim. The upper curve was shaped into a substantial thumb-piece. This type continued until the 1750s, measuring about 6 inches in diameter and 3½ inches in height. Chamber candlesticks with rectangular trays raised on four ball feet date from the 1780s. The tray now might be mechanically shaped.

Early in the 19th century the nozzle was dispensed with and the socket rim considerably extended. The extinguisher might hook to an attachment on the socket placed immediately opposite the handle. By 1820 the tray might be octagonal and from 1830 square outlines were frequent.

The Victorian chamber candlestick was usually circular, but might have a shaped outline, its rising centre supporting a socket as in the 17th century. Cast chamber candlesticks were now made: a popular type took the form of a cast lotus leaf spray, with the socket shaped as a lotus flower. Other flowers were similarly treated.

From the 1740s chamber candlesticks might be so designed that candles were protected from the draughts and the billowing curtains responsible for many a disastrous fire. The socket was enclosed within an outer cylinder of brass encircled with a double row of air vents, crosses and circles being common. Into this was fitted a candleshade of flint-glass. The cone-shaped extinguisher was provided with a rod rising from its tip, long enough to reach down the shade to the candle flame. These were made in variations for a century until they were superseded by a type in which a simple wire frame composed of four uprights and two rings was soldered to the tray, enclosing the socket. This formed a holder for a tubular glass chimney lifted slightly above tray level by four knops, thus permitting a free flow of air.

WARMING PANS

These date from the time of Elizabeth I and the frequency with which 17th-century examples come to light in provincial antique shops is surprising. Until the 1660s the ember pan was made from English brass, a hard, heavy metal difficult to work. The lid was shaped from fine quality Dutch brass

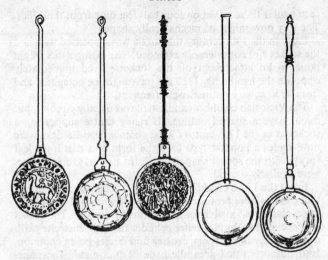

140. Warming pans, brass and copper. Latten cover, wrought iron handle, bearing the symbol of the Clothworkers' Company, about 1610. Latten cover, wrought iron handle, with punched ornament, about 1650. Brass with pierced ornament in Continental manner, and iron handle with brass mountings, later 17th century. Copper in the beefeater's hat style with brass ring handle, early 18th century. Copper, the lid fitting inside the ember pan rim, and turned wood handle, later 18th century.

sheet of attractive colour. The handle measured about 3 feet in length and might be of flat wrought iron elaborated with scrollwork or of solid cast brass, rod-turned with baluster and knop ornament and terminating in a loose shackle for hanging. During the second half of the 17th century a series of handles consisted of two 15-inch lengths of square or round iron fitted into three mountings of turned cast brass.

The handle expanded into a flat shoulder attached to a flat ring of $\frac{3}{4}$-inch wide metal. Into this was placed the ember pan, its wide rim resting upon the ring to which it was firmly fixed. One leaf of the hinge was attached to the flat shoulder of the handle, the other leaf to the underside of the lid. This pattern of warming pan continued until early in the 18th century. Ebony, oak and other hard wood such as box came into use for handles by the 1650s, carved with flutes and terminating in a large knob. Such a handle was finished merely by polishing and fitted into a tapering socket rivetted or brazed to the ember pan.

The cover at first was slightly convex and extended beyond the rim of the ember pan. It was usually embossed with ornament in relief, a favourite being the owner's coat of arms surrounded by an inscription and a circle of $\frac{1}{4}$–$\frac{3}{16}$ inch holes spaced $\frac{1}{4}$-inch apart. During the period 1620–80 it might be engraved with a portrait. It became more highly convex by 1660 and might be elaborately pierced with fret-cut designs. From 1670 it was made with a wide flat rim fitting closely against the strengthened edge of the ember pan, which itself was turned over with a similar flat rim.

The great majority of brass warming pans date from the 1720s onwards and are considerably lighter in weight than formerly and always have wooden handles. The ember pan, with almost vertical sides, measured $8\frac{1}{2}$ inches in diameter by $3\frac{1}{2}$ inches in depth and was made from better quality brass than formerly; its lid measured about 12 inches in diameter and swung loosely over it.

No copper warming pan has been noted in the early styles. The use of copper modified design. The ember pan, handraised from the copper plate $\frac{1}{16}$-inch thick, was straight sided with a lid resembling a beefeater's hat, its short sloping rim fitting snugly over the beaded rim of the ember pan. A brass ring was fitted to facilitate opening. The hinge was narrow and often three-jointed, one leg rivetted inside the ember pan, the other to the interior of the cover. Brazed or rivetted to the ember pan was a strong, tapering socket of cast brass to hold a polished wood handle of beech or ash.

From the early 1770s warming pans and their lids were stamped in copper. They were appreciably shallower than formerly and their weight about one-third of those in brass. The lid fitted closely into the ember pan and curves were introduced into the design. From 1780 the handle might be japanned. Such a warming pan sold in the shops for nine or ten shillings.

HORSE BRASSES

The whole story of old horse brasses reflects man's affection for his beasts, his wish to protect them against ill-luck and his glory in their proud display. Only in the late Georgian period did brasses begin to ornament the harness of working horses. They were then worn singly, mainly in astronomical designs such as sun, crescent moon and stars: being hung upon the foreheads of driven horses, these were known as face pieces. Ornamental brasses suspended from the leather martingale appear to date no earlier than about 1830. Saddlers', brassfounders', and other pattern books which illustrate other harness furniture make no reference to the horse brasses now collected. At this time emblems began to be framed within hand-pierced rings with serrated edges, the polished emblem being engraved with a name, crest or cypher.

Only when May Day processions became flamboyant cere-monial occasions in Victorian industrial England, however, with cart and dray horses parading in full holiday regalia, did horse brasses become more than simple amulets, crests or commemorative souvenirs. Year by year horses were increas-ingly enriched with brass harness furniture, so that by the 1860s pattern books were illustrating full complements of the brass work. More than three hundred pieces might be displayed on a single cart-horse harness, enhanced with brightly coloured ribbons plaited into mane and tail. Fifteen to twenty of these were pendant horse brasses: a face-piece on the forehead; a pair of ear-brasses hanging behind the ears; three on each side of the runners at the shoulders; and as many as ten hanging from the martingale, each weighing more than four ounces. It became the carter's duty to keep the regalia spotlessly brilliant. This involved much hand polishing, which in the course of years gave a silky surface texture to the metal.

The martingale, a broad band of leather or series of straps, extended from the girth, between the horse's forelegs, being double at the breast, with rings for the reins to pass through, so as to prevent the horse from rearing or throwing back its head. From about 1880 the brasses hanging from it might be in matching sets of gradually diminishing sizes. The lowest might feature a personal symbol or name plate. These were attached to the martingale by means of short leather straps passing through the rectangular loops of the brass and copper rivetted to the martingale.

Horse brasses may be classified into nine groups, each with subsidiary types:

    (a) Hand-worked from hard-textured latten or battery brass; to about 1800.

    (b) Hand-worked from rolled calamine brass; c. 1800–c. 1850.

    (c) Cast in fine brass alloy of the pinchbeck type; late 1830s–1860.

    (d) Cast in calamine brass; to 1860.

    (e) Cast in brass of a brilliant gold colour; 1837–60.

    (f) Cast in zinc or spelter brass; 1860–1914.

    (g) Stamped from rolled spelter brass; 1870s–1900.

    (h) Souvenirs and gift shop brasses of coarse, poorly finished cast metal; modern.

    (i) Fakes; from the 1920s.

141. Horse brasses. Acorn, cast, in stamped crescent; windmill stamped; wheatsheaf in crescent; sunflash with central dome and flat rim.

It is essential for collectors to familiarize themselves with a series of undoubtedly genuine horse brasses. Little difficulty then will be experienced in distinguishing between the various classes.

Early- and mid-Victorian horse brass makers devised emblems that had a personal association with the purchaser's trade or district. The Staffordshire knot, for instance, obviously had a regional popularity; the wool merchant's symbol was always stocked by saddlers in sheep-rearing districts; the wagoner and his whip was intended mainly for Sussex farmers; the windmill was for the Lincolnshire millers; the dolphin was always in great demand in Wiltshire, and the hooped barrels found places on all brewery harness. Towards the end of the century this aspect of horse brass salesmanship was virtually lost amid a spate of devices in no way associated with driven horses or with specific trades.

The number of horse brass designs issued during and since the Victorian period has not been computed with accuracy. Three thousand has been suggested as a reasonable total. It is doubtful, however, whether examples issued by the Victorian harness furniture makers would reach half that number.

Horse brasses intended to deceive abound. Even though tools and acids may give them a superficial appearance of age the surface patina is not even approximated. By close inspec-

260

tion of the inner corners of the strap loop the collector may note how the imitation fails to simulate the effect of brass smoothed with years of rubbing against leather. These fakes, too, omit the rubbing and consequent wear which occurred on the back of the lower edge of the brass, making it appreciably thinner.

Acorns date no earlier than the 1890s and with oak leaves are usually cast and enclosed within a crescent. One series has a stamped crescent with a cast oak sprig brazed within, The acorn usually points upward when alone, downward when in a sprig.

Agricultural emblems such as cart-horse and wagon, horse-drawn plough, windmill, sickle or the luxuriant wheatsheaf known heraldically as a garb are usually found within the horns of a crescent or enclosed in a star.

Astronomical emblems are the most common of all. One of the earliest patterns was the sun flash, a brass disc with its centre raised into a high dome, which when polished and burnished radiated beams of light and scintillated with the horse's every movement. In the 18th century they were hand-shaped from thick latten plate and extended almost across the horse's face, weighing six ounces. The dome was encircled with a wide, flat rim and after about 1820 the edge might be serrated: this brass then became smaller and weighed about three ounces. In some mid-Victorian examples the flat rim was pierced with

142. Horse brasses. Sunflash with pierced rays; sunflash with drilled rim; the sun represented as a flat disc; crescent.

143. Horse brasses. Barrel shaped in the round; swinging bell in flat plate; phoenix cast separately and mounted; heart with central cut-out heart.

twelve triangular rays extending outward to the edge. Later, the rim might be drilled with circular perforations and from about 1880 the brass might be stamped at one operation from rolled metal. A splash of colour might be given to May day sun flashes by fitting into the raised centre a boss of coloured glass or china. Colours included yellow, green, dark blue, red, and ringed red, white and blue.

In some instances the sun was displayed merely as a flat disc with rays, often contained within a frame. The crescent moon was offered by saddlers as the emblem of Diana to whom horses had long been sacrificed. Eight-pointed stars were supposed to possess a mystic influence; five-pointed, to preserve any driven horse from danger on the road.

Barrels were intended for the harness on brewers' dray horses. This motif was usually hung vertically in an elongated crescent attached by four struts. The crescent was eventually extended to form a circular frame into which a cast barrel might be brazed. These frames might be plain or pierced, and with smooth or serrated edges. Alternatively the hooped barrel remained unframed and hung horizontally as a pendant, a strap loop brazed to one edge. A group of three tuns or barrels was common, this representing the arms of the Brewers' Company.

Bells were always popular. A few early examples exist consisting of a bell-shaped plate with a bell-shaped opening in which hangs a small swinging bell. Later the plate might be of any desired shape, and fitted with one, two or three bells. Another type has a bracket projecting from the front of the plate to carry a bell.

Birds include game-cocks, pelicans and phoenixes. Peacocks may be noted, full-faced with outspread tails, and side view walking with tail trailing. Such a bird is usually enclosed in a narrow cast framework. Often this is a plain ring with a serrated edge into which the bird, separately cast, has been inserted and brazed. Souvenir birds include swans, ducks, turkeys, ostriches, emus, lyre birds, ravens and magpies.

Estate brasses usually display crests and were cast in princes metal which might be gilded after about 1850: others were cast in german silver and gilded. Heraldic brasses were the specialist work of a few harness furniture craftsmen such as Robert Hughes, Finsbury, London, who operated from the early 1830s to 1865. An estate brass might also be in the form of a cypher with or without a coronet inside a ring or a crescent. Many were assembled from three castings—frame, coronet and cypher. Later crests were also made in this way, less meticulously finished than the one-piece variety. A collector recently bought a collection of about one hundredweight of estate brasses at the price of scrap brass: they were eventually discovered to be in sterling silver and gilded. Crests or cyphers are sometimes to be noted engraved on early Victorian sunflash brasses.

Hearts appear to have been used chiefly on the check rein and are commonly stamped. A plain heart might be enclosed in a circular pierced frame: rayed piercing was popular. A heart within a heart—that is, a flat, heart shape with a heart pierced in its centre—is uncommon, as is the cast heart with a secondary heart rising in relief from its centre.

144. Horse brasses. Heart and pierced frame made as single flat disc; Pegasus or winged horse; locomotive; NER railway cypher.

Horses were among the most popular emblems. The prancing horse of Kent and the horse combatant remain in large numbers. Other models range from the graceful race-horse to the heavy dray horse, including winged and running steeds. The front view of a horse's head in a quatrefoil opening, with a circular outline is found cast in inferior metal. A fully harnessed horse cast in the round made an attractive pendant, the loop rising from the top of the horse's back. It is doubtful if these were made earlier than about 1920.

Horse shoes symbolic of good luck are found in most instances, surprisingly, hanging with the opening downward. The majority contain a profile of a horse's head and neck looking to the left. A stamped and cast horse shoe with pierced nail holes may contain a trotting horse on a slender bar joining the two horns of the shoe.

Locomotives were issued by various railway companies in more than twenty patterns usually displayed in crescents or pierced rings. In a few instances a driver is included in the design. One old series consists of a set of six locomotives illustrating development from the *Rocket* until about 1880.

Playing cards were popular horse brass emblems in the 1890s in sets of four. Each was enclosed in a flat ring pierced with pips of the same suit. A fifth brass was in the shape of an eight-pointed ring, each point cast with a pip in high relief.

145. Horse brasses. Diamond playing-card motif; club playing-card motif; Victorian jubilee issue with solid crown and pierced background; Victoria Cross jubilee issue.

Portraits are mostly of the souvenir variety. The very rare 'bun' portrait of Queen Victoria in profile, with a star-shaped inner rim and a circular outer edge, was issued early in her reign and continued until the jubilee year of 1887. Those issued on the occasion of her jubilee display an unpleasant three-quarter profile with a highly perched crown and widow's weeds. The full widow profile designed by Thomas Brock was first issued on the coinage of 1893. This portrait is found on diamond jubilee brasses. Another series issued for the diamond jubilee was in the form of a Victoria cross bearing a royal crown in relief. Edward VII is found both in full face and in profile, both as monarch and as Prince of Wales, each in several editions and always cast in a single piece. The frame might be inscribed 'God Save the King 1902'. Modern royal portraits include George V, George VI, their queen consorts, and Edward VIII.

Portraits of political celebrities of the late 19th century include Gladstone, Disraeli, Joseph Chamberlain and Lord Randolph Churchill. Early 20th-century souvenir issues include Shakespeare, Lincoln, John Wesley, Nelson, Wellington, Baden-Powell, Roberts, Kitchener, Lloyd George, and more recently Sir Winston Churchill and Field Marshal Viscount Montgomery.

CHAPTER THIRTEEN

Coins

No coins other than silver pennies were minted in England earlier than 1279: small currency was obtained by cutting pennies into halves and quarters. Edward III (1327–77) established the first permanent gold currency on 1st January 1344 and from that year until 1928 the flow of gold coins from the mint was unbroken. The first three gold coins to be minted, now valued at £3,000, were a florin of 6s., the obverse representing the king beneath a canopy; a half florin or leopard of 3s., the reverse showing a leopard sejant and banner; a quarter florin or helm of 1s. 6d., depicting a helm on a fleured field. Edward III also added groats and half groats to the silver coinage: for the next three centuries the groat was the customary gratuity.

Upon his accession Edward III decreed that his coinage should bear secret marks selected by the Master of the Mint and changed quarterly. These mint marks enable collectors to approximate the year during which undated coins were minted. The last to be used were the sun and anchor of the Commonwealth and the crown on the hammered coinage of Charles II.

The first English coin to bear a profile portrait of the monarch was the silver testoon of 1s., minted for Henry VII in about 1504. This replaced the traditional stylized head. Henry VIII (1509–47) followed tradition, and the former monarch's head remained on the coinage until 1526. Then groats were minted bearing a profile portrait of a beardless, youthful Henry VIII. The king grew a beard in about 1530, but not until 1544 was this displayed on the coinage, the golden

266

sovereign and half sovereign then showing the king full-faced and bearded: on the reverse the shield bore the royal arms with lion and dragon supporters, innovations in coinage design.

Although the fineness of English silver coins had remained unaltered since the Conquest, and gold from Edward III's reign, Henry VIII had already started a policy of lowering, year by year, the quality of the gold and silver used by the Mint. This brought about a world-wide distrust of English money: confidence was not fully restored until fifteen years after his death. During the period of debasement, when the metal consisted of one-third alloy, little wear quickly discoloured the end of the nose on full-face portraits, resulting in the king being nicknamed 'Old Copper Nose' during the last few years of his reign.

The counsellors of Edward VI (1547–53) retained the old coinage for about two years. The first coin to bear the boy king's profile was the shilling struck late in 1548 at a mint in Durham House, Strand. These were the first English shillings to be dated. Precious metals were now entering the country from south America, a hitherto untapped source of wealth. Some attempt was made towards the restoration of standard fineness, but such coins were hoarded immediately after issue, causing debasement to continue. The shilling of 1551, for instance, contained three parts of pure silver to nine parts of copper alloy. Some coins struck during the same year bore equestrian portraits of Edward VI in armour with the date in arabic numerals, and on the reverse a shield on a long cross. Others depicted the king full-faced wearing a crown and robes of state.

Gold coins struck during the reign of Mary (1553–58) were of standard quality: silver seldom reached the sterling standard. Until 1557, three years after her marriage to Philip of Spain, coins were issued in the queen's name only. The sovereign showed the queen enthroned with a portcullis at her feet, and was usually dated: on the reverse was a shield on a double rose. The sovereign and the rial, bearing a portrait of the queen in a ship, were not minted after the queen's marriage. Groats, half groats and pennies bear the profile portrait of the queen looking to the left. All silver minted during this reign was struck with dies inadequately sunk. Shillings and half shillings minted from 1557 bore the portraits of Philip and Mary face to face, following a fashion introduced on coinage by Ferdinand and Isabella of Spain: the reverse bore the Hapsburg shield impaling Tudor.

ELIZABETH I (1558–1603)

The privy marks used by Elizabeth I were: (on hammered coins) lis, 1558–61; crosslet, 1558–61; martlet, 1560–61; pheon, 1561–65; rose, 1565; portcullis, 1566; lion, 1566–67; coronet, 1566–70; castle, 1569–71; ermine, 1571–73; acorn, 1573–74; eglantine, 1573–77; cross, 1577–81; sword, 1582; bell, 1582–84; A, 1582–84; escallop, 1584–87; crescent, 1587–89; hand, 1590–92; tun, 1592–95; woolpack, 1594–96; key, 1595–98; anchor, 1597–1600; 0, 1600; 1, 1601; 2, 1602; (on milled coins) martlet, 1560–61; star, 1561–64 and 1566; lis, 1568 and 1570; pierced mullet, 1570
Gold: sovereigns of 30s. were minted during the periods 1558–61, 1584–95; rial of 15s., 1558–61, 1583–94; angel, half angel and quarter angel, 1558–61, 1566–1602; pound of 20s., half-pound, crown, halfcrown, 1558–61, 1565–71, 1593–1602.
Silver: crown and halfcrown, 1601, 1602; shilling, 1558–61, 1582–1602; sixpence, 1561–1602; groat, 1558–61; threepence, 1561–82; half groat, 1558–61, 1566–71; three halfpence, 1561, 1582 (excluding 1571 and 1581); penny, 1558–61, 1565–1602; three farthings, 1561, 1562, 1572–81; halfpenny, 1583–1602.

Elizabeth I restored English coinage to standard quality by demonetising base coin in 1561. In February of the following

146. Coins of Elizabeth I and James I. TOP: gold rial; gold angel. (Elizabeth). BOTTOM: gold crown (Elizabeth); gold unite (James I).

year Bishop Jewel was able to write to Peter Martyre of Zurich: 'Queen Elizabeth has restored all our gold and silver coinage to its former value, and rendered it pure and unalloyed: a truly royal action which you will wonder could have been effected in so short a time.' The fineness of silver coins thereafter remained unaltered until 1920.

Silver coins having current values of sixpence, threepence, three halfpence, and three farthings were issued from 1561. Because of their resemblance to groats, half-groats and pennies, they were distinguished by the inclusion of a large five-petalled rose behind the queen's head. These are the only three-halfpence and three-farthing denominations to be found in English coinage. No shillings were minted between 1561 and 1582. Probably the most handsome of Elizabethan coins were the silver crowns and half-crowns bearing profile portraits of the queen bejewelled and wearing a deep ruff.

Coins had been produced by hand-operated machinery in the Paris mint as early as 1554. Eloye Mestrell, one of the coiners, secured drawings of the apparatus and offered his services to the Tower Mint. He was granted coining facilities in 1561 and for the next ten years a very small proportion of English coinage was struck by his sway or fly presses, the planchets being made in a single operation with a cutting press worked by hand lever. He also introduced a device by which the beads encircling the coin were spaced uniformly. Although Mestrell's coinage was far superior to anything possible with the hammer, speed of production was too slow, approximating one-tenth that of the hammer. The experiment was therefore abandoned and Mestrell's employment terminated in 1572. Apart from their quality, collectors recognise such coins by four mint marks: martlet, 1561; star, 1562–64 and 1566; lis, 1568 and 1570; pierced mullet, 1571.

JAMES I (1603–25)

The privy marks used by James I were: thistle, 1603–04; lis, 1604–05; rose, 1605–06; escallop, 1606–07; grapes, 1607; coronet, 1607–09; key, 1609–10; bell, 1610–11; mullet, 1611–12; tower, 1612–13; trefoil, 1613; cinque-foil, 1613–15; tun, 1615–16; book, 1616–17; crescent, 1617–18; plain cross, 1618–19; saltire cross, 1619; spur rowel, 1619–20; rose, 1620–21; thistle, 1621–23; lis, 1623–24; trefoil, 1624.

Gold: (first coinage 1603–04) sovereigns of 20s.; half sovereign or double crown; crown, halfcrown. (Second coinage 1604–19) rose rial of 30s.; unite; spur rial of 15s.; angel of 10s.; half angel; double crown and Britain crown; thistle crown of 4s.; halfcrown of 2s. 6d. (Third coinage 1619–24) rose rial of 30s.; spur rial of 15s.; angel of 10s.; unite (laurel); half laurel; quarter laurel.

Silver: (first coinage 1603–04) crown, halfcrown, shilling; sixpence; half groat; penny. (Second coinage 1604–19) crown;

halfcrown; shilling; sixpence; half groat; penny; halfpenny. (Third coinage 1619–24) crown; halfcrown; shilling; sixpence; half groat; penny; halfpenny.

Copper: farthing tokens in various sizes and weights.

The union of the English and Scottish crowns under James I (1603–25) was affirmed by adding his Scottish title to the inscription already upon the English coinage. Also, the English shield was quartered with the arms of Scotland which, with those of Ireland, appeared upon English coinage for the first time. The title 'King of Great Britain' was added in October 1604. Some coins bear the inscription *Henricus Rosas Regna Jacobus* (Henry united the roses [of York and Lancaster], James, the kingdoms).

The first change in the new coinage produced the unite, named in allusion to the union of the two crowns. James's proclamation described this coin as 'one piece of Gold of the

147. Coins of James I. TOP: gold rose rial or thirty-shilling piece; gold double crown. BOTTOM: spur rial or fifteen-shilling piece; silver shilling.

value of Twentie shillings sterling, stamped on one side with our Picture, formerly used.' The third issue of the unite in 1619 was given a laureate bust, never before seen on English coins. These became known as 'laurels' to distinguish them from the earlier unites now referred to as 'sceptres'.

So far no English copper coinage had been issued. The silver farthing had been abandoned during the reign of Edward VI and half-pennies were rarely seen although struck periodically until about 1650. In 1615 the king granted Lord Harrington a patent giving him the right to issue copper farthings weighing six grains each: as these were not legal tender they were unpopular.

The Welsh silver mines became a considerable source of supply during the reign of James I. That powerful goldsmith-financier Sir Hugh Myddleton bought the lease of the Cardiganshire silver mines in 1621 and obtained a contract to supply this metal to the Tower mint. Coins struck from Welsh silver may be distinguished by the presence of plumes above the shield.

CHARLES I (1625–49)

Privy marks used at the Tower Mint were: lis 1625; long cross, 1625–26; negro's head, 1626–27; castle, 1627–28; anchor, 1628–29; heart, 1629–30; feathers, 1630–31; rose, 1631–32; harp, 1632–33; portcullis, 1633–34; bell, 1634–35; crown, 1635–36; tun, 1636–38; anchor, 1638–39; triangle, 1639–40; star, 1640–41; triangle in circle, 1641–43; p in two semi-circles, 1643–44; R in two semi-circles, 1644–45; eye, 1645; sun, 1645–46; sceptre, 1646–49.

Gold: unite of 20s.; double crown; angel of 10s.; Britain crown. Triple unites or three-pound pieces were struck at Shrewsbury, 1642, and at Oxford, 1643–46.

Silver: crown; halfcrown; shilling; sixpence; half groat; penny; halfpenny. Silver pounds of 20s. were minted at

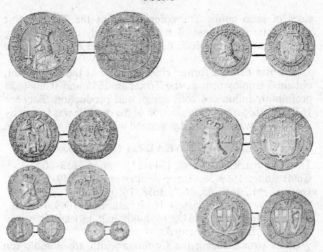

148. Coins of Charles I and Commonwealth. TOP: gold unite; gold double crown (Charles I). CENTRE: gold angel; silver shilling (Charles I). BOTTOM: silver groat and, immediately below, silver penny and silver halfpenny, all Charles I; silver sixpence (Commonwealth).

Shrewsbury, 1642, and at Oxford, 1643–46; half pounds at Truro, 1642–43.

Copper: farthing tokens, 1625–49.

The coinage of Charles I was more varied than that of any other monarch. Three groups are recognised by collectors: coins struck at the Tower Mint; those struck at provincial mints; and coins issued in towns and castles during sieges. Welsh silver continued in use at the Tower until 1637, when Thomas Bushell, lessee of the mines, was authorised to establish a mint at Aberystwyth. The plumes were struck on both sides of such coins. The coins struck at the Tower Mint varied little from those of James I. In early issues the king was shown wearing a ruff: this was replaced by a lace collar in 1632.

Nicholas Briot, a former chief engineer at the Paris Mint, obtained employment at the Tower in 1625 and from 1628 profoundly influenced coin design and production. Between 1632 and 1638 a small proportion of the coinage was struck by means of a sway and the edge grained with a knurling machine.

COMMONWEALTH (1649–60)

The privy marks were: sun, 1649–57; anchor, 1658–60.
Gold: unite, 1649–58, 1660; double crown, 1649–55, 1657, 1660; crown, 1649–55, 1657, 1658, 1660.
Silver: crown, 1649, 1651–54, 1656; halfcrown, 1649, 1651–56, 1658, 1660; shilling, 1649, 1651–60; half groat and penny undated; halfpenny, undated.

Coins struck during the Commonwealth are notable for their simplicity: except for the halfpenny they were of uniform design. These, the first English coins to bear inscriptions in English, were struck in 1649. A shield containing the cross of St George appeared on the obverse, together with a garland of laurel and palm, and the inscription: 'The Commonwealth of England.' On the reverse were conjoined shields bearing the cross of St George and the harp of Ireland with the inscription 'God With Us' and the date. Similarity of design and size enabled shillings to be gilded and passed off as ten-shilling pieces.

CHARLES II (1660–85)

(*Hammered coinage*—1660–62) Privy marks: crown.
Gold: unite or broad piece; double crown; crown.
Silver: halfcrown; shilling; sixpence; groat; threepence; half groat; penny.

274

(*Milled coinage*—1662–84)

Gold: five guineas, 1668–84; two guineas, 1664, 1665, 1669, 1671, 1675–84; guinea, 1663–84; half guinea, 1669–84.

Silver: crown, 1662–84 (the date on the edge is in words from 1667); halfcrown, 1663–84; shilling, 1663, 1666, 1668–84; sixpence, 1674–84; fourpence, threepence, twopence, penny, 1670–84 (1668 twopence only).

Copper: halfpenny, 1672, 1673, 1675; farthing, 1672–76, 1679.

Tin: farthing, 1684, 1685.

The designs on the hammered silver coinage of Charles II followed the crowned and robed figures used by Charles I: in gold the king was armoured and laureated. Jan Roettiers, Dutch medallist, was engaged by Charles to prepare dies for the new milled coinage, on which the king's bust was undraped on gold, draped on silver. The reverse on higher values displayed a cross composed of the four shields containing the arms of England, Scotland, Ireland and France. On gold the spaces between the shields were occupied by sceptres: on silver by linked C's.

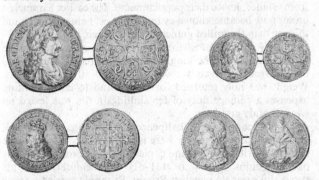

149. Coins of Charles II. TOP: milled coins. Gold guinea and gold crown. BOTTOM: silver shilling; copper halfpenny.

150. Coins of James II.
TOP: crown. BOTTOM:
halfpenny.

In 1663 the Mint was authorised to coin golden twenty-shilling pieces 'in the name and for the use of the Company of Royal Adventurers of England trading with Africa: these pieces are to bear the figure of a little elephant below the monarch's head.' These coins were struck from gold imported from Guinea, hence their popular name. The earlier hammered unites now became known as broad pieces, being broader and thinner than the milled guinea minted in their stead.

In 1667 the Mint lost the privilege of charging seignorage (a commission for the king) and brassage (coining expenses) for converting privately owned gold and silver into coins. Weight was now returned for weight and to cover minting expenses a coinage duty of ten shillings a tun was levied on wine, brandy and beer.

The first copper coins, halfpence and farthings, to be struck in England as legal tender were issued in 1672. Their reverse displayed Britannia, a figure copied from the bronze sistertius of Antoninus Pius (A.D. 131–61) commemorative of his successful campaign against Britain. Britannia carried a spear and sat on a throne resting upon the earth: the head was a

151. Coins of William and Mary.

TOP: silver crown.
BOTTOM: shilling.

portrait of Frances, Duchess of Richmond. An exergue containing the date appeared for the first time on English coinage. Much silver coinage of this period was struck from metal mined in the west of England: this was marked with the Tudor rose. Coins struck from a mixture of English and Welsh silver were marked with rose and plumes.

JAMES II (1685–88)

Gold: five guineas, 1686–88; two guineas, 1687, 1688; guinea, 1685–88; half guinea, 1686–88.
Silver: crown, halfcrown, shilling, sixpence, 1685–88 (excluding crown and sixpence, 1685); groat, threepence, half groat, penny, 1685–88 (excluding groat and half groat, 1685).
Tin: halfpenny, 1685–87; farthing, 1684–87.

WILLIAM AND MARY (1688–94)

Gold: five guineas, 1691–94; two guineas, 1691, 1693–99; guinea, 1689–94; half guinea, 1689–94.

152. Coins of William III. Copper halfpenny; shilling.

Silver: crown, 1691–92; halfcrown, 1689; shilling, 1692–93; sixpence, 1693–94; maundy groat, threepence, half groat and penny, 1689–94 (half groat omitted in 1690).

Upon the accession of William and Mary in 1689 Mint officials solved the problem of placing two portraits on a single coin by selecting jugate busts, bare on gold, draped on silver, reverses displaying various forms of the arms of England and Orange-Nassau, sometimes with the royal monogram W & M. After the death of the queen in 1694 the head of William appeared alone.

WILLIAM III (1694–1702)

Gold: five guineas, 1699–1701; two guineas, 1701; guinea (eight variations) 1695–1701; half guinea (four variations) 1695–98, 1700–01.

Silver: crown (five variations) 1695–97 and 1700; halfcrown (twenty-one variations), shilling (twenty-three variations), sixpence (twenty-nine variations), 1695–1701; maundy groat, threepence, half groat, penny, 1698–1701.

Copper: halfpenny, 1695–1701; farthing, 1695–1700.

The last demonetisation had taken place in 1562 and since then nearly the whole of the hammered coinage had been clipped and worn smooth. By 1695 twenty-eight shillings' worth of hammered silver coin was needed to acquire a guinea in milled silver. The government decided to embark on a recoinage and hammered coins were no longer legal tender after 1696: old coins were exchangeable at face value, however worn or clipped. The loss to the Mint was made good by a seven-year property tax graded in accordance with the number of windows. To replace the coinage temporary provincial mints were established at Bristol, Chester, York, Norwich and Exeter. Here were minted halfcrowns, shillings and sixpences, recognised by the initial letter of the town mint beneath the king's head.

ANNE (1702–14)

Gold: five guineas, 1703, 1705, 1706, 1709, 1711, 1713 and 1714; two guineas, 1709, 1711, 1713, 1714; guinea, 1702–14; half guinea, 1702, 1703, 1705–14.

Silver: crown, 1703–08 and 1713; halfcrown, 1703–14; shilling, 1703–14 (excluding 1711); sixpence, 1703, 1705, 1707–08, 1710–11; maundy groat, threepence, half groat and penny, 1703–10 and 1713 (except penny of 1704 and penny of 1707).

Copper: farthing, 1714.

153. Coins of Queen Anne.
TOP: pattern halfpenny in silver and copper; silver crown. RIGHT: shilling.

154. Coins of George I.
TOP: silver crown; copper
halfpenny RIGHT: shilling.

Queen Anne began the custom, continued by succeeding monarchs, of turning her portrait in the opposite direction from that of her predecessor. The bust on her coinage therefore faced to the left. There were two issues of coinage in gold and silver, before and after the union with Scotland in 1707. Denominations remained unaltered: before the union the arms of England and Scotland were shown on separate shields and afterwards impaled on a single shield. Scottish money was called in and recoined at Edinburgh: such coins are recognised by the letter E beneath the queen's portrait. The presence of the word VIGO in a similar position indicates that the coin was struck from gold or silver captured at the port of Vigo from the Spanish treasure fleet in 1702.

GEORGE I (1714–27)

Gold: five guineas, 1716, 1717, 1720, 1726; two guineas, 1717, 1720, 1726; guinea (seven variations) 1714–27; half guinea (three variations) 1715–27, excluding 1716; quarter guinea, 1718.
Silver: crown (two variations) 1716, 1718, 1720, 1726; half-

crown (four variations) 1715, 1717, 1720, 1726; shilling (six variations) 1715–27; sixpence (two variations) 1717, 1720, 1726; maundy groat, threepence, half groat, penny, all values 1723–27, groat, threepence, half groat, 1717–21, half groat and penny, 1726, penny only 1716, 1718, 1720, 1725.

Copper: halfpenny and farthing (each two variations) 1717–24, except farthing of 1718.

GEORGE II (1727–60)

Gold: five guineas (four variations) 1729, 1730, 1731, 1735, 1738, 1741, 1746, 1748, 1753; two guineas (three variations) 1733–35, 1738–40, 1748–53; guinea (eleven variations) 1727–40, 1743, 1745–53, 1755, 1756, 1758–60; half guinea (five variations) 1728–40, 1745–60, except 1754 and 1757.

Silver: crown (six variations) 1732, 1734–36, 1739, 1741–43, 1746, 1750, 1751; halfcrown (six variations) 1731, 1732, 1734–36, 1739, 1741, 1743, 1745, 1746, 1750, 1751; shilling (seven variations) 1727–29, 1731, 1732, 1734–37, 1739, 1741, 1743, 1745–47, 1750, 1751, 1758; sixpence (seven variations) 1728, 1731, 1732, 1734–36, 1739, 1741, 1743, 1745, 1746, 1750,

155. Coins of George II.
TOP: silver shilling; silver crown.
LEFT: halfpenny.

1751, 1757, 1758; maundy groat, threepence, half groat, penny,
1729, 1731, 1732, 1735, 1737, 1739, 1740, 1743, 1746, 1760,
half groats and pennies, 1746–59, pennies only, 1750, 1750–52,
1757, 1759.

Copper: halfpenny 1729–40, 1742–54; farthing, 1730–37,
1739, 1741, 1744, 1746, 1749, 1750, 1754.

Little change was made in the coinage of the first two
Georges, apart from the portraits and inscriptions. Portraits
were given older features on gold in 1739, on copper in 1740,
and on silver in 1743. The gold crown of George II displayed
a crowned shield on the reverse, and silver coins four shields
placed crosswise as formerly. The spring rolling machine,
invented in 1729, was introduced into the Mint during the
mid-1730s; this gave to the metal strips an exact uniform
thickness. No regal copper coinage was issued between 1754
and 1770: then the Mint produced a very inadequate issue of
halfpennies followed the next year by a scanty issue of farthings. Coin shortage was met by the Birmingham counter-
feiters: Lord Liverpool, Master of the Mint, estimated that
more than half the copper coinage in circulation was false.

GEORGE III (1760–1820)

Gold: guinea, with early shield, 1761–86, excluding 1762 and
1780, first head 1761, second head 1763–64, third head 1765–
73, fourth head 1774–86, spade and shield 1787–99, gartered
shield 1813; half guinea, 1762–66, 1768, 1769, 1772–79, 1781,
1784–91, 1793–98, 1800–04, 1806, 1808–11, 1813, first head
1762 and 1763, second head 1764–75, third head 1774–75,
fourth head 1775–86, fifth head and spade shield 1787–1800,
sixth head and gartered shield 1801–03, seventh head 1804–13;
third guinea 1797–1804, 1806, 1801–11, 1813; quarter guinea
1762; sovereign, St George and half sovereign, shield, 1817,
1818, 1820.

Silver: crown, 1818–20; halfcrown, 1816–20; shilling, 1763 (with young bust and known as the Northumberland shilling), 1787, 1798, 1816–20; sixpence, 1757; 1816–20; maundy, all values, 1763, 1766, 1772, 1780, 1784, 1792, 1795, 1800, 1817, 1818, 1820; groat, threepence and half groat, 1765; groat, threepence and penny, 1770; groat, half groat and penny, 1776; groat 1797; threepence, 1762; penny, 1779 and 1781.

Copper: twopence (cartwheel), 1797; penny (cartwheel), 1797; penny, 1806, 1807; halfpenny, 1770–75, 1799, 1806, 1807; farthing, 1771–75, 1779, 1806, 1807.

Little coinage was issued by the Mint during George III's reign, currency consisting chiefly of worn silver dating to 1696, privately issued copper tokens, countermarked foreign

156. Coins of George III

TOP: spade guinea, 1789–99.
CENTRE: maundy money for 1792.
BOTTOM: 'cartwheel' penny of 1797.

157. Coins of George III.

TOP: silver token dollar struck by the Bank of England, value 5 shillings, 1804 (George III). BOTTOM: crown, 1818 (George III).

coins, and forgeries. In 1797 George III issued Spanish dollars countermarked with the head of the king. The punch mark was small and oval, similar to that used by the Assay Office to indicate that duty had been paid on silver plate. These dollars were current for 4s. 9d. In 1804 the Bank of England struck silver token dollars worth 5s.

For twelve centuries silver pennies had been an essential denomination of English coinage. Not until 1797 were copper pennies issued and these were struck, not by the Tower Mint, but by Matthew Boulton's private mint in Soho, Birmingham. A twopenny piece was also issued, the two coins being popularly known as cartwheels. Boulton represented Britannia with olive branch and trident, the earth of the former design being replaced with waves and a ship in the background. The ship has been omitted since 1895.

When pressure was brought to bear compelling the Mint to continue its function of recoining, legislation in 1816 declared gold to be the legal standard of coin: silver became token coin and legal tender only to the value of 40s. The guinea, last minted in 1813, was replaced by the golden sovereign. Silver coins of the old denomination were redesigned and for the first time engravers not actually on the pay roll of the Mint were employed for this work. Benedetto Pistrucci designed the beautiful St George and the Dragon for the new sovereign and the crown piece. The same engraver also produced the realistic portrait of the aged George III, used on coinage from 1817.

GEORGE IV (1820–30)

Gold: double sovereign, 1823; sovereign, 1821–25 with St George and the dragon, 1825–30 with crowned shield; half sovereign, 1821 with shield and emblems, 1825–30 with ungarnished shield and emblems beneath, 1826–28 with garnished shield.

Silver: crown, 1821 and 1822 with St George and the dragon; halfcrown with shield and emblems 1820, 1821, 1823, with gartered shield 1823–25, helmed shield 1824–29, excluding 1827; shilling,, with shield and emblems 1820–21, with gartered shield 1823–25, with lion 1825, 1826, 1827, 1829; sixpence, with shield and emblems 1820, 1821, with gartered shield 1824–26, with lion 1826–29; maundy money (four values) 1822–30.

Copper: penny and halfpenny, 1825–27; farthing, 1821–30, excluding 1824.

George IV was dissatisfied with Pistrucci's portraits for the coinage and commissioned another set from William Wyon.

158. George IV shilling. 1826.

These were minted from 1823, in which year the new denomination of the double sovereign was issued. Shillings from 1825, and sixpences from 1826, were struck on the reverse with the British lion supported by a royal crown. Half, third and quarter farthings were minted for use in colonies using other English coins. Half farthings became regal coinage in Britain in 1842.

WILLIAM IV (1830–37)

Gold: sovereign, 1831–37, excluding 1834; half sovereign, small size, 1834, large size, 1835–37.
Silver: halfcrown, 1834–37; shilling, 1834–37; sixpence, 1831, 1834–37; fourpence, 1836, 1837; maundy money, 1831–37.
Copper: penny and halfpenny, 1831, 1834, 1837; farthing, 1831, 1834–37.

William IV issued a silver fourpenny piece for general circulation from 1836: this was the first silver coin to display Britannia on the reverse.

VICTORIA (1837–1901)

Gold: sovereign, with shield, 1838–74, excluding 1840 and 1867; with St George, 1871–1901; excluding 1875, 1877, 1881, 1882, 1897; half sovereign, with shield, 1838–93, excluding 1840, 1862, 1868, 1881, 1882; with St George, 1893–1901.
Silver: crown, 1844, 1845, 1847, 1887–1900; double florin, 1877–90; halfcrown, 1840–46, 1848–51, 1874–1901; florin, 1849, 1851–60, 1862–81, 1883–1901; shilling and sixpence, 1838–46, 1848–1901; fourpence, 1838–55, excluding 1850; threepence, 1845–1901; maundy money, 1838–1901.

159. Groat. 1838.

286

Copper: penny, 1841, 1843–49, 1851, 1853–60; halfpenny, 1838, 1841, 1843–48, 1851–60; farthing, 1838–60; half farthing, 1839, 1842–44, 1847, 1851–54, 1856.

Bronze: penny, halfpenny and farthing, 1860–94, excluding farthing 1870, 1871 and 1889. Without ship and lighthouse, 1895–1901.

Victorian coinage until 1887 bore a portrait of the 18-year-old queen engraved by William Wyon. The silver threepenny piece, struck as Maundy money by each sovereign from 1662, came into general circulation during 1845. Influential propaganda demanding a decimal coinage caused the florin to be introduced in 1849. The first issue was known as the godless and graceless florin because the words DEI GRATIA and FIDEI DEFENSOR, which had appeared on the coinage since Edward II, were omitted. The design of the gothic florin issued from 1851 was based on medieval motifs in accordance with the gothic revival of the period. The double florin dates from 1887, but was withdrawn after three years owing to its confusion with a crown. Bronze was substituted for copper coinage in 1860.

The jubilee year of 1887 brought many changes to the coinage. Except for Pistrucci's St George and the dragon remaining on the sovereign, the new design received much criticism, particularly Joseph Boem's portrait of the queen with a tiny crown high on the head. In 1893 this was replaced by Thomas Brock's better known and more distinguished portrait of the widowed Queen Victoria.

Reproductions: copies of outmoded regal coinage were struck in base metal by Birmingham button makers between the early 1850s and 1872. These were in base metal and intended for use as games counters. In wrong hands, however, they were electroplated in gold or silver. Old English coin collecting was fashionable at that period and some of the tools were used for striking coins in gold and silver. Inspection of many shows that care was taken that these bogus coins did not bear dates shown on genuine coins, and none later than 1800. For instance, bogus Charles II sixpences are dated earlier than 1674, the first year this denomination was issued. Vast numbers of bogus coins of the Roman occupation exist.

CHAPTER FOURTEEN

Prints

Beginner collectors of prints find some difficulty in distinguishing one kind from another. It is essential, then, to be fortified with information regarding the method which has produced the print. This is indicated by the appearance of the lines, dots and surface tones which form the picture. Examination through a magnifying glass is necessary to find out the nature of the instrument—tool or acid—which has been used. All prints are made in one of three ways: by intaglio, relievo or planographic processes. The intaglio prints are the line, steel, and stipple engravings, etchings and dry points and aquatints; in the relievo class are wood-cuts and wood engravings; and in the planographic group the most common process is lithography.

Aquatint. An engraving process invented in 1768 by Jean Baptiste Le Prince (1734–84), and introduced to London in 1775 by Paul Sandby. Few were printed after 1840. Aquatinting resembles etching in that acid was used, but areas instead of lines were bitten into the copper plate, the effect produced being that of a wash of sepia or Indian ink. It was also possible to print in colour, but this was usually hand applied. As many as two thousand impressions might be taken from a single plate. Some aquatints of landscapes exhibit the beauty of water colours. English aquatint engravers include Thomas and William Daniell, Thomas Malton, F. C. Lewis, Samuel Prout, J. C. Stadler, R. and D. Havell, and Richard Golding.

Baxter prints. These were made under a patent granted to George Baxter in October 1836, and extended to 1855. The picture was first engraved on a planished steel plate, using aquatint for general tones, etching for delicate lines, stipple for flesh tints. Impressions taken from this key plate were overprinted with colour blocks which numbered between eight and thirty.

In addition to innumerable commonplace prints Baxter issued four hundred of high quality: it is these that the collector seeks. The first of these was 'The Departure of Camden' in 1838. In 1841 Baxter made his reputation with 'The Coronation of Queen Victoria' containing about two hundred recognisable portraits, and 'The Opening of Her Majesty's First Parliament'. His flower pictures are always in great demand, but 'The Gardener's Shed' and 'Hollyhocks' have been widely reproduced.

After 1849 Baxter licensed his process to others, including Abraham le Blond, Joseph Mansell, William Dickes, and J. M. Kronheim and Company. Le Blond issued about one hundred and thirty colour prints in the Baxter manner and in 1868 he acquired sixty-nine sets of Baxter plates and blocks. Prints from these are poorly finished and known as Le Blond-Baxters.

Dates may be approximated from the lettering and the addresses given therein. Baxter prints were imprinted in the picture itself, or, after 1848, embossed on the mount with the inscription: 'Printed in Oil Colours by George Baxter Patentee' or 'Printed by G. Baxter, the Inventor and Patentee of Oil Colour Printing', together with his address. In 1830 he was at 29 King Square, Goswell Road; in 1835 he moved to 3 Charterhouse Square, moving in 1843 to 11 Northampton Square. In 1851 he acquired the adjoining premises and used the address 11 and 12 Northampton Square until his retirement in 1860. Until 1849 his pictures were surrounded by a fine, blue hand-ruled line border. The imprint known as the 'Baxter seal', a red oval containing the title of the subject with Baxter's name and address, was first used in 1849. This was changed, during 1850, in favour of a white seal.

Crayon. This type of engraving is closely allied to stipple, but endeavours to produce results resembling chalk drawing. Stipple and crayon engraving were often combined in a picture, the face of a portrait, for instance, being finished in pure stipple as in a miniature, the remainder was then lightly sketched in the crayon manner. Some of the finest engravers in this medium were the late 18th-century mezzotint engravers, such as John Jones, J. R. Smith, William Ward and William Walker.

Dry-point. These engravings have a velvety softness, the deeper parts of the lines having a somewhat blurred effect. They were made by drawing or scratching the design directly to the surface of a copper plate with a pointed steel needle and without the application of wax composition or acid as in etching. The needle threw up a slight burr or turned-over ridge on each side of the line. This burr held the ink during printing: if removed a delicate line resulted. Dry-point was often used by etchers to touch up a plate. The real effect is seen only on the first fifty or so impressions, as the burr was soon flattened by the pressure of printing and this reduced the effect.

The collector might look for dry-points by Thomas Worlidge (1700–66); Benjamin Wilson (1721–88); Andrew Geddes (1783–44); David Wilkie (1785–1841).

Etching. In an engraving the lines are cut entirely: in an etching they are partially cut with a needle into a copper plate covered with waxed varnish. The ends of the lines are more nearly square than are lines from the graver or dry-point which gradually taper to a point as the tool comes to the surface of the copper. The metal exposed is then bitten into to the correct breadth and depth by the application of aquafortis, producing the peculiar 'furry' appearance which distinguishes the lines from those produced by the engraver's burin. Proofs, or states, have to be taken from time to time to enable the

291

160. Etching.
Rembrandt,
1639

etcher to gauge the quality of his work. Parts which are correct in shade value are 'stopped out', that is, covered with varnish impervious to acid; those which are not dark enough are deepened by another biting, while those which are too dark are lightened by an application of charcoal.

Several prints are usually taken before the work is considered perfect, and these unfinished 'states' are often highly valued.

Among British artists whose etchings are highly valued are Samuel Palmer (1805–81); Charles Keene (1823–91); Sir Francis Seymour Haden (1818–1910); Andrew Geddes (1783–1844); David Wilkie (1785–1841); James Whistler (1834–1903); J. M. W. Turner, R.A. (1775–1862).

Line engraving. Finely polished plates of copper have been used for line-engraving on paper from the mid-15th century. Lines were cut into the surface of the plate, the plain areas which were left becoming the whites in the pictures. Shading was accomplished by varying the depths of the grooves and

the spaces between them. The plate was inked and all except
that retained in the engraved lines was removed by wiping.
The great pressure required to transfer the inked lines to the
paper caused the well-defined plate mark. The lines of ink
standing in relief on the surface of a line engraving can be
felt by gently drawing the finger-tips across the print. Examined
under a magnifying glass, a line engraving will show the lines
to be wider, with softer edges, than the lines of a print from a
steel plate. The copper was so soft that only a limited number
of impressions, about two hundred, could be taken from a
plate.

During the 18th and 19th centuries large numbers of copper-
plate line engravers established studios and brought the art
to a high technical level. Almost all paintings of any conse-
quence were immediately copied and multiplied and a constant
flow of engravings was produced from old masters. Turner
had many engravers such as W. B. Cook, E. Goodall, J. T.
Willmore, Robert Wallis and John Pye. There were many

**161. Line
engraving.**
Sir Robert
Strange, 1770.

others celebrated for the delicacy and crystal clarity of their work. Rosa Bonneur found excellent engravers in J. Landseer, H. J. Ryall and C. G. Lunn. There was no lack of second-rate engravers such as James and Charles Heath. (*See* Steel Engraving.)

Lithograph. A surface print taken from stone, a process invented in the late 1790s and practised by many celebrated artists until its commercialisation in the 1850s. The picture was drawn upon the surface of a specially treated stone with a pencil composed of greasy chalk or ink. The stone was then drenched with water so that only the lines made by the chalk were capable of picking up ink from a roller passed over its surface. The appearance of a lithograph is that of a drawing made with a very soft pencil. Towards 1820 English lithographers began printing on tinted paper, the high-lights being added by hand painting with flake white. Colour lithography was developed by 1830, the process being known as chromolithography.

William Nicholson was the earliest English artist to utilize lithography to any great extent: he sketched some outstanding landscapes on stone. He was immediately followed by William Prout (1783-1852) and James Duffield Harding (1798-1863). Prout's vigorous pencilling, combined with broad effects of light and shade, proved highly effective. Harding gave greater finish to his work and his copies of sketches by R. P. Bonington are glowing masterpieces of light and colour effects produced only in black and white. Bonington's own lithographs are of excellent quality. Richard Lane, A.R.A. (1800–72) produced lithographs unequalled in delicacy of tint and clarity of deep shades.

The collector will look also for Lowes Dickinson's spirited versions of George Richmond's portraits, and for lithographic copies of portraits by Dixsie, Fairland, Hamberger, Maguire, Edward Morton, William Sharp, Slater, and Templeton, as well as the profiles cleverly drawn and lithographed by Count d'Orsay. Also desirable are flowers by Bartholomew; landscapes by George Barnard, J. C. Bourne, H. W. Burgess, George Childs, T. C. Dibden, Andrew Picken and William Walton; architectural views by Allom, Dighton and Hawkins.

Ornithological works by Gould were among the most attractive contributions to the study of natural history; the parrots and tortoises of Edward Lear, the kangaroos of Richter, mammalia of Waterhouse and Hawkins, insects of Humphreys and Wing, form a remarkable array of lithographs.

Mezzotint. These engravings were made in England as early as 1660 and declined with the introduction of early Victorian mechanical print-making processes. Their distinguishing feature is absence of lines, the picture consisting merely of

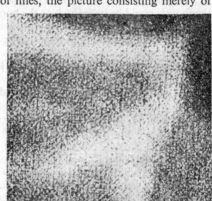

162. Mezzotint.
P. Pelham, 1720

masses of velvety half-tones cleverly arranged and contrasted to form light and shade, making a more exact representation of the subject depicted than was possible by other methods.

The process consisted of roughening the surface of the copper plate with a rocking tool, an instrument of the chisel type with its cutting edge in the form of a segment of a circle containing a hundred or more small ridges. This was rocked backwards and forwards methodically over the polished plate in different directions until the whole surface had been gone over about eighty times, forming thousands of crossed lines. Every crossing caused a tiny depression with a corresponding raised burr which would print a deep black. The picture was formed upon this roughened surface by forcing the burrs back into the depressions in varying degrees. Where light tones were required the burr was pushed almost right back and for high-lights the surface might be burnished, while a burr was left for depth of tone. The plate was smeared with ink and the surface wiped off. As the burr held the ink according to its depth, beautiful gradations of tone could be produced. Few copies could be impressed, as the burr quickly wore during printing. Later mezzotints were usually finished with a certain amount of etching to reinforce line and texture.

English mezzotinting developed in the late 17th century under Isaac Beckett, John Smith and J. Faber, all of whom worked into the 18th century, but received greater impetus when it was proved how specially adapted it was for portraiture. It is computed that more than a hundred mezzotint engravers, including such names as James MacArdell, John Raphael Smith and Richard Earlom worked on the portraits of Sir Joshua Reynolds; and the works of great painters such as Gainsborough and Romney were made more widely known by John Raphael Smith and Valentine Green. The works of Turner and Constable and the nature subjects of Morland were similarly treated by Charles Turner, T. G. Lupton, S. W. Reynolds the elder, David Lucas and James Ward.

Steel engraving dates from the early 1820s when burins of hard steel cut into plates of soft steel. This innovation increased ten-fold the number of impressions it was possible to take from a plate. The closely set lines or meshes used in background sky tones were obtained by using special instruments. Steel engraving prices thus became lower and its cheapness almost ousted engraving as a fine art.

The necessity of working on a steel surface became obsolete after about 1850, when a method was invented of covering the engraved copper plate with an infinitesimal layer of steel.

Stipple. Engravings in which tone values are rendered by pricking with an etching needle a conglomeration of dots or short strokes through a coating of waxed varnish over the copper plate. An acid was then floated over the plate and allowed to bite into the metal. The subject was finished and given brilliance by dotting or flecking on the surface of the plate with a stipple-graver. In pure stippling the tiny dots were close together in the style known as grained. This engraving was at its best in various shades of red and brown: although black was used it was not a favourite. A combination of blue and red in various tints with the addition of black produced richly soft effects.

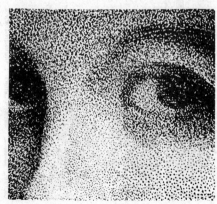

163. Stipple engraving.
J. Jones, 1785.

The chief exponent among English stipple engravers was Francesco Bartolozzi, an Italian who established himself in London early in 1764 and was immediately appointed engraver to George III. Bartolozzi was responsible for an exceptionally attractive series of portraits, notably Lady Betty Foster, Jane, Countess of Harrington, Lord Thurlow, and Lady Smith and her children, all after Reynolds. Bartolozzi also produced portraits after Gainsborough, Romney and Downham. Other principal engravers in stipple were W. W. Ryland (1730s–83); Thomas Burke (1749–1815); Charles Knight (1740s–late 1820s); Thomas Cheesman (1760–late 1830s); Charles Wilkin (1750–1814); J. P. Simon (late 1740s–1810).

Woodcut. The oldest form of producing prints, which reached its height as a means of artistic expression under Albert Dürer (1471–1528): many of his original blocks are in the British Museum.

There is no plate mark upon a woodcut impression. The woodcut is a printed reproduction of a black line drawing, the

164. Woodcut.
J. Amman, 1568.

165. Wood engraving.

T. Bewick, 1789.

design being drawn directly upon a plank (as opposed to end-grain) of sycamore, apple, pear, beech or other fairly soft wood, and the unwanted background being cut away with a knife and gouge. By a wood engraving the collector generally means the form of woodcut in which the design outlines are cut away with a graver so that they appear white in the print against the shaded background. For this technique end-grain of boxwood was preferred. With delicate 'tint-tool' gravers the wood engraver could make a series of delicate lines in the background mass, resulting in considerable range of tone. Thomas Bewick (1755–1828) popularised this process but was not the inventor.

The collector will rarely discover woodcuts dating earlier than the late 18th century. Among the well-known English woodcut engravers are: Thomas Bewick; William Blake (1757–1827); Charles Nesbit (1755–1838); Luke Clennell (1781–1840); A. R. Branston (1778–1827). Many book illustrations were executed on wood in the late 19th century.

Definitions

LAID DOWN: prints pasted on paper and usually rejected by collectors as flawed.

ORIGINAL ENGRAVING: a print in which the engraver is also the artist.

PLATE MARK: the indentation caused by the edges of the metal plate in the printing.

PROOFS: a term generally indicating the first few copies taken off the plate or stone before it is worn: these are usually signed by the painter and the engraver. These were followed by 'proofs before letters' which have the name of the artist and engraver printed upon them. They are not signed. 'Lettered proofs' are printed next and bear the title of the subject as well as the names of the artist, engraver and publisher. Lettered proofs are in two groups: those with the title printed in open letters are the earlier and were followed by ordinary thick letter proofs.

STATE: the condition of a plate in its successive stages of development. The engraver constantly takes impressions or proofs to prove his subject before completion. These are taken from the first, second, third state and so on, according to the alterations and additions made by the engraver.

TITLE: the lettering below the engraved portion of a print. This differs in minor details in various states and assists in their identification.

Technical terms in the lettering on prints

AD VIVUM: often found following the name of the engraver in portraits, showing that the work has been done direct from the sitter and not from a painting.

COMPOSUIT: designed by.

DELINEAVIT (delin., del.): drawn by.

DIVULGAVIT: published by.

EXCUDIT (excud., exc.): printed.

FECIT (fec., f.): etched or engraved by (literally, made by).

FIGURAVIT: drew.

FORMIS: printed.

INCIDIT (incid., inc.): engraved.

LITH: drew, or printed on stone.

LITH BY: lithographed by.

PINXIT (pinx): painted by, painter.

PUBLISHED ACCORDING TO ACT OF PARLIAMENT: referring to one of the various Acts of Parliament associated with the copyright of engravings from 1735.

SCULPSIT: engraved by, engraver.

Glass pictures. Known contemporaneously as 'mezzotinto painting on glass', these date from the late 17th century, reaching their zenith during the third quarter of the 18th century, and continuing with increasing crudeness to about 1815. Briefly, such a picture is the block print of a mezzotint cemented to glass and coloured by hand. The soft paper bearing the print was removed as pulp leaving only the mezzotint outline which was then given several coatings of translucent varnish before being coloured, so that no paint touched the glass. So cleverly were the three layers combined that a complete picture resulted.

Many of the engravings seen on glass pictures display the original lettering with the engraver's name. During the early years the painting was done by the actual engravers of the mezzotints. The earliest now found bear the names of John Smith, Francis Place, or William Sherwin. Georgian names seen on glass pictures include John and Joseph Boydells, John Faber, Valentine Green, Richard Houston, J. MacArdell, J. Payne, J. R. Smith and some forty others.

Only the finest examples of glass paintings are worth collecting, such as portraits of celebrities engraved after Kneller, Lely, Hudson, Reynolds, Highmore, Ramsey, Zoffany and others. Engravings after such artists as Watteau, Boucher and Fragonard are astonishing in the delicacy of their colouring. Sporting pictures, mythological scenes and decorative pictures generally are collected: the Biblical subjects made in quantity after 1790 are of little intrinsic value, being crudely painted.

Forgeries have been made, but these are on smooth modern glass, thicker than the thin, light-weight old crown glass whose imperfections of surface and slight warps cannot be copied.

CHAPTER FIFTEEN

Portrait Miniatures

Portrait miniatures were defined by Nicholas Hilliard, miniaturist to Elizabeth I, as 'small portraits which are to be viewed by hand.' They were fashionable costume ornaments from the time of Henry VIII to that of George III. The purpose was to provide a true likeness of the sitter whose face dominated the picture. The collector has to realise that miniatures by master artists are comparatively rare. It was customary for copyists to be employed, often distinguishable by less perfect technique and by the fact that their work is not signed. The number at work during the Georgian period (1714–1837), most of them anonymous, cannot be guessed; the number of sitters must have been prodigious. George Engleheart, for instance, painted 4,853 miniatures between 1775 and 1813.

Materials. Miniatures are found painted in and on various materials and these must be distinguished and identified by the collector. *Vellum* was used for some of the earliest: Nicholas Hilliard in *The Art of Limning* (about 1601) stated that miniatures were painted upon playing cards covered with fine vellum 'smoothe as any satine, pure, without specks or stains', and were known as tables. The off-white vellum surface was cleansed, polished by rubbing on a flat stone, and finally burnished. Miniaturists became more numerous in the 17th century and specialists prepared the vellum-covered cards ready for the artist. Some miniaturists preferred to paint on a thick, smooth-faced parchment.

Gouache. The *gouache* used for painting vellum and parchment miniatures consists of opaque earth-colours ground in water and thickened with gum and honey. The substance was applied to the vellum with fine, continuous brush strokes. It was an elastic and enduring medium which did not crack upon the flexible vellum. Early specimens show a hard, niggling style but by the mid-17th century broader, stronger, more sweeping brushwork became the accepted style, more closely resembling oil painting.

CARTOON PAPER. This may be noted instead of vellum for some early 18th-century gouache miniatures, before ivory became established as the finest basis for miniature portraits. The surface of the paper was primed with isinglass thickened with pearl white and the portrait painted over this.

IVORY SLIPS. Oval in shape, these were introduced to London miniaturists in about 1705, when it was discovered that a delicate lustre suggestive of flesh could be achieved with ivory under translucent water-colour paints. Old ivories are seldom if ever found polished on both sides: some appear slightly roughened to enable the paint to 'bite'. The bleached ivory was rubbed with garlic juice before painting. Old ivories appear yellow on the reverse and stained at the edges where touched by the protective gold-beaters' skin of the framing.

The majority of existing miniatures are on ivory in transparent water colours, applied with the stippling technique first used early in George II's reign. The pin-point dots of colour, applied with fine brushes, sometimes appear entirely round, sometimes as casual flecks. Only miniaturists to whom speed of production and bold effects were essential, such as copyists, used hatching—that is, short strokes crossing each other in every direction. The size of ivories tended to increase during the 1770s, possibly to enable the artists to include the flamboyant hair styles of the period.

The art tended to decline in the 19th century although some exquisite portraits were produced. Richer colours may be noted and a solidity of style reminiscent of oil painting.

OIL PAINTING. This technique has been practised by many celebrated portrait painters and may be noted throughout the collector's period, these miniatures, too, being worn as pendants. A collection of 530 examples exhibited in London in 1928 showed the majority painted on copper and a few on brass or pewter. Nearly all the celebrated portrait painters in oils were represented.

ENAMELS. Miniatures in this technique may be notably fine, and appear as fresh to-day as when painted. Almost invariably they are on plates of 22 carat gold, as impure gold and base metals reduced the lustre of the colours. The miniaturist applied opaque colours with minute delicacy to a ground of white enamel, the flesh colours being stippled. In England this work dates back to the reign of Charles I, but the majority of specimens that remain were painted in the 18th century up to the 1780s. There was a revival in the first quarter of the 19th century. The majority of enamellers copied portraits in oils by contemporaneous artists; others were themselves water-colour miniaturists who copied their own work in enamels. A third group in the early 19th century specialised in painting portraits of royal and celebrated personages and miniature copies of old masters. Most enamel portraits are signed on the back, frequently with the date and address of the artist. Such signatures are usually burnt in black on the back of the enamel.

Playing card miniatures may be regarded too highly by the beginner-collector. Some portraits were painted in gouache directly on to such cards in the 16th century, but such cards painted in water-colours are either 19th-century productions or forgeries. It is essential to have a working knowledge of contemporaneous playing cards so that their period may be recognised from texture and printing. Playing cards suitable for water-colour miniature painting were not made until about 1830.

Eye portraits are sought by some miniature collectors. The fashion may have been introduced to London by Richard Cosway who painted a miniature of the right eye of Mrs Fitzherbert as a love token from her to the Prince Regent. Such paintings appear on ivory and set in jewelled mounts such as rings, bracelets, brooches, stock pins and ivory and tortoiseshell snuffboxes. Eyes painted by late 18th-century miniaturists appear clear and liquid, their colours beautifully modulated. Later eye miniatures are coarser. George Engleheart painted a large number of eyes, the first in 1783. Each eye might be the subject of a separate miniature: in 1796 he painted Mrs Mitchell's right eye and her left eye a year later.

By the 1830s eye portraits painted in enamels could be bought from jewellers who stocked them in a wide range of colours and shapes and set them to order. Such eyes were illustrated in a jeweller's catalogue published in 1890. The life-size eye was a Victorian vogue, to be set in a frame of pearls on the mantel and appearing to follow one about the room.

Signatures. Works by master miniaturists are usually signed with a full name, monogram or initials. The full signature is usually on the reverse of the ivory or vellum: the surname may be inscribed on the portrait itself, but usually only monograms and initials are written there. These are often microscopic and may be mingled in the hair or concealed in a fold of the dress so that search with a strong glass is necessary to detect them. When gilding or lead pencil has been used it is essential to hold the portrait at the correct angle to the light. Sometimes the signature is found on the thin edge of the ivory.

Initials and monograms with the names of the artists who used them were listed some years ago by J. H. Yoxall. Dates are given for the more important artists and asterisks indicate those who worked before ivory was introduced.

A.B.L. Andrew Benjamin Lens
*A.C. Alexander Cooper, d. 1660?
A.G. Andrew Grazlier
A P (*very small, plain or in monogram*) Andrew Plimer, 1757–1822
A R (*in monogram*) Andrew Robertson, 1777–1845
*B.G. Balthazar Gerbier
*B.L. (*in monogram*) Bernard Lens, 1662–1724
*C.B. Charles Beale, 1660–89
C.F. Charles Fox
C.F.Z. (*plain or in monogram*) C. F. Zincke, 1684?–1767
C.P. Christian Richter, 1678–1732
C.R. (*monogram*) Richard Cosway, 1740–1821
*D.D.G. David des Granges, *c.* 1611–*c.* 1675
*D.L. David Logan
D.P. David Paton
E. George Engleheart, 1752–1829
*F Thomas Flatman, 1635–88
F.C. (*in monogram*) Francis Cleyn, but sometimes Thomas Flatman
G.C. (*in monogram*) George Chinnery, 1774–1852
G.E. George Engleheart, 1752–1829
G.S. Gervase Spencer, d. 1763
*H. John Hoskins, senior and junior
H.B. H. Bone
H.E. (*in monogram*) Henry Edridge, 1769–1821
H.H. Horace Hone, at work 1750–70
I.B. John Bogle, 1768–1805
*I.H. (*in monogram*) John Hoskins senior, d. 1665
*I.H. fc John Hoskins junior
*I.O. Isaac Oliver, 1565?–1615
I.T.B. John Thomas Barber or Beaumont, 1774–1841
J.B. John Bogle, 1746?–1803
J.S. John Smart, 1741?–1811

J.S. JUNR.   John Smart junior

J.T.B.   John Thomas Barber or Beaumont, 1774–1841

L.C. (*in monogram*)   Lawrence Crosse, d. 1724

L.S.   Luke Sullivan, 1705–71

M.B.   Mrs Bradney, Mary Beale

M.L.   Lady Lucan

N.   James Nixon

*N.D. (*in monogram*)   Nicholas Dixon, at work 1667–1708

N.H.   Nathaniel Hone, 1715–84

*N.H.   Nicholas Hilliard, 1547–1619

N.P.   Nathaniel Plimer (brother to Andrew Plimer)

O H (*in monogram*)   Ozias Humphrey, 1742–1810

*P.C. (*in monogram*)   Penelope Cleyn

P.J.   Paul Jean

*P.L.   Peter Lens

*P.O. (*in monogram*)   Peter Oliver, 1594?–1647

R.B.   Rodolphe Bel

R.C.   Richard Collins

R.C.   Richard Crosse, 1742–1810

R.C.   Richard Cosway (rare), 1740–1821

R.D.   Richard Dudman

S (*very small*)   James Scouler, 1740?–1812

S.   Pierre Signac

S.A.   Sarah Addington

S.C.   Usually Samuel Collins or Samuel Cotes, 1734–1818, rarely *Samuel Cooper

*S.C. (*in monogram, usually in gilt*)   Samuel Cooper, 1609–72

S.P.   Samuel Polack

S.S.   Samuel Shelley

*T.B.   Thomas Betts

*T.F. (*plain or in monogram*)   Thomas Flatman, 1635–88

W.B.   William Blake

W.G.   William Essex

Forgeries. Miniatures have been reproduced by the thousand, but most of them are not difficult to detect after examination of museum specimens. Technique is clumsy; the portraiture characterless with poorly drawn eyes and lips; Chinese white over-used; stippling faulty; the ivories polished on both sides. But in some instances endless time has been expended in forging a valuable miniature.

CHAPTER SIXTEEN

Silhouettes

From about 1780 to 1850 the profile shade was the most popular style of 'likeness' this country had ever known, patronised by royalty from George III to Victoria, yet offering for the first time a recognisable, lasting portrait for shillings or pennies instead of pounds. As a result, a collector may acquire such profiles of at least a few recognisable, famous sitters and a few still greater treasures bearing the initials or the printed labels of known profilists. A few more may be identifiable by details of technique. But most silhouettes found to-day are disappointingly anonymous, and the collector must set his own standards, choosing only those in perfect condition and finely executed. Some of the most attractive are conversation pieces containing several figures in an appropriate setting. There is no chronological order for the methods used to produce the profile and some well-known profilists used several techniques, but the work tended to deteriorate after about 1820 and the collector is unlikely to find many really fine specimens among the commonest late scissor-cut work.

Techniques to look for include:

1. Profiles painted on ivory, vellum, card or white composition in Indian ink or an intensely black pine-soot medium, with thinned black for softer detail and sometimes with highlights in gold or bronze. Coloured backgrounds—red, blue and yellow—are rare.

2. Painted on the back of clear glass and thus, when framed, automatically protected. The glass may be backed in various ways, with card, with gold leaf, silver foil or tinsel paper

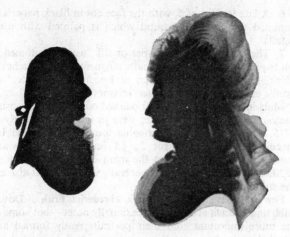

166. Silhouettes by J. Miers. Lord McLeod; Mrs Siddons.

protected by wax and a second sheet of glass, or directly with a wax composition.

3. Painted on the inner surface of slightly convex glass. This may be closely backed as above, but a particularly attractive result is achieved with a flat back of white plaster or chalk: the profile outline, raised a little above the background, is softened by the shadow it throws upon the plaster.

4. Painted on glass but in outline only, to detail features, hair, clothes, and surrounded by a background of solid black: pigment introduced behind the black then shows the profile in colour. **W. Spornberg** of Bath used bright brick red for this somewhat crude style.

5. The profile painted but with only the flesh in black, the head-dress, etc., being in lighter tones and the draperies in colours.

311

6. A late variant of 5, with the face cut in black paper and gummed to the white ground which is painted with dress details.

7. The black cut-out of paper or silk, usually gummed to white pasteboard and occasionally augmented with touches in black, gilt or bronze with pen or brush. The 18th-century profile cutter used a knife; later, scissors were preferred.

Machines to guide the cut or painted outline, and to ensure some resemblance to the sitter were in use from as early as 1775, when **Mrs Sarah Harrington** toured England making machine-guided profiles for 2s. 6d., cut out in white and mounted on black silk. But the main development came in 1820 when a machine became generally available that also cut the silhouette.

Few profilists signed their work—**Frederick Frith** of Dover, **Gibb** and **Lincoln** are names occasionally noted—but some of the more important sold their portraits ready framed and labelled.

John Miers (1758–1821) painted profiles in black on card and on solid white composition medallions with superb evanescent detail such as lace and hair. He moved from Leeds to London in 1788 and his Leeds work is rare and most valuable, distinguished by the different styles of label as his prices rose from 2s. 6d. to 3s. and 5s. Some of his London labels indicate the introduction of his son: the most familiar are those of **Miers** and **Field** when his son was working with John Field. His labels declare him to have been 'Profile-Painter and Jeweller', and exquisite silhouette jewellery may be found, occasionally signed J. Miers under the bust. Later work, labelled Miers and Field, may be pencilled with bronze paint.

Francis Torond (1743–1812) was the name adopted by a Huguenot refugee. He painted profiles in black and colour, bust and full-length, but is best known for his conversation pieces of family groups, fascinating to-day for their details of

312

SILHOUETTES

dress and furnishings. He moved from Bath to London in 1784 and employed several assistants. **William Wellings** was a London profilist who produced late 18th-century conversation pieces.

Charles Christian Rosenberg (1745–1844), who worked at Bath, painted in intense black (guaranteed not to fade) on the inside of convex glass, so that the profile was shadowed upon the intense opaque white of a flat plaster backing. He also painted on flat glass backed with pink (now faded) card to suggest marble and in colour and made profiles for jewellery. He came to England as a page with Queen Charlotte and printed the royal arms at the head of his label.

A. Charles of Bath and London painted in intense black with translucent detail. He claimed the convex glass painting as his invention and charged as much as a guinea for a full-length profile on glass or ivory, and 3s. 6d. for a bust on paper.

167. Silhouettes by Mason and W. Holland. H.R.H. the Duke of Sussex by Mason, touched with gilding; unknown sitter painted on glass by W. Holland.

H. Gibbs of Bristol and Chelsea was among the profilists who backed their glass with wax.

Mrs Isabelle Beetham of Fleet Street, London, also used a wax composition to protect her dress-conscious profiles, but this has tended to crack. Others are painted on ivory, and later Beetham specimens may be noted cut in black paper pasted on card and finished with softening lines of brushwork. Her labels are dated 1785, the date of their printing.

William Holland painted profiles in Dublin 1774–86 and a signed specimen may be found painted on glass backed with silk. He claimed that his water-colour composition was better than the usual on plaster or oil colour on glass.

Colour in painted profiles was used before 1788 by **W. Phelps** of Drury Lane, who introduced blue and green in his sitters' dresses and coloured the hair under dark lines of shading.

William Hamlet of Bath, painting on flat and convex glass, 1780–1815, put touches of colour to his guinea and half-guinea figures and claimed to be 'Profile Painter to Her Majesty and the Royal Family'. His son Thomas worked at Bath and Weymouth.

Edward Foster of Derby (1762–1864) made his profiles in rusty red heightened with gold, and in the 19th century **J. Buncombe** of the Isle of Wight painted the grand uniforms of naval and military officers in full colour with only the faces in black silhouette.

William Hubard (1807–62) of Whitchurch, Shropshire, is among the best-known cutters as distinct from painters of silhouettes, working professionally from the age of 13, always in full-length, pasted on card and often touched with gold— sometimes with white. He used neither drawing nor machine, as may be noted embossed on the mounts of early specimens; later London portraits (1829–34) were on mounts embossed 'Taken at the Hubard Gallery'. Many Hubard shades were intended for scrapbooks and include pictorial scenes such as

168. Silhouette by A. Edouart.
Part of a conversation piece, 1831.

Oxford High Street, and Epsom races with some 200 tiny figures. In general, scrapbook cuts are seldom worth collecting. Hubard went to America and became a portrait painter. Another English prodigy, 'Master Hankes', joined his Hubard Gallery out there.

August Edouart, at work 1825–60, made a conspicuous success of the craft—when it was becoming a cheap sideshow—with **J. Gapp** at work in his booth on Brighton chain pier and **J. Dempsey** of Liverpool offering memento likenesses for emigrants at 3d. and 6d.—colours 1s. 6d. Edouart cut about a quarter of a million profiles, some set against painted backgrounds or lithographs. His charge for a full-length rose to 5s. (7s. seated) and he sold profiles of celebrities for 3s.

J. Smith of Edinburgh, **Paskin** of Colchester and **W. F. Godfrey** were among the makers of silhouette jewellery—

brooches, scarf pins, bracelet clasps, highly valued memorial rings, and playing card, patch and snuff boxes. Watch discs for the backs of watch cases date to the 1840s and are now very rare.

Frames are important details. Rich 18th-century work was framed like a miniature in an oval gilt metal mount with a border of paste or pearls. Less rare, but desirable, is the early frame of thin brass stamped in gadroon patterns. The typical early 19th-century frame is of black papier mâché with an inner oval rim of brass and brass acorn-and-ring hanger. The most usual alternative is the rectangle with deeply mitred corners, in pearwood or the Victorians' favourite bird's-eye maple.

CHAPTER SEVENTEEN

Maps

Colourful maps of England and the counties have been important accessories to the interior decorator since James I set the fashion. Inventories taken in 1626 show that '8 Mapps' enhanced the withdrawing room walls at Kimbolton, and the great parlour at Hatfield was graced with three framed maps. These double folio maps, too large for glazing, were protected from dust and daylight by curtains of taffeta.

Collectors of old English maps must necessarily know something of the paper which received the engraved prints and colours used to illuminate them. Early maps were printed on strong, thick hand-made paper of watermarked quality. Until about 1610 suitable paper was imported from France and English maps of the period show one of the numerous French watermarks when held to the light. Elizabethan maps have clear, vertical watermarks caused by wires used for drying the paper, $1\frac{1}{2}$ inches apart. Early in the 17th century these spaces were reduced to 1 inch, with close horizontal lines, twenty to the inch, at right angles. These have faintly ridged the paper and the untidy fibre surface has been overcome. The original maps of Christopher Saxton (d. 1596) were printed on a thick, soft-textured paper, its surface an irregular mass of wrinkles and watermarked with a stalked bunch of grapes surmounted by A F, or a small bunch of grapes lacking both stalk and initials.

French paper imports were drastically reduced after the establishment of paper mills in England late in the 16th century, but French quality was still required by map makers. Variations of the arms of France are consistently found on

317

169. Watermarks on maps. Camden's Britannia, 1637; G. & J. Blaeu's Atlas of the Netherlands, 1644; G. & J. Blaeu's England folio, 1647.

this 17th-century paper, appearing as late as 1688 on a re-issue of Saxton's *Atlas of the Counties of England and Wales*.

Watermarks in the form of bogus coats of arms characterised English-made map paper until the mid-18th century. Many were mere heraldic distortions accompanied by the papermaker's initials and a date. Adaptations of the Amsterdam and Strasbourg arms were commonly used. The pseudo-Strasbourg coat of arms watermarked the Saxton-Webb map of 1645; Moore's map of the Fens, 1650; Speed's Atlas, 1676 and Petty's Atlas 1683 and 1730.

The fleur de lis variously outlined watermarked some English-made map-paper from 1615. In Speed's *Theatre*, 1616, it is accompanied by a crowned shield with initials below; in Porter's Atlas, 1665, the petals are shaded; with the addition of the maker's name or initials the fleur de lys watermarked Speed's Atlas, 1666; Blome's Atlas, 1670; the Moxon Atlas, 1670; Wells's *Sett of Mapps*, 1700; Senex's maps, 1721; Rocques's *London*, 1746.

Monogram watermarks appeared on map-paper from 1660 and continued until 1770 or even later. From 1750 monograms were designed with cursive capitals. Paper-making processes improved, and maps were engraved on smooth, ivory-tinted, hand-made paper until 1800.

The old cartographers until 1700 enthusiastically decorated their maps with fabulous animals and wonderful monsters on land, with gigantic ships, leviathans and fish on the sea. Before 1520 cartographers represented the sea by swirling

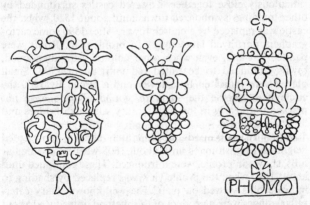

170. Watermarks on maps. G. Hole's map of Worcestershire (arms of Burgundy) 17th century; Kip's map of Westmorland, 17th century; the arms of France and Navarre, constantly used throughout the 17th century.

lines. Gradually the water along the coast-line came to be depicted in calm washes of colour until after 1550 when stippling indicated water. The water surfaces on many pre-1620 maps are indicated by conventional wavy lines which appeared dingy unless coloured. Coast-lines during the 16th century were represented by hatching. This was abandoned early in the following century, but re-appeared from the mid-1690s.

Gigantic trees symbolized forests on manuscript maps, line engravers adopting the same convention in a smaller size, making them more numerous with shadows cast to the east. After about 1750 woods were indicated as clumps of foliage viewed from above.

Towns were usually shown disproportionately large, thus dwarfing distance and having the effect of bringing them ridiculously close together. Towered castles surrounded by other buildings symbolized towns until about 1520, when the castle was replaced by a church tower. After 1590 some carto-graphers portrayed large towns in profile-plan. Roofs were painted red and, even when other colours were abandoned, towns continued to be tinted red until about 1790. Small places were indicated by a tower and a circle. By 1800 the circle had become the standard symbol. Roads were not marked until early in the 17th century, although bridges and fords were shown.

Gently rising mounds, appropriately shaded, represented height on English maps until about 1605 when more angular hills, shown in profile, were introduced. These continued until about 1690 when the profile view was replaced by shading to indicate hills viewed on plan. The well-known 'hairy cater-pillar' ranges were a product of this method, introduced about a century later.

English maps are often dominated by elaborate cartouche decoration. The earliest style, adapted from the Italian, was the strap-work frame curling forward round the inscription. Late Gothic designs interspersed with flowers and fruit, animals and birds, were added by Saxton. The fashion then changed to a rectangular frame engraved in imitation of carved wood picture frames. Cartouches became less formal, early in the 17th century displaying much scrollwork. Cherubs and garlands of flowers were added, nobles and their ladies figured on the scrollwork, signs of the zodiac and scenic views were incorporated in the space originally devoted to the title. During the 18th century the scroll might be replaced by a banner, shield, ribbons—all manner of designs being tried out as backgrounds for map titles.

Engravers' initials in script, too small to detect without a glass, are found in cartouche designs. Here, too, the only date on a map may be concealed among the folds of ribbon. When engraved copper map plates were sold, the new owner usually erased names and dates: close examination of a map will sometimes reveal a poorly erased date or name.

171. Watermarks on maps. R. Morden's map of Durham, 1695; Sir William Pety's Atlas of Ireland, 1720; Camden's Britannia (2 volumes), 1722.

172. Watermarks on maps. Hermann Moll's New Description of England and Wales, 1728; Thomas Kitchin and T. Jeffreys Small English Atlas, 1775; Carrington Bowles' Atlas folio, 1785.

Many old English maps are set in attractive borders, at first ornamental surrounds resembling narrow carved wood picture frames. Speed set the fashion for borders displaying town plans and gaily costumed men and women. These were succeeded by the 'margent' or 'square stick of degrees' coloured red, crimson or yellow.

Map-painting became a recognised occupation. Elizabethan

322

cartographers made their maps brilliant, but paints were carelessly applied. With the increasing demand for finely bound coloured atlases during the first half of the 17th century cartographers tended to send uncoloured engravings to Amsterdam, where map painting was considered an art rather than a craft. This desire for perfection was short-lived and English map painting quickly settled into a skilful but stiff uniformity governed by precise rules. The process thus lacked any spark of originality, the quantity of colour varying with cost.

The following pointers will assist collectors in recognising modern reproductions. Standard colours incapable of running or sinking into the paper were mixed by map painters according to established formulae, unchanged until the second quarter of the 18th century. Red lead tempered with gum water was liberally applied. Unfadable copper-green, which in a thin wash became transparent willow-green, was a mixture of French verdigris and cream of tartar. Other colours included stone colour from tincture of myrrh, crimson, indigo, gamboge, ultramarine, carmine, scarlet and burnt umber. These were given a slight glaze and essential transparency by blending with gum water.

The Art of Map-Painting by John Smith, 1665, describes the map-painter's routine. First, forests and woods were coloured in grass-green, a mixture of copper-green and gamboge; towns were accentuated with red lead; 'sea-shoars' and lakes in thin indigo. Boundary lines were next painted and where they passed through already coloured woods or towns the duck-quill brush was lifted. In town plans houses were coloured in red lead, tiles in vermilion, castles in tincture of myrrh with leaded towers in slate blue and spires in thinnest red lead. Unfortunately much fine engraving was lost to view behind a thickly applied red lead. Water immediately beneath ships sailing the ocean was tinted a deeper indigo than the surrounding waves; hulls were coloured amber; sails with tincture of myrrh, and flags with vermilion or blue bice. Fire from guns was shown in red lead, smoke with thin blue. Colours on framed maps have become gently softened by the passage of time: those preserved in the closed pages of atlases have retained their original brilliance.

CHAPTER EIGHTEEN

Playing Cards

Five centuries of English modes and manners are recorded
with uninhibited enthusiasm on innumerable thousands of
playing cards. Here is a fascinating subject for collectors
with a love of social history and the patience to hunt down
the rarer but by no means prohibitively expensive specimens.

Playing card packs printed between 1712 and 1862 may be
dated by their aces of spades. During this period excise tax
was levied on each pack and the Commissioners of Stamp
Duties required that one card in every pack should be
'stamped on the spotted or printed side' with a distinctive
mark showing that duty had been paid. The ace of spades,
printed in black, was selected for this purpose. Wrappers were
also sealed and stamped.

This created an illicit trade in bogus aces which grew to
such magnitude that in 1756 legislation made it a felony to
counterfeit or forge duty aces. An engraver was executed in
1762 merely for possessing a copper plate engraved with duty
aces. The Stamp Commissioners endeavoured to frustrate
forgery by limiting the number of playing card manufacturers,
by confining their trade to the cities of London, Westminster
and Dublin and by issuing licences under two £500 securities.
The trade was prohibited in Scotland.

The aces themselves were printed by the Commissioners at
Somerset House. Manufacturers requisitioned duty aces as
required, usually drawing a ream of 9,600 aces. When playing
cards were ready for sale an excise officer visited the workshops and sealed each pack with a stamped label. Cards for

export were exempt from duty, the aces bearing a special stamp and the packs being enclosed in distinctive wrappers.

The duty levies stamped on playing cards may be summarised as follows:

Until August 1712: plain aces of spades without duty marks.

1712–14: a duty of sixpence was levied on each pack. The ace of spades and the wrapper were both stamped in red with the crowned monogram AR. The red ink is now so faded as to be scarcely visible. There was no statement as to amount of duty.

1714–56: the duty remained at sixpence and the ace of spades was stamped with the monogram GR.

1756–65: the duty was increased to 1s. and the ace was stamped with the amount.

1765–76: the duty continued at 1s., payment of half the sum being indicated by stamping the wrapper. The ace of spades was designed in an expansive, complicated pattern. The spade was surrounded by a garter wreathed in laurels and inscribed HONI.SOIT.QUI.MAL.Y.PENSE, surmounted by a royal crown and G.III.REX. Beneath was the plate number and a ribbon inscribed DIEU.ET.MON.DROIT with the name of the manufacturer below.

1776–89: duty was increased to 1s. 6d. and the ace surmounted by the words SIXPENCE ADD^L DUTY.

1789–1801: the duty was raised to 2s., the extra levy being indicated by stamping around the sides SIXPENCE ADD^L DUTY.

1801–15: the duty was raised to half a crown, a third inscription ADD^L DUTY SIXPENCE being stamped below the ace.

1815–20: duty continued at half a crown. The design of the ace remained unaltered, but no longer counted as having a sixpenny value. The lettering, in a different type from that used since 1765, was changed to DUTY at the top, ONE

SHILLING vertically to the left with AND SIXPENCE to the right. The remaining shilling was made up by impressing two sixpenny stamps on the back and front of the wrapper.

1820–28: duty remained at half a crown. The monarch's cypher was changed to G.IIII or G IV REX and the ace stamped DUTY ONE SHILLING AND SIXPENCE and the wrapper impressed with two sixpenny stamps. At this time the duty approximated 200 per cent. the cost of manufacture plus a paper duty of 6d. a dozen packs.

1828–62: duty was reduced to 1s. A fresh duty ace was designed, delicately engraved on steel plate and incorporating a mass of intricate flourishes responsible for the nickname of 'Old Frizzle'. This ace of spades contained the royal heraldic quarterings supported by the lion and the unicorn and marked DUTY ONE SHILLING.

1862: duty was reduced to 3d. and denoted on the wrapper: the duty ace was abandoned. Fanciful aces of spades continued and some late 19th-century and early 20th-century examples carry the inscription DUTY THREE PENCE WHEN USED IN GREAT BRITAIN AND IRELAND.

Playing cards of even a hundred years ago now seem difficult if one really tries to play with them. The backs, with few exceptions were quite plain, rough surfaced and easily soiled until 1840, when intricate patterns were printed with a glossy surface. Figure indices date no earlier than 1862 and with letters from 1884; round corners from 1862 and double-headed court cards from 1867.

CHAPTER NINETEEN

Fans

Plumed fans of ostrich and peacock feathers with long, heavy handles of jewel-encrusted gold, silver or exotic wood were fashionable at the English Court until the early Stuart period. Every man of importance possessed at least two fans—one for walking, the other for full dress.

These fans were eventually outmoded by folding fans introduced in the early 1580s, with mounts or leaves of vellum delicately cut in open work patterns rivalling the finest needlepoint and edged with gold or silver lace. The cutting of these découpé fan mounts in fine vellum became a favourite pastime among dilettantes. The seven to ten blades or sticks, elaborated to carry the flamboyance of the lace effects, were at first in ivory and later in tortoiseshell trimmed with gold and precious stones, or in Levantine mother of pearl carved and engraved with mythological subjects.

The size of fans. This varied with fashionable dress. In the 17th century they measured about 4 inches in length, increasing to a foot or more during the reign of Queen Anne, and reverting to the 9-inch standard during the 1720s and 1730s, increasing to 'the size of a portable firescreen' during the 1740s. The *London Magazine*, 1744, noticed that 'fans are wonderfully increased in size from three-quarters of a foot to a foot and three-quarters or two feet.' In the 1750s fans reverted to about 9 inches for the remainder of the century. From about 1815 11 inches was the fashionable length.

Fan spread. The shape and arrangement of the fan changed chronologically down the years. Until the mid-17th century the fan-spread extended to about one-third of a circle, reaching 160 degrees by 1650, the early mount covering about two-thirds of each of the fourteen to sixteen shouldered sticks. The full semi-circle was reached ten years later, the mount still concealing two-thirds of the length of the blades which then numbered twenty-four to twenty-six, reduced to eighteen or twenty-one by the mid-18th century and without visible shoulders. The brin—the lower part of the blade—had been lengthened by 1720, thus reducing the space for the mount. At the same time and until 1760 the spread reverted to 160 degrees, afterwards increasing to rather more than the semi-circle.

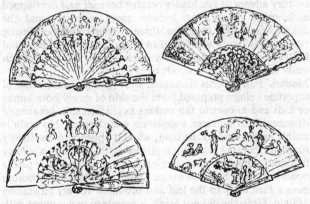

173. Fans. TOP LEFT: early Georgian. Richly-worked fan of the 1720s–30s, with small mount on long, shouldered sticks, each similarly decorated, opening to a full half-circle. RIGHT: somewhat larger fan of the 1740s, with mount and sticks about equal length and each pair of sticks making a pattern. BOTTOM LEFT: mid-Georgian specimen of about 1760, the more elaborately carved sticks making a unified pattern and opening to more than the half-circle. RIGHT: fan of the 1780s, the sticks carrying a secondary figure scene.

The blades. A wide range of materials was used for fan blades, ivory and mother of pearl being favourites: in the 18th century tortoiseshell, horn, bone and fine-grained woods such as ebony, sandal-wood, holly and laburnum, were also used. Early ivory blades were long and narrow and widely spaced with well-balanced outlines, each enriched with a separate near-identical design painted in brilliant colours. Early in the 18th century the fan blade became straight without a visible shoulder and the ornament might be carved, pierced, painted, stained or gilded. Each stick carried a complete pattern, but several patterns might be introduced in a single fan. As the century advanced fan blades became broader and overlapped each other. Decoration became more elaborate and the design was carried over two, three or four sticks, and finally right across. Ivory was found to be an extremely fine ground for gold encrustations, such as ribbons and bows conspicuously studded with diamonds or brilliants.

Mounts. Fan mounts decorated with painting were often of superfine vellum prepared from the skin of newly born lambs or kids and known to fan makers as chicken skin because of its exceptional thinness, suppleness and strength. No grain is visible unless held to the light, when it appears to be slightly mottled. Painting was accomplished with gouache, a widely favoured substance consisting of glue and water-colour paints opacified with white lead oxide. This extremely elastic medium gave a firm body to the leaf and produced velvety reflections of light. Gouache did not crack, a necessary requirement with paint used on folding fans.

Chicken skin mounts from 1660 were painted with full, bright colours but with a delicacy that was never gaudy. Subjects included classical scenes and portraits. The inventory description of a fan presented by Charles II to the Duchess of Portsmouth is typical of court fans of the period: 'skin mount, finely painted and finished, with figures, slaves and camels,

174. Fans. TOP LEFT: fan of the end of the 18th century, with a more compact central figure scene on the mount and narrow, separate sticks, with simple ornament. RIGHT: Regency fan with neo-classic pattern on the wide-opening, very deep mount and plain narrow sticks. BOTTOM LEFT: 19th century. Combination of lace and carved ivory. RIGHT: mid-19th century specimen that might be confused with earlier work.

foliage and buildings. Sticks and guards of mother of pearl carved with emblematic subjects, inserted with gold ornaments. On the reverse a landscape, minutely detailed.'

Fan painting. In London this became a highly skilled craft. Towards the end of the century pastoral subjects predominated, but portraits of celebrated beauties remained fashionable. Georgian fans display the rococo influence, and treble gilding was introduced to the mount and to the carved figures, urns, shell and dolphin designs, garlands and scrolls on guards and sticks. For each court fan painted on chicken skin in the 18th century there were thousands of commercially made fans with mounts of hand-made paper effectively decorated with gouache.

The demand for low-priced fans early in the 18th century prompted engravers to print fan mounts on a special quality paper imported from France. The subjects engraved included topical events and passing fancies of the day and were used as propaganda pieces for vilifying politicians, glorifying generals, advertising plays and actors and popularizing ballads of the day. Some were printed with full instructions for the figures of popular dances. Others were impregnated with perfumes, a treatment which would quickly have destroyed gouache paintings. The mounts were inexpensive enough to be replaced to meet the needs of the moment.

The most prolific maker of engraved mounts was M. Gamble, at the sign of the Golden Fan, St Martin's Court, London: many were printed on the lower edge with the publisher's name and date of issue in accordance with the law. The quality of engraved mounts improved from about 1760: some delightful work was engraved in line and stipple. Classical and mythological subjects were in black and white or sanguine, or overpainted with water-colours. Fan mounts in lithography date from about 1815 onwards, and were often used as a base for overpainting: it is often difficult to detect the lithographed foundation.

TYPES OF FAN

A curious type of fan decorated with Biblical subjects was evolved in the late 1720s for church-goers, intended to turn their thoughts on Sunday from worldly matters, and receiving special sanction from the Bishop of London. These sometimes beautiful fans point a moral rather than illustrate a story, the soft colouring of the mount being repeated in the blades and guards. Fans for chapel-goers were made during the second half of the century.

Mourning fan. This appeared in grey and black overlaid with white, the ivory blades darkened with brown stain to unify the general tone, sometimes burnished with a simple design of silver, blending with the grey tones of the leaf.

Quizzing fan. This fan had become popular by the mid-18th century. It was designed with large peep-holes covered with transparent material, so that when open the fan showed a series of perforations around its upper border. Behind these its owner could present a modest pose, yet miss nothing of the risqué play of the period. Later a quizzing glass was inserted above the rivet.

Cabriolet fan. This type was fashionable from the 1770s to the 1790s, the name derived from a light-weight two-wheeled carriage. The fan generally exceeded 9 inches in length but not more than 11 and was fitted with two or three narrow arc-shaped bands of chicken skin or silk. The top mount, measuring twice the depth of the others, was usually painted with a

175. Fans. TOP LEFT: fan of the second half of the 18th century, its whole pattern of mount and guards designed to render unnoticeable the peep-holes included in the pattern on the sticks. RIGHT: cabriolet fan, the outer mount showing a scene involving the fashionable carriage. BOTTOM: detail from the cabriolet fan above right, with fallen horse and broken wheel—an early gibe at the lady driver.

176. Fans. TOP LEFT: medallion fan with the narrow, wide-spaced sticks of the late 18th century. RIGHT: another version of the medallion fan but in the brisé manner, the sticks threaded with ribbons and carved and painted to suggest a mount. BOTTOM LEFT: early brisé fan with narrow painted border and the sticks carved in two contrasting patterns. RIGHT: simple, delicate work in a brisé fan of the mid-19th century.

scene incorporating a cabriolet, its occupant a portrait of the fan's owner. The exposed parts of the blades were perforated, carved and gilded, and tiny mirrors might be inserted in the guard sticks and a minute telescopic glass fitted into the blade pivot.

Medallion fan. Contemporaneous with cabriolets. The mount of finely woven silk was painted with a light-coloured ground ornamented with three medallion subjects. The central medallion might be elliptical, rectangular or circular, the fan's symmetry emphasised by a flanking pair of small medallions. The paintings were the work of highly skilled miniaturists, detail being displayed quite as cleverly as on the more costly chicken skin. Late in the period tiny Wedgwood jasper cameos

334

were set in the blades, many of which were overlaid with gold or silver work, often in the form of a cartouche extending over the central six or eight blades.

Brisé fan. Composed solely of flexible blades in ivory, tortoise-shell or horn, without a mount, this fan was introduced in the early 1680s, becoming popular in about 1715 and continuing until early in the 19th century. The twelve to twenty-four blades were joined by coloured silk ribbons, seemingly in one continuous length passing through the whole fan, but in reality consisting of many short lengths, each attached separately to a blade. Each blade was cut to wafer thinness, the upper part being saw-cut with patterns so exquisite as to resemble the finest lace and enriched with burnished gilding: the brins might be worked with an armorial device. Equal care was given to both sides of the blades.

Another type of brisé fan consisted of overlapping, unperforated blades. These formed a plain field for decoration, each side enriched with an oil painting. Towards the end the ivory and tortoiseshell were superseded by flexible blades of whalebone, scented sandal wood, laburnum wood or cut steel. In their final phase brisé fans might have plain medallion shapes among the piercing: these were painted or covered with engravings.

CHAPTER TWENTY

Musical Boxes

Musical-boxes chimed and tinkled their melodious little accompaniment to the life of drawing-room, boudoir and nursery throughout almost the whole of the 19th century. They first appeared during the Regency, the mechanism consisting of a driving spring which set in motion a revolving cylinder of brass set with projecting steel pins arranged to pluck a resounding metal comb with 15 to 25 teeth tuned to scale. The tunes on these early machines lack volume of sound and notes are inclined to chatter. The first of a long sequence of improvements was made shortly after 1820 and by these it is possible to date examples.

An early comb needed detailed work in fixing teeth to a brass bed-plate, at first singly and then in groups of three to five. From 1820 makers began to cut it from a single plate of steel. Chattering was prevented from about 1825 by introducing dampers in the form of tiny feather quills.

Efforts to increase the range of tone led to the appearance of the first considerable musical-box in 1833. Known as the Cartel music-box, this shows the first of many developments in tone. Five years later Nicole-Frères of Geneva introduced the two-comb or Forte-piano musical-box. This was an immense improvement, playing loudly or softly as the music required. The movements, larger than anything hitherto, have combs fitted with flat steel wire dampers, with the exception of short high notes which retain feather quills.

A mandoline effect was evolved at about the same period for fitting to a large musical-box. A dominant note is repeated at regular intervals like a well-played mandoline. Greater volume of sound was obtained by using five combs, each having eight or ten notes of the same pitch, in the centre and the treble end. Large, deep-toned combs tuned to chromatic scale produced really good music on costly machines from about 1840, and at about the same time appeared cylinders 18 inches to 22 inches long.

Innovations in automatic music made around 1850 included the addition of a drum and bell accompaniment. In an early example the brass drum is screwed to the bottom of the case, concealed beneath the bed-plate. The six or more bells hang in a cluster on a small gantry beneath the movement and are struck with little brass hammers. From about 1860 drum and bells were placed in full view and these add greatly to the appearance of the box. Less melodious drum and bells were included in most cheap musical-boxes from 1875.

The Flutina, or reed musical-box, made its appearance in 1850. Flute effects were obtained by the introduction of air-vibrated reeds. The organ notes are arranged in the centre of the cylinder with a comb on either side. The combined effect of comb music and flute is excellent when the cylinder exceeds 17 inches in length. Later came the orchestra musical-box: in this an orchestral effect is produced by the introduction of wooden or metal whistles.

An important advance was made in 1854 with the invention of the re-change musical-box, so designed that the cylinders may be replaced by others containing fresh programmes of music. As far as expensive musical-boxes were concerned this ended the era of boring repetition. The changing mechanism was improved in 1862 and the telescopic cylinder, expanding as the tune played, was evolved. By 1870 a series of cylinders might be arranged on a rotating shaft, with a device enabling any one to be brought into playing position.

The Sublime Harmony musical-box appeared in 1870. Similar notes striking together in a chord produce greater volume and richer tone than any former type. This contains two or three combs of equal length having excellent base tones. The Sublime Harmony piccolo gives a clear, distinct accompaniment to the melody of the long comb.

An introduction of 1875 was the musical-box with four springs. This was capable of playing for three hours with a single winding. The tune-changer was devised in 1881, enabling the cylinder to be lifted into as many as ten slightly different positions. Manufacturers then inserted pins so closely that a one-tenth of an inch shift in the mechanism brought a fresh tune into operation.

Steel pins were inserted in the cast brass cylinder, a process costly in labour and materials. Only skilled musicians could be employed for this work. In 1883, however, it was discovered that dents punched into a cylinder of sheet brass served the same purpose.

Circular card discs were introduced to musical-boxes in 1885. Known as the Symphonium, this design was patented and could be made far more cheaply than the cylinder type, and a wider range of tunes was possible. This machine is fitted with tiny levers for plucking the combs, perforations in the card disc bringing the levers into operation. By 1890 metal discs were in use, measuring $15\frac{1}{2}$ inches in diameter. The invention of the metal disc had a devastating effect upon the sales of cylinder musical boxes. The music was clear and up-to-date tunes were in the shops shortly after production in the London theatres.

Accompanying changes in their mechanism came changes in the appearance of musical-boxes. Early examples are enclosed in perfectly plain cases of fine quality oak or mahogany. These were followed from the mid-1820s by cases of polished rosewood. From this period, too, cases might be made to order, matching the purchasers' furniture. At first a large movement had key-wind, stop-start and change-repeat levers projecting through the side of the case. From about 1835 a hinged flap concealed these control levers.

Few, if any, inlaid cases were made earlier than about 1840. At first the lid only was enriched in this manner, plain lines of inlay following its edges. The interior lid of plate glass appeared in 1843 to protect the movement from dust and accident. From 1850 this might be enriched with an elaborate wheel-engraved border. Ratchet winding came at the same time, the key being placed beneath the glass lid which had to be opened for the winding.

Elaborately inlaid cases appeared in large numbers after the Great Exhibition, 1851, handsome examples of the cabinet-maker's craft. The inlay decorates the four sides, the lid, and the frame of the inner plate-glass lid. Walnut, rosewood, mahogany, satinwood, burr elm, cherry, maple, amboyna and coromandel may be noted among favourite woods and may be inlaid with colourful fruit woods of contrasting tones, silver, ivory, mother of pearl, brass or zinc. The centre of the lid may be enriched with a trophy motif composed of trumpet, tambourine, music sheet and olive branch; other musical devices may be noted. Cases of oak were plain at first, then hand carved from the mid-1820s; from 1850 they were mechanically carved. Golden oak, lavishly embellished with applied decorations of cast bronze, was made from 1880.

The lid interior usually displays a numbered programme of the repertoire of airs available. This is usually a card with an engraved border enclosing the names of the tunes in copper-plate handwriting. Sometimes the programme is engraved on a silver or brass plate. Occasionally, from about 1860, the lid might display a colourful painting in oils and bronze.

The music produced by these fascinating mechanisms went through various phases too. Until about 1835 it consisted chiefly of operatic selections. Ballads and patriotic folk songs were fashionable between 1835 and 1850, six or eight tunes being played; other, less popular, musical-boxes played three or four overtures. Airs from oratorios were included in musical-box repertoires from about 1845.

During the period 1850–75 the musical-box most usually played six or eight waltzes. Popular tunes were the rule, with an occasional operatic overture included by way of variety. From 1875 music-hall tunes predominated in cheap musical-boxes, classical music being used extensively in the more costly machines.

Index

341

345